Loss, Hurt and Hope

Loss, Hurt and Hope
The Complex Issues of Bereavement and Trauma in Children

Edited by

Sandra L. Bloom and Lorelei A. Vargas

CAMBRIDGE SCHOLARS PUBLISHING

Loss, Hurt and Hope: The Complex Issues of Bereavement and Trauma in Children, edited by Sandra L. Bloom and Lorelei A. Vargas

This book first published 2007 by

Cambridge Scholars Publishing

15 Angerton Gardens, Newcastle, NE5 2JA, UK

British Library Cataloguing in Publication Data
A catalogue record for this book is available from the British Library

Dedicated to
the memory of
Larry Jamal Warren and Peter Woodruff Ment,
whose untimely passing has brought the Andrus Children's Center
a deeper, more personal understanding of loss and bereavement;
and in honor of the children in our care who work through loss and
hurt to find hope and healing.

TABLE OF CONTENTS

PREFACE

NANCY WOODRUFF MENT

If you have ever felt your heart slip at a newspaper photo of a young girl reaching tearfully for a dying mother; cried at the frozen faces of children whose village was upended by an earthquake; or clenched your jaw when your neighbor yanked his whining son's arm – then this volume has been prepared for you. You may be a professional teacher, clinician, youth worker; you may be a community volunteer; you may once have been a child who lost someone who mattered to you very much. If you are reaching for this book, something inside you is open to the pain and suffering that children feel but rarely can define. This is a book about children who know loss and hurt in forms that even adults cannot absorb. This is a book for people who want to care for these children by grasping the dimensions of their pain. This is a book for people who want to nurture hope that the future can be different from the past.

I feel privileged to be writing this introduction to a volume that has a deep personal resonance for me. A core of the papers you will read originated in presentations at a conference held in October, 2005 at the Andrus Children's Center in Yonkers, New York. For 20 years I have been associated with Andrus, a haven for vulnerable children founded in 1928 by philanthropist John Emery Andrus whose wife, Julia Dyckman, had been orphaned as a young child. Mr. Andrus believed that children should be treasured and given opportunities to succeed in spite of the losses they had endured. Over the years, our mission has stretched to encompass residential and day treatment for seriously emotionally disturbed children, community-based mental health services and home-centered family strengthening. Like many mental health and social service organizations, we have seen children struggling against increasingly formidable odds: mental illness, developmental discontinuities, family disruption, poverty and community violence. As new theories emerged in our field, we came to understand that trauma was a rich concept to capture the stunning effects of life experiences on our children.

In 2001, we began working with Sandra Bloom, M.D., to adapt her *Sanctuary Model* of trauma-informed care for children. We committed ourselves to perfecting our craft in caring for children whose lives were derailed by single devastating losses, by the steady accretion of hurts, or by the pain of being chronically outside. Early in our work together, September 11 became a flashpoint. Suddenly what had been "out there" for our children came "inside" for all of us. Trauma and loss became vivid, deeply felt experiences for all of us. Unlike our children, we could find words to convey how dislocated and vulnerable we felt. And yet, like our children, we could *not* find hope.

In time, because we could rely on each other, we came to believe that we could move forward. But life continued to happen to us. In February, 2003 our small community at Andrus was shattered when the beautiful son of Larry Warren, one of our Program Manager's was murdered. Larry Jamaal Warren grew up dearly loved and protected by his father who himself has devoted his life to protecting other people's children. Young Larry, always a role model, intervened in a fight between two young men. A short time later, he was shot in the head, allegedly by one of these young men, but justice has never been served.

In August of 2004, my son Peter Woodruff Ment, died in an accident in Costa Rica where he had been pursuing his latest passion, surfing. He was a joy to me every day of his life. For both Larry and me, the loss of our boys is the worst thing that has ever happened to us. And yet, both of us have come to know safety in our memories of wonderful sons who were loved and cherished. As we have made our way through grief, we have been lifted up and carried by family, friends and colleagues. We have come to benefit from personal resources of language, mature thinking and adult perspectives. We know how to solve problems and to ask for help. We have had reliable incomes, food, clothing and stable homes. But still, we have barely made it through.

Being adults who have endured unspeakable loss has given us a unique perspective on what loss is like for children who cannot apply a sense of reason or self-efficacy. Although we did not believe it could be possible, Larry and I have survived and we have come to know joy again – even in our sadness. The conference *Loss Hurt and Hope* was dedicated to our treasured sons. This volume is dedicated to all the children who have known loss and hurt, all the children whose lives we and you will touch, in the hope that they will master sorrow to know joy and love.

INTRODUCTION

LORELEI ATALIE VARGAS, MPP, MA

Each year millions of children experience some form of trauma. A car accident, a fire, rape, physical abuse, abandonment, homelessness, the loss of a parent, friend, or pet, a natural disaster, domestic violence, community violence — all can leave a child with scars, usually unseen by the human eye, but often more devastating than any physical wound. When left untreated, childhood trauma crosses generational boundaries, developing risk factors that far outpace the threat of any other childhood disease, and yet, most children who have lived through a significant traumatic experience, usually do not get the care they need to begin their healing process. This book gathers the collective wisdom of professionals who have spent years on the front lines of working with children victimized by trauma. Its purpose is to share and celebrate the knowledge and best practices that have proven successful in healing the most vulnerable among us.

In chapter one, "Beyond the Beveled Mirror: Mourning and Recovery from Childhood Maltreatment", Dr. Sandra L. Bloom shares her years of experience working in an inpatient psychiatric unit, how she and colleagues came to understand childhood trauma. Bloom discusses the long-term outcomes of unresolved grief that stem from chronic childhood maltreatment. She outlines the various losses that a child experiences from "loss of wholeness" to "loss of the capacity to establish safe and trusting relationships" to "loss of self esteem". Using anecdotes from her work in the field of psychiatry, Bloom discusses how these losses must be confronted and dealt with in the recovery process.

Kenneth V. Hardy's "Untangling Intangible Loss in the Lives of Traumatized Children and Adolescents" defined tangible and intangible loss. In chapter two, Hardy unveils why most individuals, including mental health professionals, find it difficult to deal with loss. Hardy draws the distinction between tangible loss – "loss of a loved one, a sweater or a limb" and intangible loss – "emotional psychological loss that is usually attached to a tangible loss". Using vignettes from the field, Hardy highlights why intangible loss is often just as devastating as tangible loss.

In chapter three, "Walking Together: A Child Therapist's Journey through Loss", author Kathryn Kehoe-Biggs uses a case study approach to illustrate the complex variations of loss and how multiple losses are layered in a child's life and influence his perception of past, present and future. Using the lens of the therapist, this chapter provides an appreciation of the significant role of the therapist in developing a non-verbal exchange that can often become the basis of interactions between the therapist and the client — with each client having their own non-verbal code. Kehoe-Biggs shares the intricacies of understanding the value of these non-verbal exchanges with children who have experienced loss, as a way to further the healing process.

Chapter four, "Responding to Trauma, Violence and Bereavement Overload in the Lives of Young African American Men: Trauma-Informed Approaches to Health Care" provides a cultural lens through which chronic trauma and loss can be understood. Dr.'s Theodore J. Corbin and John Rich utilize their unique vantage point of working in urban medical emergency rooms and primary care clinics, to discuss the role of trauma in the lives of young African American men who are victims of trauma. Two programmatic efforts shed light on community level prevention and intervention models that were geared to provide more than medical care within a healthcare system. The authors share learned lessons on these approaches, including the importance of having trauma-informed framework to structure their programs, dedicated staff and support from the host institutions.

In chapter five, Valerie Anderson provides a respite from the intensity of trauma and grief in her poem entitled "Acceptable Losses". Anderson reminds the reader of the natural losses that compose life from the "The loss of childhood to adulthood" to "The loss of being under to rising above". This poem offers a simple and approachable understanding to life and loss.

David McCorkle and Sarah Yanosy Sreedhar's work in chapter six, entitled "When Loss gets Lost: Using the SELF Model to Work with Loss in Residential Care", presents considerable insight to the world of residential care. Residential treatment programs offer children 24-hour care in a therapeutic environment. Presenting with a history of failed placement, oftentimes, children entering residential treatment have repeatedly exhausted all other less-restrictive and community-based options. McCorkle and Sreedhar share the perspective that residential treatment is rooted in loss. This chapter illustrates the use of the Sanctuary Model's — a trauma-informed treatment method — SELF acronym (Safety, Emotional management, Loss and Future) in a residential setting. Using a case study approach, the authors share how SELF is used to mitigate grief among children who have experienced severe and chronic trauma.

In chapter seven, "Loss in Human Service Organizations" Dr. Sandra L. Bloom offers an in-depth look at how organizations that are charged with caring for the most vulnerable populations, manage loss and grief within the organization. Bloom's development of the Sanctuary Model provides the backdrop of this chapter as she shares the delicate balancing act that organizational leaders must endure in managing vulnerable children in a vulnerable environment. Her conversations with the leadership of organizations shed some new light on how personal and organizational loss gets managed and grieved collectively.

Together theses chapters help to identify the numerous individual and contextual factors that should be considered in helping children who have experienced loss. They also provide a broad etiological context in which to consider how loss can be better managed in children, and how professional healers can begin the process of creating hope for the future.

CHAPTER ONE

BEYOND THE BEVELED MIRROR: MOURNING
AND RECOVERY FROM CHILDHOOD
MALTREATMENT ACROSS THE LIFESPAN[*]

SANDRA L. BLOOM, M.D.

Introduction

I had this thing when I was a child, this fantasy. My parents had a beveled mirror
in their room and the regular mirror was in the center. I thought that everyone in
the world must see me as in the beveled part of it, the part that was screwed up,
with the eyes over here and the nose separate, in pieces, in shards, because that is
how I felt – disconnected.. . .Before I came to Sanctuary, I never really knew
what these symptoms were about because the grief was like something separate
from me. Now I am feeling it in my body as well. Now it is all inside of me and I
can feel the grief bubbling instead of just being outside of me somewhere.

—Jodie, adult survivor of child maltreatment

When someone close to us dies, society generally accepts and even
expects us to undergo a process of mourning. Death presents a tangible and
comprehensible loss. Throughout history, cultures have built traditions and
customs to provide a passage for the bereaved that enables us to let go of those
who have died, in order to prepare us to create new attachments.

But society has yet to recognize the necessity and value of grieving for
other kinds of losses besides those associated with death. A common
denominator among the thousands of adults treated in the inpatient program we
called Sanctuary, are the "little deaths" – of hope, of innocence, of love and of
joy. For some, the sources of grief constituted the loss of already established
assumptions and beliefs about self, home, family and society. For others, the

---

assaults to their integrity began when they were so young that they had no time to even develop a coherent assumptive world before their lives were shattered. Complicating the process of grieving for adult survivors, is the fact that the losses that accompany child maltreatment are cloaked in silence, lost in the shrouds of history, and largely unrecognized. In general, their grief for these losses is unaccepted, rejected, denied and stigmatized. But these "little deaths" remain as unremoved splinters in the survivor's psyche for decades, as Jodie's description illustrates. Although new protective psychic tissue may form over these wounds and new experiences may allow the child to develop assumptions about the world that contradict the traumatic and abusive experiences, the psychic splinters remain, surfacing again in adulthood, often triggered by a new insult to their well-being. Child neglect represents particular challenges for adult survivors because they must grieve for things they never had, and thus never had the chance to lose.

This chapter will focus on these losses. From 1985-2001 my colleagues and I specialized in the treatment of adult survivors of child abuse and neglect in our inpatient treatment programs and we followed many of them as outpatients[1] We have learned about how difficult it is to form healthy attachments as an adult when your childhood attachments have been so scarring that the pain of the past continues in the present. Attachment theory and our growing understanding of the impact of trauma and traumatic grief provided ways to understand how trauma and loss in childhood affects adult relationships and impacts the capacity to grieve.

The lessons they taught us have helped us to understand loss through the eyes of the children they once were. They taught us about the difficulties they encounter in grieving for the omissions that accompany child neglect as well as the more flagrant commissions of physical, emotional, and sexual abuse. In this chapter I will detail many of those losses through the testimony of several people who agreed to be interviewed and describe the process of recovery that for many begins in childhood and continues throughout their lifetime. Our treatment model uses an acronym to describe the phases of recovery that trauma survivors must work through in the process of their recovery: S.E.L.F. The four letters stand for "Safety", "Emotional Management", "Loss" and "Future"[2]. This chapter focuses on the "L" in Loss and we will look at the losses – and the discoveries – that accompany the healing process.

---

[1] Bloom, *Creating Sanctuary: Toward the Evolution of Sane Societies;* Bills and Bloom, *From Chaos to Sanctuary*
[2] Bloom, Foderaro, & Ryan, *S.E.L.F.: A Trauma-Informed Psychoeducational Curriculum;* Foderaro, *Creating a nonviolent environment*

Attachment and Grief

The losses that accompany childhood exposure to terror and violence can only be grasped within the context of attachment theory. One of John Bowlby's great contributions was to recognize that attachment behavior is a fundamental part of our evolutionary heritage and therefore is critical to survival. Primates – including humans – need to attach from "cradle to grave" and any disruption in normal attachment relationships, particularly those being established in early childhood, is likely to cause developmental problems[3]. He recognized that "grief and mourning occur in infancy whenever the responses mediating attachment behavior are activated and the mother figure continues to be unavailable"[4]. He went on to discuss how "the experience of loss of mother in the early years is an antecedent of relevance in the development of personalities prone to depressive and other psychiatric illnesses and that these conditions are best understood as sequelae of pathological mourning"[5]. He identified four main variants of pathological responses by bereaved adults: 1) anxiety and depression, which he saw as the persistent and unconscious yearning to recover the lost person, originally adaptive because it produced strong motivation for reunion; 2) intense and persistent anger and reproach expressed towards others or the self and originally intended to achieve reunion with the lost relationship and discourage further separation; 3) absorption in caring for someone else who has also been bereaved, sometimes amounting to a compulsion; and 4) denial that the relationship is permanently lost[6]

Since Bowlby originally made these astute observations, other clinicians and researchers have been busily extending his work to show the relationship between disrupted attachment in childhood as a result of maltreatment and the development of adult pathology[7]. As far back as 1963, Khan discussed the idea of cumulative trauma, and the impact of protective failures: "cumulative trauma is the result of the breaches in the mother's role as a protective shield over the whole course of the child's development, from infancy to adolescence"[8]. He went on to discuss how this can leave a person vulnerable to breakdown later in life. There is a long-established connection between childhood loss and depression[9] and between suicidal behavior in

---

[3] Bowlby, *Development psychiatry comes of age*
[4] Bowlby, *Grief and Mourning in Infancy and Early Childhood,* p.9
[5] Ibid, p.11
[6] Bowlby, *Pathological Mourning and Childhood Mourning*
[7] De Zulueta, *From Pain to Violence*
[8] Khan, *The concept of cumulative trauma*
[9] Bowlby, *Attachment and Loss*

adolescents as well as adults and disrupted attachment[10]. In the last decades, other workers have concretized the relationship between insecure forms of attachment in childhood and the evolution of personality disorders[11]. Fonagy and colleagues have helped illuminate the important relationship between disrupted attachment and borderline states[12], while Liotti has written about the development of dissociative disorders within an attachment framework[13]. Others have looked at both highly conflicted families and violent couples from the point of view of disrupted childhood attachment relationships[14], while other investigators have provided abundant theoretical and evidence-based data showing how the disrupted childhood attachment relationships of parents can be carried over into the ways in which they parent their own children[15].

Complex Post-Traumatic Stress Disorder

Of the adult patients we treated, most had been victims of severe physical, psychological, sexual abuse and neglect. Some had experienced only one form of child maltreatment, many had experienced two or more. Childhood maltreatment is associated with a wide variety of physical, psychological, and social dysfunction in childhood and in adulthood and there is now a significant body of literature reviewing various aspects of comorbidity[16]. There are well-established connections between chronic depressive disorders, somatization disorder, anxiety disorders, and various personality disorders especially borderline personality disorder and childhood exposure to overwhelming and

---

[10] Adam, *Suicidal Behavior and Attachment*

[11] West & Keller, *Psychotherapy Strategies for Insecure Attachment in Personality Disorders*

[12] Fonagy, et al, *Attachment, the reflective self, and borderline states*

[13] Liotti, *Disorganized/Disoriented Attachment in the Psychotherapy of the Dissociative Disorders; Disorganization of Attachment as a Model for Understanding Dissociative Pathology*

[14] Henry & Homes, *Childhood Revisited: The Intimate Relationships of Individuals from Divorced and Conflict-Ridden Families;* Roberts & Noller, *The Associations between Adult Attachment and Couple Violence;*

[15] Main and Hesse, *Parents' Unresolved Traumatic Experiences Are Related to Infant Disorganized Attachment Status:*

[16] Ellason and Ross. Childhood Trauma and Psychiatric Symptoms; Koss et al. Deleterious Effects of Criminal Victimization on Women's Health and Medical Utilization; Grady. Posttraumatic Stress Disorder and Comorbidity: Recognizing the Many Faces of PTSD; Leserman et al. Impact of Sexual and Physical Abuse Dimensions on Health Status: Development of an Abuse Severity Measure.

traumatic events[17]. However, many of the patients we see enter treatment carrying two, three, or even more psychiatric labels, many of the same diagnostic categories that have been implicated as the long-term results of disrupted attachment relationships. In many ways, the trauma-related disorders can be seen as disorders of disrupted attachment.

Children can be maltreated in a number of different ways and it is common for maltreated children to have multiple victimization experiences. In a large survey of an HMO adult population performed by the Center for Disease Control in Atlanta and Kaiser Permanente of San Diego, a third of respondents reported belonging to at least one category of exposure to adverse childhood experiences or "ACE's". The categories of adverse childhood experiences included: psychological, physical, or sexual abuse; emotional or physical neglect; witnessing violence against mother; or living with household members who were substance abusers, mentally ill or suicidal, or ever imprisoned.

The overlapping symptoms and complex clinical picture characteristic of adults who have experienced childhood maltreatment is more comprehensible if we formulate the problem as one of "complex post-traumatic stress disorder"[18]. Field trials for DSM-IV, demonstrated that there are significant differences between survivors of disasters who suffer from post-traumatic stress disorder and childhood survivors of maltreatment[19]. These differences fall into seven major categories of dysfunction: alterations in regulating affective arousal, alterations in attention and consciousness, somatization, alterations in self-perception, alterations in perception of the perpetrator, alterations in relations to others, and alterations in systems of meaning. These symptom clusters have been demonstrated to differentiate acute adult onset trauma syndromes associated with disaster victims from adult victims of childhood interpersonal violence and abuse.

When viewed from the point of view of the grief literature, difficulties with managing affect and alterations in attention and consciousness may reflect two of the final adult personality outcomes of two of Bowlby's sequelae of pathological mourning. The unrelenting yearning and searching for the lost love relationship, and the defenses built up to protect against this yearning can be seen as an underpinning for many of the symptoms that lead people to seek treatment. The persistent anger and reproach originally intended to achieve reunion and discourage more separation are common problems for our patients in all of their relationships and strongly color the nature of the therapeutic alliance.

---

[17] Kessler et al, *Posttraumatic Stress Disorder in the National Comorbidity Survey;* Solomon & Davidson, *Trauma: Prevalence; Impairment; Service Use; and Cost.*
[18] Herman, *Trauma and Recovery*
[19] Roth et al, *Complex PTSD in Victims Exposed to Sexual and Physical Abuse*

Alterations in self-perception, in perception of the perpetrator and in relationships with others all can be understood in the context of an expectable developmental outcome in the face of disrupted early attachments. It is well established from studies of captive victims of all kinds – political prisoners, torture survivors, hostages, and both adult and child victims of family violence – that when people are placed in situations of inescapable danger for prolonged periods of time, they may develop very strange relationships with their captors and alter their perception of themselves. This phenomenon has become known as "trauma-bonding"[20]. Trauma-bonding is a relationship that is based on terror and the twisting and manipulation of normal attachment behavior in service of someone else's malevolent intent. People who are terrorized experience the perpetrator as being in total control, the source of pain but also the source of pain relief; the source of threat but also the source of hope. Victims come to internalize the experience of helplessness and the role of perpetrator and then later in life, unconsciously recreate the pattern of these early and traumatizing relationships in new relationships. Successful grieving means letting go of these patterns as well as letting go of the former abusive relationships, even though these relationships are also associated with a deep sense of fear and foreboding at their loss.

Somatization may represent not just the effects of prolonged stress but also the long-term effects of suppressed grief on the body. In the ACE's study, there was a graded relationship between the number of categories of childhood exposure and each of the adult health risk behaviors and diseases that were studied. People who had experienced four or more categories of childhood exposure, compared to those who had experienced none, had 4- to 12-fold increased health risks for alcoholism, drug abuse, depression, and suicide attempt; a 2- to 4-fold increase in smoking, poor self-rated health, and greater than or equal to fifty sexual intercourse partners, and sexually transmitted disease; and 1.4- to 1.6-fold increase in physical inactivity and severe obesity. The number of categories of adverse childhood exposures showed a graded relationship to the presence of adult diseases including ischemic heart disease, cancer, chronic lung disease, skeletal fractures, and liver disease[21]. In another study looking at the connection in women between childhood adverse experiences and physical health, a history of childhood maltreatment was significantly associated with several adverse physical health outcomes including perceived poor overall health, greater physical and emotional disability,

---

[20] James, *Handbook for Treatment of Attachment Trauma Problems in Children*
[21] Felitti et al, *Relationship of Childhood Abuse and Household Dysfunction to Many of the Leading Causes of Death in Adults.*

increased number of distressing physical symptoms and a greater number of health risk behaviors[22].

Disrupted systems of meaning can be understood as the logical outgrowth of growing up within intimate childhood contexts of mistrust, deceit, hypocrisy and cruelty that are embedded within a larger social context that insists that children are to be valued, loved, cherished and protected from harm. A child's exposure to deliberate malevolence at the hands of a primary caretaker powerfully confuses the ability of the child to correlate his or her own experience of reality with the realities of other people. The contradictions are shattering. Most importantly, perhaps, this bears on the issue of justice, a fundamental human striving, rooted in our primate-derived sense of reciprocity, the basis of all social relationships. If children are treated unjustly, they will seek justice for their hurt. If their family or their larger society denies them justice, then they will seek revenge, either against themselves, others, or both. When children discover that the adults who hurt them were never held accountable for the infliction of harm by the society, not only does this cause disruption in the attachment relationship with the perpetrator, but also with the self, the other members of the family and the society at large. As Charny points out, *"The avoidance of defining perpetration of evil as a disturbance in its own right reaches its bizarre extreme in the classic literature on child abuse – violence to the child. According to the prevailing definitions, the majority of parents who abuse children are not emotionally disturbed. . . it is utter nonsense to ignore the fact that anyone who seriously abuses his or her child is seriously disturbed"*[23].

Traumatic Grief

While attachment theorists have been carefully formulating theory and analyzing data from the perspective of developmental psychopathology[24], clinicians and researchers in the overlapping fields of traumatic stress studies and thanatology have been broadening our understanding of what happens to people who are traumatized and the ways in which traumatic bereavement differs from normal bereavement. Jacobs has described traumatic grief in relation to any death that is personally devastating and is characterized by traumatic separation. Traumatic grief has been shown to be associated with impaired role performance, functional impairment, subjective sleep disturbance,

---

[22] Walker et al, *Adult Health Status of Women with Histories of Childhood Abuse and Neglect.*
[23] Charney, *Evil in Human Personality*, p. 483
[24] Cichetti & Lynch, *Failures in the expectable environment and their impact on individual development*

low self-esteem, depression and anxiety, as well as a high risk of cancer, cardiac disorders, alcohol and tobacco consumption, and suicidal ideation[25]. Other authors have looked at the various ways that traumatic bereavement and exposure to death and dying affect various populations and age groups[26], while still others have looked at the way entire communities grieve after mass tragic events[27].

Rando has written extensively about the treatment of complicated mourning and has connected unresolved grief to many of the symptoms of chronic and complex post-traumatic stress disorder. She has also looked at the difficulties survivors encounter mourning someone who has victimized them, as is so often the case in survivors of childhood maltreatment[28]. At least since Lindemann's seminal work[29], the connection between the normal somatic manifestations of grief and symptoms of complicated mourning have been recognized[30].

Although the literature is by now rich and persuasive in conceptualizing the relationship between traumatic loss and disrupted attachment, relatively little has been detailed about the losses the do not involve actual death, but that do represent extraordinary loss for adults who were maltreated as children. These "little" losses occur in the context of a long-standing pattern characterized by the absence of sustaining and loving caregiver behavior. As children, our patients often had parents who were physically present, but the nature of their parenting was so abusive and/or neglectful that their losses are not even seen as losses at all, but a way of life.

Nonetheless, recovery from loss requires the working through of a mourning process. Ochberg has described some of the necessary tasks required to complete the process of grief[31]. Mourners must be able to express their emotions, understand the meaning of the lost person or object, be able to surface and work through the ambivalence in the relationship, all of which will eventually free them up to attach trust and love to new significant others and find appropriate replacements for the lost relationships. These tasks are very difficult to complete for adult survivors of child abuse and neglect. Being raised in abusive homes characterized by disruptive attachment relationships almost guarantees that people will have difficulty in managing their emotions. The

---

[25] Jacobs, *Traumatic Grief*

[26] Figley, *Traumatology of Grieving;* Figley et al., *Death and Trauma*

[27] Zinner and Williams, *When a Community Weeps*

[28] Rando, *Treatment of Complicated Mourning*

[29] Lindemann, *Symptomatology and Management of Acute Grief*

[30] Engel, *A Challenge for Medical Research;* Rando, *Treatment of Complicated Mourning*

[31] Ochberg, *Post-Traumatic Therapy and Victims of Violence*

problems associated with disrupted meaning schemas will make it difficult for them to understand the meaning of the lost person, lost experience, lost self. Trauma-bonding may make it feel very unsafe to deal with the ambivalence in the earlier relationship, even if it occurred decades before. The consequent lack of resolution interferes with the capacity to establish new, safe, and loving relationships, to even find appropriate people to love in order to replace the old abusive ones. Some people will stay aloof from relationships altogether so as not to become involved in more abuse. Others, having no other internalized standard, use the abusive relationships as their only norm. In this way the past becomes the present.

As has long been pointed out in the field of grief studies, failure to complete the tasks of grieving can impair future development and adaptation. Lack of grief resolution can also impact on physical health. The ACEs study mentioned earlier may provide connecting links between traumatic grief, traumatic stress, disrupted attachment and childhood maltreatment[32].

Recovery From The Impact Of Child Maltreatment

There is by now an extensive literature on the treatment of people who suffer from the complex syndromes related to a past history of child maltreatment. Since Janet first talked about the process of trauma resolution and the need to "liquidate" traumatic memory, there has been an understanding that trauma treatment progresses in stages, or perhaps more accurately, phases[33]. Like the descriptions of bereavement, however, these phases are dynamic, interpenetrating and spiraling, rather than indicative of a clear stepwise progression.

We use the acronym "S.E.L.F." to describe the way we understand this dynamic movement. Our patients have helped us develop the concepts over the last fifteen years, and as a result the S.E.L.F. model has become a practical and useful way for our patients and their therapists to map out a road to recovery. "S" represents "Safety" – the starting point for all efforts at healing. We understand that there are four levels of safety: physical safety or the ability to be safe from physical or sexual harm; psychological safety or the ability to be safe with oneself; social safety or the ability to be safe with others; and moral safety or the ability to live and work within a personal and professional context whose guiding value is a respect for life[34].

---

[32] Edwards et al, *Adverse Childhood Experiences and Health-Related Quality of Life as an Adult*
[33] Van der Kolk & van der Hart, *Pierre Janet on Post-traumatic stress.*
[34] Bloom, *Creating Sanctuary: Toward the Evolution of Sane Societies*

In practical terms, adults generally enter treatment because in any of a number of ways, they are not safe. They may be self-mutilating, have attempted or are threatening suicide. They may be abusing drugs or alcohol, have an eating disorder, or are becoming increasingly nonfunctional because of escalating anxiety. They may be in dangerous relationships or placing themselves at unnecessary risk without understanding why or feeling able to control their behavior. Whatever the reason, the first step in recovery is to confront existing issues of safety, develop a plan for the restoration of safety and implement that plan.

In the course of learning to manage safety by inhibiting dangerous or damaging behavior, however, it quickly becomes obvious to people that their unsafe behaviors have been serving a useful purpose. The behaviors have helped them exert control over emotions that are otherwise overwhelming, toxic, oppressive and extremely painful. In order to be safe, they must learn how to manage emotions in health-promoting ways. This process is reflected in the "E" phase of S.E.L.F.: Emotional Management. With enough social support, cognitive restructuring, skill development, inner fortitude and perseverance, our patients allow themselves to trade in their self-destructive behaviors for healthier relationship. But the very act of taking such a relational risk with therapists, teachers, friends, and family opens the door to the next phase of S.E.L.F: Loss.

Unresolved, Stigmatized, Disenfranchised LOSS

Adults who were maltreated as children carry around with them the impact of delayed, unresolved, "stigmatized" loss[35]. According to the descriptions of stigmatized grief, the incidents giving rise to the loss happen suddenly, are associated with violence, result in others fearing contagion and blaming the victim and result in victims believing they should have done something to prevent the events, or that they deserve what happened. Several of the characteristics of stigmatized grief describe the situation of abused children. In some cases, as in sexual abuse, the loss of a secure relationship with the parent can be quite sudden and unexpected. Child abuse is clearly associated with violence and the victims are usually told that they have done something to deserve the violence. Their parents and society-at-large tends to blame them and frequently they are told that if they had behaved differently they could have prevented it. Social denial of the magnitude of the problem is still a prominent feature of our social environment.

---

[35] Sprang and McNeil, *The Many Faces of Bereavement*

Victims' grief is delayed because most abused children learn how to adapt to even astonishingly difficult circumstances in order to survive, but they do pay a price. A later crisis or loss in adult life may unmask an underlying vulnerability that has been lurking beneath the apparently normal surface of their lives for years. The losses they sustain are unresolved because for most survivors of childhood abuse, there is no clearly established and socially acceptable pathway for grief resolution if actual physical death has not been involved. Their losses cannot even be acknowledged as loss. Their grief is stigmatized because it is seen as a "blemish of individual character"[36]. The losses associated with childhood maltreatment that are only recognized or surfaced in adulthood are not considered legitimate reasons for grief, by the larger society. They are not "legitimate" mourners.

According to Doka, who has written about "disenfranchised" grief, there are three general types: those individuals whose relationships are socially unrecognized, illegitimate, or in other ways unsanctioned; those persons whose loss does not fit the typical norms of appropriateness; and those people whose ability to grieve is in question or who are not considered to be legitimate grievers[37]. Victims of child maltreatment experience many losses that carry with them no social legitimacy. In the case of victims of sexual abuse, the losses they sustain are often not only unrecognized but are denied by the perpetrator and by other family members. Victims of other forms of maltreatment are frequently labeled as "whiners" or "complainers" who manipulate others with their "victim mentality". As for normative appropriateness, the society at large barely is willing to deal with death as a legitimate cause for bereavement behavior. The social attitude towards most other losses is generally, "get over it". And even among therapists and otherwise supportive others, there may be great resistance to empathizing with the grief victims feel at finally having to give up a relationship with someone who has been abusive, dangerous and cruel or letting go of a behavior that has helped them cope and feel in control, even if that behavior appears "crazy". They are not legitimate grievers because the losses they experience are usually not considered appropriate causes for grief. After all, they survived, didn't they?

Bearing Witness to Childhood Loss

The seven categories associated with complex post-traumatic stress disorder are a useful way to classify the various losses our patients experience. In the following pages, several people were willing to share their experiences of

---

[36] Goffman, *Stigma*
[37] Doka, *Living with Grief after Sudden Loss*

loss secondary to childhood abuse and neglect. When interviewed, each person was at a different point in her personal recovery and each one had suffered unique experiences. All, however were able to relate to the concept of loss and the questions I asked them in the interview. I have changed their names and identifying information and after transcribing their conversations, received their permission to use the quotations I have included.

Samantha (S) is in her thirties and has been diagnosed with schizoaffective disorder. She has a history of self-mutilation, suicide attempts, multiple hospitalizations, substance abuse and has been considered to be chronically mentally ill. Along with everything else, she episodically has a thought disorder and has difficulty separating reality from her paranoid ideation. She has been tried on many medications and is currently on antidepressants, antianxiety medication, and antipsychotic agents . She is living in a sheltered apartment, is no longer self-mutilating, and is determined to get well. Despite her long history of mental health problems, Samantha managed to complete college. She recognizes that she is currently grieving for the many losses she has sustained throughout her life as the result of her extremely abusive, chaotic, neglectful, and dangerous home life. She was sexually abused by her father, physically abused and neglected by both parents, both of whom were and still are, active alcoholics.

Jodie (J) is also in her thirties. College-educated, she has a responsible position in business. Sexually abused by a relative beginning at a very young age, she lived with a number of symptoms until seeking treatment. She originally sought treatment because of post-traumatic symptoms secondary to her involvement in a violent relationship.

Helen (H) is thirty-seven years old, college educated and employed by a state government agency. She suffered physical abuse at the hands of her father, emotional abuse by her mother, and severe neglect from both parents. One of five children, her graduate school trained father, refused to spend money on the family home or his children so that there was not even sufficient clothing or shoes or heat in the house when they were growing up. Neither Helen nor her siblings were given sufficient health care as children, and these tangible omissions were paralleled by a complete lack of affection, love, or empathic regard for the children. She originally sought treatment because her frequent negative encounters with authority figures and co-workers made it impossible for her to hold a job.

Rachel (R) is in her early forties and runs a successful hair salon with her husband. She was raised by a mother who she describes as a hippy who ran with the avant-garde set in New York City in the 50's and 60's and left her children to fend for themselves emotionally, while at least providing for them financially.

Losses Secondary to Child Maltreatment

Alterations in ability to manage emotions

Children require loving and empathic relationships in order to develop properly. The immature central nervous system needs caregivers who are willing to serve as protective shields against overwhelming arousal. The hallmark characteristic of all forms of child maltreatment is empathic failure[38]. When exposure to abuse and neglect corrupts the family environment, children lose – or fail to develop – the ability to modulate their own level of emotional arousal and as a result they are forced to use whatever coping skills they happen to hit on that calms them down. Often those coping skills are self-destructive – drugs, alcohol, aggression, self-abuse – but these behaviors within the child or the adult's control are preferable to the noxious experience of overwhelming distress. The inability to manage emotions in a relational, constructive way means that later you must grieve for how much more difficult life is and has been for you than it is for other people. It means that you lose a sense of being safe and secure in the world, if you ever had it in the first place. The prolonged effects of exposure to overwhelming stress means that it is very difficult to finish the grieving process that enable you to make more successful relationships because being able to grieve means being able to tolerate and work through very painful emotional experiences.

✓ Loss of ability to manage emotions like other people

Samantha has great difficulty in managing her emotions, especially now that she has given up self-abuse as a way of coping. Samantha provides us with an example of one way in which maltreated children, without supportive adults to help them adequately express themselves, may fail to develop the ability to associate feelings with words, also known as alexithymia[39]. As a result, she lives with what is now a state of pain and finds verbal expression difficult. People from more secure homes learn how to use other people as resources to help manage feelings when they are overwhelming, but children deprived of empathic care have great difficulty relying on others or even knowing how to get the help they need.

> **S.** My day-to-day living now is so painful because I never really felt anything and now I am. I had no words to attach to even asking for help. Even now I struggle with feeling and talking.

---

[38] Weil, *Early Deprivation of Empathic Care*
[39] Krystal, *Integration and Self Healing*

S. There was nothing else, nothing else but self-abuse. Anytime I felt anything I had to dissociate. I couldn't handle feelings at all.

✓   Loss of a sense of safety

A basic sense of safety is what serves as the foundation for all developmental achievements. Children who grow up in violent homes are robbed of this basic necessity. For them, emotional, intellectual and creative energy must be put in the service of protecting their minds and bodies from assaults at the hands of the people they are supposed to be able to trust. Samantha's home was so chaotic, violent and deprived that the listener is more amazed at her capacity to go on, despite her limitations, then the extent and magnitude of those limitations. Rebecca talks about the terrible and pervasive anxiety that accompanies a child without context, a child living with emotional neglect, while Helen focuses on the daily fear of living with the violence of physical and verbal abuse.

S. All my life I had to worry about things like how early in the day I should wet my pants so I could go home and check on what was happening at home. It was pure chaos – addiction to drugs and alcohol, sexual and physical abuse. I had to be one step ahead all the time.

S. My sister's best friend was killed in the house too – she was 12 and I was 10. They were playing with guns and it went off accidentally. The girl and my sister were getting high, they got out the gun, I had the gun and my sister went to get the gun from me and the girl was shot in the head. Then my father started shooting at all of the kids to teach them a lesson.

R. I remember always feeling afraid. I was always afraid of going out to the playground for recess at school, but things were even worse if it rained. Then we would have to go to the cafeteria and I would be terrified. I would get so distressed that the teacher would send me home with my brother and I would miss more time from school and make my brother miss school as well.

H. I was always afraid of my father because of his violence, his angry outbursts. My mother was verbally abusive but not violent, just haranguing. I was not safe in those regards. Did I fear for my life? Not really, but there was never a sense of safety or comfort.

✓ Loss of ability to complete mourning

The disruption in the developing ability to manage emotions makes enduring and working through loss extremely difficult. Our patients have great difficulties in tolerating the painful affects that accompany the resurfacing of unresolved grief. As a result of the process of therapy Samantha has learned about the importance of grieving and is allowing herself to grieve as best as she can. She is even struggling to educate the staff of the transitional living facility where she lives about the importance of the grieving process. Jodie has come out on the other side of the mourning phase of her treatment, at least for now, and has come to recognize how much her failure to grieve has impacted on her developmental progress. Helen has not yet really even begun to grieve. Before she can allow herself to work through her losses, she must allow herself to feel the emotions associated with the losses in the first place. Helen's protective mechanism as a child was to detach herself from relationships and from her own emotional states and now those states have become foreign to her.

S. My doctor and the staff of Sanctuary encourage me to work through my grief, but even with them it feels too big to manage sometimes, especially in front of someone. With my doctor, I have to take care of how she is going to manage my feelings and I feel protective of her. With where I live now, a lot is going to be about me educating them. They seem to miss the whole grieving piece. And that makes it harder for me to deal with it, because I need them to understand. I am still struggling to put words to how I feel. I don't have words. One of the things I am working on is staying in the present, keeping the past and the present separate. I get pissed off, because why should I have to educate them when they are supposed to be helping me?

J. I am not avoiding grieving any longer but it took a long time to get to it – about twenty-nine years.

H. I don't like people seeing me sad or emotional in any way. It is embarrassing to have emotions in front of people. Particularly crying in front of someone. People tell me that I should have sadness about not having a relationship with my parents. I don't talk to them. But I don't feel it. They are probably right. This male therapist I was seeing kept telling me that I have a lot of anger towards my parents and one day I had an explosion of anger towards them. I guess you could be quite debilitated by it, if it is bad enough. But that is just conjecture. Like people don't let themselves get angry because they might do something violent. But that is all intellectual.

Alterations in Attention and Consciousness

Exposure to chronic states of physiological hyperarousal interferes with the capacity to learn, to voluntarily direct attention, and to maintain focus[40]. Traumatized children have little ability to self-protect. Confronted with the

---

[40] Putnam, and Trickett, *Child Sexual Abuse;* Perry, *The Boy Who Was Raised as a Dog*

massive physiological hyperarousal that accompanies exposure to violence, there is little they can do to fight back or to flee. But they can dissociate – fragment their experience in a way that protects them against the very real danger of physiological overload. But the price they pay for this protection is substantial – the loss of a sense of wholeness, of an integrated self that adults from functional families simply take for granted.

✓ Loss of wholeness

Jodie's experience gave me the title for this chapter. She offers her childhood experience of fragmentation up as a way of helping us understand what this "beveled mirror" effect looks like, feels like. And then she goes on to describe the separateness, the state of dissociation she felt that she now understands as grief.

J. I had this thing when I was a child, this fantasy. My parents had a beveled mirror in their room and the regular mirror was in the center. I thought that everyone in the world must see me as in the beveled part of it, the part that was screwed up, with the eyes over here and the nose separate, in pieces, in shards, because that is how I felt – disconnected. I had this fantasy that my parents must be paying doctors all over the world to fix everyone's eyes so that they would see me as they would see a normal person because nobody knew really, what was going on inside of me. I was around seven or eight.

J. Before I came to Sanctuary, I never really knew what these symptoms were about because the grief was like something separate from me. Now I am feeling it in my body as well. Now it is all inside of me and I can feel the grief bubbling instead of just being outside of me somewhere. I thought of this separate entity as a kind of blackness that was separate from me. It held so much power that it could control me and turn me against myself like wanting to kill myself or wanting to starve myself or just doing negative things to myself. I really thought about it as a separate thing. I knew it had something to do with my trauma – that the trauma was still controlling me. I could tell by the power and the impact it had on me that it had something to do with the past.

Alterations in Relationships

Abused children lose relationships. Some maltreated children, have no one to relate to from the very beginning. But many parents are adequate in supplying an infant's basic needs but cannot handle the demands of a growing, active child. For such a child, the loss of the formerly nurturing parent can be experienced as a death for which there are no words. The loss of early attachment relationship is devastating in its impact upon the capacity to establish safe and trusting relationships as an adult. And it is not just individual relationships that are affected. It is within the family that we first learn about political, social and economic arrangements between people. Dysfunction in the family relationships will directly carry over into school, the workplace, and the community-at-large. As a result, many survivors of systematic abuse do not feel a sense of place in their social system, and they do not know how to achieve such a place without paying a price similar to the one they have already paid in their families. History repeats itself in the life of the individual inside and outside of the family and then history repeats itself on the part of the whole group.

✓ Loss of attachment relationships

As Samantha's story illustrates, children can lose siblings, friends, pets and other important relationships secondary to the abuse. Her story about the puppy, below, is particularly poignant because in responding with understandable rage to her father's perfidy, she becomes complicit in his murderous behavior, yet another loss that she cannot begin to touch. The priest's failure to respond is another way that her capacity to trust other human beings is compromised, based on a realistic notion of what she could expect from other people. When Jodie's parents failed to protect her from the sexual proclivities of her mother's stepfather, even though he had previously molested her mother, she experiences a secondary empathic failure, one that is possibly even harder to resolve than the original abusive incident. For abused and neglect children, relationships with animals can take on an even greater significance than the usually deep attachment that secure children have with their pets. In Helen's case, the pets were as neglected as the children and there was nothing she could do to help herself or them. Sometimes siblings can serve as buffers against the abuse of the parents, but in cases like Helen's, the children are turned against each other, competitively struggling for what little affection and care that is available.

S. My older sister was removed from our home when she was ten by Child Protective Services. I was 8 at the time. I was responsible for the younger children. My little sister that died was my baby doll. My father made me watch while he smothered her. I still have flashbacks about that. I was afraid about what was going to happen next. I got in the crib with her and tried to wake her up afterward, and then when my mother came home, my father blamed me, said I had killed her. Mother didn't believe him. They called it a crib death.

S. I had gotten a puppy for Christmas and my father knew it meant so much to me, after my sister was killed. I could attach to the puppy. But he would destroy anything I liked. He took the puppy and me into the bathroom, put peanut butter between my legs and had the puppy lick it. I put rat poison in the honey my father used in his cereal and he gave some to the puppy. The puppy died, but my father didn't. He got sick, that's all. I had my father's baby when I was in 8th grade. I already had had one abortion. I went to the priest for help and told him who the father was. The priest told me to keep going to church and did nothing else about it.

J. I remember longing for protection from my mom, that she would act like a parent instead of a sibling that I was supposed to take care of. I had a longing for a dad that didn't rage and try to make us something we weren't and a longing for a grandfather who didn't use me for whatever he wanted

H. I remember losing one particular teacher in third grade who was really good to me. This teacher recognized my plight. And I lost pet cats that died. They were sickly because my parents wouldn't pay for veterinary care and they would die off. They were very important to me. Also, I had a close relationship with my younger sister and when I was about 9 or 10, my older sister convinced her I was the devil incarnate. I had five brothers and sisters but no one would play with me. My older sister had this practice of taking away my friends and one of them was my younger sister. It happened several times. I also lost two very close friends because of her. I have had devastating experiences when boyfriends broke up with me over the past fifteen years – a number of times. In the last ten years, three have broken up with me. The last one was that we couldn't agree on children – I didn't want any and he did.

✓ Loss of the capacity to establish safe and trusting relationships

Children who come from abusive and neglecting homes may have no models for relationship other than the ones they experience at the hands of their parents. Without such a model it is extremely difficult to establish trusting and safe relationships with others. We are conservative creatures and we tend to repeat the past because we so easily adapt and form habits. If the definition of relationship that we behaviorally experience is one based on empathic failure, it will be difficult for us to establish any other kind of relationship, even as adults. Samantha's tentative moves to create a friendship in college is brave, and for awhile effective, but even so, the course of normal endings or change takes on a significance for her that is overwhelming because of all the unresolved experiences of loss from the past. She has no pathway for knowing how to lose and begin again. Her extreme vulnerability to the disorganization of loss manifests as eruptions in clearly symptomatic behavior. Jodi, aware of the dangers of vulnerability, spends most of her life keeping herself away from confronting the demands of intimacy, although she is aware of her fear and clearly wants to overcome it. Helen stays away from intimacy as well, and what relationships she has now are with men. She overtly declares that she cannot trust women. Although both parents were abusive, her mother emotionally violated her with verbal abuse, manipulation, deception, and cruelty.

> *S.* It makes me so sad to remember trying to keep one step ahead of what was going to happen. The energy that took deprived me of ability to have any relationships myself. I now realize that is almost the biggest part of what I have to deal with now. At least now I can make a connection with someone, but I cannot transfer it to friendships. It has affected my ability to make attachments – once they are gone they are gone. My doctor is the first person that I can't say that about. So, never having the opportunity to have friends, to go through that process of finding out that you can work through conflict, that has been a big loss.

> *S.* I was in college and I had made a friend who was older than me. I felt very attached to her and when she graduated I felt that she was leaving me. I was hospitalized shortly after that for the first time. I was drinking a lot at the time. The closer it got to the feelings about this woman, the more the drinking increased, along with blackouts, terrible flashbacks, reliving everything. I was sure my father was there, chasing me.

> *J.* I have been shut down emotionally and socially from people for my whole life. Also, whenever I reached out to people I felt like my self would be lost if I was rejected.

> *H.* No, I don't have a best friend. I did have one for fourteen years, between age 18 and 32, but she had a multiple personality disorder of sorts and once I got into therapy and she didn't, we stopped being able to identify with each other. I don't have a boyfriend, or close relationships with my siblings. I have a couple of friends that I can call for some support and some intimate conversations. If you add them together, they are like having one best friend – all men.

✓ Loss of feeling like a meaningful part of the community, of society

Feeling like a member of society is about feeling related. Victims of child abuse often experience themselves as "beyond the pale", stigmatized, outsiders, aliens. Neglected children may have particular holes in their comprehension of what is expected of them, how they are to behave. Peers commonly reject neglected children and as a result these children may miss out on a particularly important facet of the socialization experience. Helen talks about how as an adult, she has had to learn how to live in society, how to get along with others in order to even function in a job.

H. I am avoiding it [grieving] and I'm not there yet. I don't think I have much grief experience. The last nine years have been about learning how to live in society. I am learning how to do that after coming from a family that couldn't do that. How to relate to people I work with, how to have friends, how to accomplish something.

Alterations in self-perception and perception of the perpetrator(s)

We develop a sense of self-esteem in the context of our significant relationships. The baby learns to view himself or herself with the same regard that he or she sees mirrored in the mother's and father's eyes. Likewise, abused and neglected children come to believe the image of themselves that their parents create, an image that usually has very little to do with the reality of the children's abilities, skills, or dispositions. They are told they are bad, evil, or worthless, just like their faithless Aunt Sadie or Uncle Bill. Repeat a lie frequently enough and people come to believe it. Children are particularly vulnerable to this kind of parental systematic brainwashing because of the large power imbalance that exists between parents and children.

As adults, people often maintain the same connection with their parenting figures as they had as a child and consequently, experience similar fears, powerlessness and helplessness in the face of their parents, or in the face of their internal image of their parents. We may experience that internal image as "the voice of conscience" and have taken it on board as our own, without fully realizing that it is the internalized voice of an abusive parent. As a result, even within our own minds we continue to reenact the childhood trauma between ourselves and our parents. As outsiders, we may look at a young, six-foot-two man, intimidated and quivering before a frail old man, half his size and fail to understand that the grown man is experiencing the same terrors as when his now frail father would beat him into submission every day after school. Our perceptions of ourselves do not just automatically change as we mature, nor do our perceptions of the people who have perpetrated violence against us. Without working through the grief and the anger connected to the relationship we can remain terrorized and humiliated by past figures in our lives, even though they may be out of sight or even dead. In the process we lose our sense of self-esteem, we lose any role models that guarantee our success in the world, we lose the capacity to figure out how to resolve problems without violence, we lose the ability to let go of the past and move on as a whole person, and along the way we miss out on many important educational and vocational opprortunities that could have led our lives in very different directions.

✓   **Loss of self-esteem**

Helen talks about how her childhood impacted – and is still impacting – her self-esteem. The physical and emotional impoverishment of her childhood, deliberately induced by her parents – profoundly affected her view of herself in a multitude of ways. She has been struggling for years, and with great perseverance, to reclaim her natural birthright, but she knows she still has years to go. In the conversation she reveals her continuing relationship with the perpetrators she no longer sees and how their influence, now deeply embedded in her psyche, continues to exert a powerful influence over the way she treats herself.

H. The way I was raised had a terribly devastating effect on my self-esteem. It is getting better because I have been in therapy for nine years. I still have years ahead to repair the damage. It is now to the point that I can at least hold a job. For the longest time I couldn't hold a job without being fired. People like me more now. I had abusive relationships for a long time. I deprived myself of basic things, that most people have, even though I can afford them – like a decent place to live. I still live in a seedy place. I don't have a microwave, or a computer or a VCR, even though I could. I don't take nice trips to places. My self-esteem was really bad ten years ago, but there is still significant headway to be made. I realize that in not allowing myself to have things I am repeating the pattern of my parents. Money does play a factor. Not having money growing up, I tend to put a lot away.

✓   **Loss of successful role models**

Human beings are great imitators. "Children will do as we do, not as we say" is an expression we have all grown up with. Having viable role models for normal human development is vitally necessary for every child. Unfortunately, this is one of the mechanisms for the intergenerational transmission of faulty attachment relationships. Abusive and neglectful parents provide lousy models for how people are supposed to behave – as parents, as adults, as citizens. Rebecca puts it most succinctly and perhaps cynically. Jodie talks about how difficult it has been for her to develop anything resembling a healthy relationship with a man. Helen's role models were astonishingly barren of any redeeming human qualities.

R. "I was raised by wolves".

J. My mom is a very asexual, very inhibited person and I also grieve about that because I had nobody to look up to for that type of a role model. It is hard trying to create a self or a person that you don't really know since there is no one to model yourself after. At least you can know enough to say, "I don't want to be like that", but if you don't have something there to work with, you can't really say that. I also had no positive male role model that is actually a good human being. I have had a hard time relating to men in general because of that. I haven't been able to see men – I have basically negated half of the population because I was so afraid of them. Or I shut them out because of knowing I was going to be rejected and not knowing how to be a woman because I never saw that either. I was always looking for that as a child.

H. My father is highly intelligent but he has some kind of a personality disorder. He was very cheap. He wouldn't buy clothing for his children, didn't want to pay to fix a furnace so we had to live without heat for years. He wouldn't take us for medical care. He had his master's degree in microbiology, was very smart, but did not have a single friend. I lived my whole life in complete, abject, poverty. He did and still does insist on the house being in a state of disrepair to keep the taxes down and puts junk in the yard to keep the taxes down. It was too embarrassing to bring friends home. He was violent towards his kids, although he didn't drink. It was meted out based on how much a threat you were to him. My brother was intelligent and he got 80% of the violence – he would break chairs over his head. I was ambitious and so I got about 15% of the violence. He is not a nice person. Very opinionated and feels he can tell the world how to run their lives. My mother is a schizoid personality and cannot form relationships with anyone, even with her children. She is bright, but incompetent in life. She is verbally abusive to her own family, but outside of the family she puts on an act of a loving mother, then she is nasty.

✓ Loss of ability to resolve problems or conflicts in a positive way

How do we learn to resolve problems or conflicts? As children, we watch how the adults around us resolve problems and if they are successful, we develop the confidence that we can do that too. If we don't expect the world to mistreat us, we often create self-fulfilling prophecies and we don't get mistreated. Children raised in abusive families have very different experiences. They learn that the way adults resolve conflicts is through abuse, violence, or denial. The child who refuses to imitate the behavior of his or her violent family will be faced with an empty spot where good judgment and problem-solving skills should be. In Helen's case, this meant that she became overly reliant on the judgment of others, even though she had no guideposts for how to choose people to relate to who have good judgment and conflict resolution skills. In situations of conflict, it is vitally important that people know what their boundaries are, and know how to protect them without over-reacting or under-reacting. Helen has had to gradually develop such skills – it didn't come "naturally".

H. There are many ways I have had problems in my ability to resolve problems or conflicts. My mother was very big on telling us how stupid we were, so I grew up thinking I was stupid, so whenever I was in a disagreement with someone I would go with their way of doing things because I thought they were smarter than me, including men who wanted to date me. Other things too, like people advising me to get into dangerous or unsuitable situations - I would go along with them because I thought, "I am stupid!" therefore, they must know more than I do. Only in the last three or four years have I realized that I can use my own judgment. It is not because I am stupid, it is often because they are.   And also, I would just do what other people wanted. I had a lack of boundaries, difficulty in setting my own boundaries. I was prone to have problems in work situations, trouble with authority figures. I would get petulant and resentful. Of course you don't like authority when the authority figures you know are so abusive. I would tell my boss off, and so then I often had to quit before I got fired. That was one of the first things I was able to change as a result of psychotherapy.

✓ Loss of capacity to individuate/separate/let go of the past

The compromised ability to handle emotions that accompanies childhood abuse leads to the inability to mourn. The inability to mourn means that it is very difficult to let go of the past. The past remains a living, haunting presence instead. Helen is beginning to understand that depriving herself of material goods, when she does not have to do so, is a form of reenactment, a way of not grieving for what has been lost in the past and will never be restored. She still reacts to people in the present as if her mother was talking to her and cannot fully differentiate her reactions in the present from the triggered memories of the hurtful past. It is as if her mother is still with her much of the time, even though she has not spoken to her parents in years. In this way, her mother could be dead but still continuing to influence her behavior in the present as if she were right by her side.

H. I have a big problem with people who are histrionic or have any kind of affect or phony behavior. I have to put my hands over my ears and walk away. My mother used to put on an act of being a good mother and if I am in a store and someone waits on me who is overly nice, I walk away. My mother had an affected air in public and then when she would come home she would be terribly nasty. I can't say "good morning" because it is too phony. I sometimes see it on TV and I have to walk out of the room. It is a sincerity factor, not an emotional factor. I can pick up lying too, but for years I never paid attention to it – I felt too stupid to know better. It has 100% to do with the other person's intention – that is the issue. It all goes back to my mother. I also live in the past by generally depriving myself – I haven't let go of that. There are a lot of things but it would take some time to think them out. For example, allowing myself to be successful at something. Often I will find myself sabotaging myself. I just feel uncomfortable, conflicted about being successful.

✓ Loss of educational/vocational opportunities

If, as a child, people who are older and bigger than you, repeatedly tell you that you are stupid, worthless, ugly, or crazy, the brainwashing takes hold and it becomes difficult, if not impossible, for you to face with confidence, the challenges that life brings. But every human being needs an identity and for too many adults abused as children, their identity becomes that of – as Samantha puts it – "a professional mental patient", or as Helen explains it, "a person too stupid to make good judgments". To relinquish such an identity and claim a new and better one, the survivor must be willing to tolerate the grief associated with all of the lost opportunities that will never be restored and Samantha has begun to wrestle with her own personal losses. Helen made some critical life decisions based on a desperate attempt to get from her parents what they were and are unable to give – love and acceptance. In doing so, she sacrificed many opportunities and has lost educational and vocational time that she can never get back.

S. I am just now getting in touch with all the losses of my adult life. I have no clue about all of the opportunities I have missed, all those lost years. I have been stuck for fifteen years. I have been a professional mental patient. I was forbidden to go away to college by my father even though I had full scholarships to Bucknell and Duquesne. But I did go to community college.

H. All my choices in life were formed by those experiences. I majored in something I didn't want to – chemistry - because I thought it could get my parents to like me. My father was a microbiologist and my mother was interested in environmental concerns. But I had no interest in chemistry, and I am an environmentalist but largely because I am a moral person. I would have majored in history and English. But I had to choose something that would get them to like me. That was not where my aptitude lay so it took me seven years instead of four. Now I am basically a writer. If I had had any sense of self I wouldn't have done that. I would have gone away to college, but I thought we were too poor. I have led a very restricted life, went to a state college. Not that my parents paid for anything, I did. But I didn't see how I could go from abject poverty to going into debt for college. When you don't have money you don't feel you can pay it back.

Somatization

Descriptions of the mourning process have always been strongly colored by the somatic presentation of grief. But our patients are grieving events from the long buried past and grieving for events that may not be considered "appropriate" causes for grief. Nonetheless, their descriptions of their own grieving processes reveal to us that when loss is worked through, the body does a great deal of the work along with the mind. The body remembers what the mind forgets, "the body keeps the score"[41]. In the case of chronic grief, this can mean the loss of health and well being. In the particular case of sexual abuse, it can also mean the loss of a healthy and fulfilling sexuality.

✓ Physical sensations associated with grief

Samantha talks about her experience of grief as utterly paralyzing and powerfully physical. She also must contend with her conflicts about crying, so typical of the abused and neglect child who is not allowed to express normal and appropriate affect without shame and punishment. As in Jodie's case, it is quite typical for victims of child abuse to describe themselves as having died or as being dead, or a part of them as being dead. The grieving process is one of restoring life, an internal sort of resurrection. Jodie also can now talk about the transformative process of moving the grief out of her psyche along with an associated feeling of badness and hopelessness, and into her body to be available to be worked through.

S. I am in the midst of it now. I feel heavy. Almost like I can seem ok, just feeling really sad and then I become paralyzed and unable to move. The people at the apartment try to get me out of bed but I cannot move. It gets into my body so much because I cannot get it out. They are trying to figure out how much is real and how much is isolation. I am holding back the tears because if they come they won't stop. I can't let anybody see me that way. My body gets so involved and that has surprised me – I feel so overstimulated and overwhelmed. My muscles start to spasm, my body feels like it is on fire, I have no clue how to get through that. It feels like there should be openings in the ends of my fingers so it can come out. I also have a thought disorder so if I get overstimulated, I can confuse reality with the sensations. Crying can bring a sense of relief.

J. The abuse started when I was two. When I was working with [her therapist] in a therapy session about another traumatic experience, I was holding my arm and he asked me why I was holding my arm and it was because I wanted to strike out at my grandfather, like my grandfather was in the room, but only in those ways, not in fantasy ways. Like a body memory. It was when my body was finally waking up for the first time and everything was being integrated and all these feelings were flooding in and I was still trying to find a balance between being completely overstimulated and being shutdown and dead and that was one of the things that came up.

---

[41] Van der Kolk, *The body keeps the score.*

J. Just recently I have been having experience with it physically, but in the past it was just an overwhelming sense of badness and hopelessness combined with that little inkling of wishing and hoping that things had been different.

✓ Loss of physical health and well-being

The state of chronic hyperarousal associated with post-traumatic stress disorder puts a terrible burden on the body as is demonstrated by the stress-related comorbid conditions that accompany trauma-related syndromes. We also know something about the impact of acute grief on physical health and mortality. But we are only beginning to comprehend what the impact of chronic and unresolved grief may be on the well being and health of the physical body, including the immune system. Jodie connects her previous eating disorder, stomach problems, and migraines to her sustained grief. Helen is convinced that her physical problems are related to chronic stress.

J. My body would always feel things, like I had an eating disorder and always had stomach problems and migraines. I never really knew what these symptoms were about because the grief was like something separate from me. Now I am feeling it in my body as well. Now it is all inside of me and I can feel the grief bubbling instead of just being outside of me somewhere. I felt physically disconnected and dead both spiritually and physically until I started to the work at Sanctuary. Only in the last two years have I been able to integrate the emotions and the physical aspects of myself.

H. I have my theories about the connection between stress, anxiety, and autoimmune disorders. I had a lot of anxiety and for most of my life didn't even realize I was anxious. I think that had physical effects. I had muscle spasms in my back that have gone away since I started therapy. I had endometriosis, which I think was related to anxiety, though doctors would say that's not possible. I had to be operated on to take care of that - a cyst was removed ten years ago. I have had hormone treatments and birth control pills to treat the problem. However anxiety affects your body. For awhile I was underweight, in my late teens, early twenties, because I was too anxious to eat.

✓ Loss of sexual function

Sexual abuse is particularly damaging to one's capacity to engage in loving, enjoyable and relational sexual behavior. Some sexually abused people avoid sexual relationships altogether, as in Jodie's case. Others engage in promiscuous sex without enjoying it or without being able to establish true intimacy. Helen, physically abused but not sexually abused used sex as a form of exchange because she was bewildered about the nature of establishing healthy and reciprocal relationships. As she is struggling to achieve a better state of health, she has stopped the former behavior but has not yet learned how to achieve an intimate, loving sexual relationship.

> *J.* I have not been able to have satisfying, successful physical relationships with either sex.

> *H.* Before I got into therapy my relationships with men weren't productive but at least I knew how to relate on a dysfunctional level, so I could relate to them. In my twenties I had lots of relationships. Because I was so deprived of basic necessities, when someone would do something for me, I felt I owed them something, including sex.

Alterations in Systems of meaning

Human beings are meaning-making animals. The structure and function of our minds compels us to make sense of our reality. In a very real way, we need to put everything we know and experience into some kind of logical, coherent, and integrated framework. Out of this framework, we develop a philosophy of life and derive the basic principles and assumptions that guide our decisions. It is exceedingly difficult to make sense of the world when you have not been cherished and protected as a child, when the very people who were supposed to love you were the people who abused, neglected, and abandoned you. This is particularly true when you grow up embedded in a society that routinely instructs you that children are to be cherished and protected. Victims of childhood abuse must grieve for the childhood that was stolen from them, that they are given to believe is their birthright. More subtle issues of neglect mean that survivors must grieve for what they did not have and should have been there. Early in their lives, victims of childhood abuse and neglect are exposed to the commission of deeds on the part of their caretakers that are deliberate, harmful and wrong. This early exposure to uncontrollable evil can have grave impact on the child's moral development and make discovering moral clarity even more difficult. As a result of all of these experiences, many adults abused as children make conscious or semi-conscious decisions not to "inflict" themselves on another vulnerable human being and so they sacrifice their own desire to have children and in doing so, their own future. The compounded result may be a joylessness, difficulty in finding purpose or meaning in life.

✓ **Loss of innocence, loss of childhood**

The innocence and protection that cherished children receive serve as a protective buffer, a stable foundation, for whatever storms a person must survive later in life. While maltreated children are young, they may not even recognize that their childhood was missing something. Only later as they grow and compare themselves to others do they come to recognize the pain of all they missed.

S. The most basic losses are easier to face. Like never being a kid, realizing all the jobs I had in my family related to protecting my parents and taking care of them and my siblings. Never being a kid – never having time to even think about me or how I felt.

J. The loss that has most affected me has been the loss of innocence in childhood. And the grief in coming to terms with the childhood that I never had and the hopes and dreams that were destroyed along with it that every child is supposed to have and carry into adulthood and grow out of in a natural way when they get their hard knocks in life, but not when they are two.

✓ **The loss of what wasn't there and should have been**

The losses one feels as a result of childhood neglect pose a particularly difficult problem because, as Jodie puts it, it is "grieving for what you don't know". It is hard to make sense of, hard to feel you have a right, hard to get anyone else to understand the sadness of losing something you never had. There are empty holes where meaning, purpose and fulfillment should be. There are things you can't do, ways of relating that are absent and arduous to discover as an adult.

J. Neglect is grieving for what you don't know. Some fantasy that what you don't know is supposed to be there. And then there is the fantasy of what you see in the movies or television of what other families show to the outside world, which of course isn't reality either. So you really don't have any idea, you just know something is missing, something that is not there that should have been, something is missing inside of you but you don't really know what it is.

H. To lose something you have to have it first. I never had a family member die that I was close to. But some people would say I experienced a loss in having no parental affection, no material support from my parents, no medical support, or a decent place to live. The basic fundamentals of living were not provided.

✓ **Loss of moral clarity**

A particularly challenging problem for many survivors is making some sense out of the role they were forced to play – actively or passively – in the violation of others. Here, Samantha touches on the choices she was compelled to make between self and others. Samantha was made to witness and be the victim of the most serious criminal behavior on the part of her father, while neither her mother, nor other bystanders, did anything to stop him. And for those of us who listen to these stories, even more puzzling is this question: How does a child like Helen or Samantha still develop concepts of ethics and morality growing up in conditions of such depravity?

S. He was sexually abusing me and he would threaten to hurt the other children if I didn't cooperate with him and let him do whatever he wanted

H. I am actually a very moral person. But why is that? Because one of my brothers turned out to be very immoral but he has turned himself around. My parents were like law-abiding sociopaths. You dare not do anything against the law, even things that people commonly do. Like cheating on financial aid packages. They were bluntly honest when they didn't have to be. So, I am on the highly responsible moral end – that has been my approach in life.

✓ **Loss of ability/desire/willingness to have children**

For most people, starting a family, being able to create a future is not perceived as a gift but a right. For abused children such a "right" can be instead funneled into the fervent desire not to reproduce, often for fear of reproducing the same trauma, grief and rage that the children have themselves experienced. If a child's parents took no joy in parenting, it is difficult to even comprehend the possibility of joyous engagement with a child. Helen begins by speaking very rationally about her decision not to have children, having previously admitted that her last significant relationship stopped seeing her when the man she was seeing ended it because he wanted to have children and she did not. As she describes her relationship with his nephews, she lights up and talks about how special they were, but when she actually imagines children for herself its, "not for me".

H. I know I don't want children. Or at least I don't think I do. It just does not appeal to me. I find nothing attractive about that scenario. I am not really sure why. I know one factor is that I dislike the loss of freedom involved. But the other reason is that it seems like a dreadful experience. I don't see kids as being appealing types of people. They seem to have negative attributes about them. I did meet a few kids in my life that I really liked, including my ex-boyfriend's nephews. They were really cute but that does not sway my opinion. When I imagine my own, it's not for me.

✓ Loss of purpose, meaning, joy in life, will to live

Samantha describes the utter emptiness of her life before she got into treatment and contrasts that later with how much better she feels. Helen describes her recognition that she is "stuck" between being dysfunctional and being functional, as she calls it, still not feeling much purpose or joy in her life. But it is Rebecca who is most revealing about her experiences of neglect and how she remains unable to find much purpose in living, to view her life as a precious gift.

S. There was nothing else, nothing else but self-abuse.

H. Basically, the reason I got into therapy was because I was having trouble making career decisions, though I had some insight based on watching TV that my family was dysfunctional. But then I realized how screwed up I was, I couldn't keep a job, my friends were crazy, I had no focus in my life. So what happened was, I was in therapy for a long time and it helped me learn to relate to society better, and I realized that I was out of focus and in disarray. And it helped me understand just how much in disarray. I am going from being dysfunctional but I'm not functional yet. I am in the middle, so I don't feel much purpose and joy – because I am stuck there.

R. As a result of the neglect I experienced as a child, I am unable to "view life as a gift" but instead I experience life as a burden that I didn't ask for.

Process of Recovery

Samantha, Jodie and Heather are all very different people, with different problems, coming from very varied backgrounds. But all three are in the process of recovery. They, as well as others, have helped us begin to understand the nature of that process and some of the tasks that must be completed, particularly as these tasks relate to the grieving process.

Recognizing the problem

People suffering from chronic, unresolved grief can present for treatment in many different ways. The most obvious and probably frequent manifestation is chronic depression that responds only partially or episodically to antidepressant medications. These patients are high utilizers of psychiatric and medical services, repeatedly seeking out some kind of direction or relief.

Because of current changes in the health care system minimizing any form of therapy except medication, these patients are likely to receive inadequate or poor care. Chronic suicidality and a preoccupation with death may be indicators of the same problem. It is not uncommon for patients to make early progress in treatment and then "hit the wall" of grief without knowing that is what is happening. Progress in treatment slows, the patient appears to be continually circling around the same issues that go nowhere, and the therapist may becomes increasingly frustrated, bored, and angry. The resort to a change in medication or adding medications is a frequent response to this situation.

Chronic somatic complaints often accompanied by the overuse or abuse of prescription pain medications is common. When physical symptoms are a manifestation of unresolved grief, the pattern may be one of "doctor hopping" or drug-seeking while the person and their health care providers seek a physical solution to a nonphysical problem. The result is bound to be an increasing level of frustration, chronicity, and compounded rage on the part of everyone involved.

Continuing to behaviorally reenact negative relationships despite insight and a commitment to treatment can also be a sign that the survivor is avoiding taking on the task of grieving. The yawning dark chasm that grief represents may feel overwhelming, endless, a bottomless pit, particularly when those feelings are not identified as what they are − feelings of bereavement − and legitimized as part of the normal process of mourning. Here Jodie points out how important it was to have someone support but not interfere with, her process, someone wise enough to know that not all human problems can be fixed with a pill.

> *J.* In the process of my treatment, I was stuck for about three months. My doctor helped me so much. It looked like depression on the outside but on the inside I was doing all this processing and little bits and pieces would come out, of very distinct emotion and very compact emotion, but it looked on the outside as if I was depressed. Other people might have treated it with medicine to get me out of it but she knew I was going through the grieving stage, and I was. The internal processing that I was doing was leading me towards grieving and towards putting the pieces together. If I had been in a different program I don't know what would have happened because I felt very stuck. If the only treatment I had received was medication at the time, I could have been stuck there for years rather than months.

Experiencing the grief

The hardest part of the grieving process may be allowing the process to begin. People whose attachments have been disrupted are so ill-equipped to process loss and have confidence that the pain will come and will go again, that they often spend decades doing everything they can think of to avoid confronting the pain of the past. Having toyed around the edges of grief for so many years, they may view it as something they can keep at bay and never have to resolve, not fully realizing just how much the past is robbing them of a vibrant present. So the first task is letting the experience happen, feeling the enormity and uncontrolled nature of grief, and then, as Jodie has, coming to recognize that in struggling to control an act of nature, you are simply prolonging and being controlled by a process that would otherwise, pass on.

> *J.* It was more like a welling up from inside of very, very strong feelings – sadness and despair. But now I know that it is inside me and that it cannot control me and I can control it or work with it. I still have body reactions. I still have stomach problems. But I pretty much can know where it comes from. Writing about it helps a lot.

Loss of previous coping skills

Grieving for the past losses that accompany childhood abuse means giving up reliable coping skills. As long as the survivor is not safe with himself or herself, s/he cannot learn to manage affect and without learning how to safely manage affect, it is impossible to safely work through the grief. But this does mean sacrificing habits that have helped manage overwhelming affect for decades – things like drugs and alcohol, compulsive working, smoking, destructive eating behaviors, and as in Samantha's case, self-mutilation. Coming out the other end of the tunnel, Jodie is able to recognize how comfortable it was to repeat the predictable past, how safe even if it was miserable.

> *S.* Today, there was a group session. A younger person had overdosed as a manipulation and a lot of the group focused on self-harm and suicidal behavior. I couldn't stay for it. I was so upset because three and a half years ago I was a self-abuser and I made a commitment to no self-harm and that option is not available to me anymore. I got so sad and felt so alone in the group. I was the only one who totally gave it up. It's another loss. It's so much easier to cut yourself, to scratch and stop the feeling. If that was available to me, then I wouldn't be in pain now. I am not sure you can grieve without giving up the self-harm. If you haven't, there is really danger. The more subtle danger is having compartmentalized everything in my life and then I get stuck in another repetitive pattern, especially with a thought disorder.

> *J.* The unknown used to be very scary to me just because at least in my old patterns of reenactment I knew how I was going to react to things. I knew I was going to be left alone and that is just how it was going to be. So the only danger or fear I have now is, what is going to happen next, but it is more exciting than scary to me. Right now at least.

Fearing loss of attachments

For many adults who were abused as children, the key to recovery is the restitution of the capacity to attach. But in allowing oneself to attach there is also the fear of losing that precious attachment. Implicit in the process of therapy is that inevitable loss, because therapy cannot substitute for the creation of a long-lasting support system that you don't have to pay for. Samantha, having allowed herself to attach to her therapist, recognizes that the love is not unconditional. Her therapist has structured the relationship so that now, for Samantha to continue with the relationship, she has to value herself at least as much as the therapist does. Balanced properly, the fear of losing attachments, of losing a potentially better future than the awful past, can be a powerful incentive for positive change.

S. It wasn't until I decided I was going to live - that's what has made the difference. The thing that changed things was video work – I had tried to hang myself and came into the hospital. I was doing video work about my mother – her voice was so dominant and internalized that I could not separate from it. My doctor came back from vacation and found me in the hospital after trying to hang myself and she was totally pissed off. I knew I had to get pretty serious pretty quick. So I worked really hard at the video stuff, really hard.

Losing attachments

Recovery can mean losing attachments as well, and although the relationships may be highly pathological, they are all the person knows, and something is better than nothing. Jodie describes how working towards her own recovery necessitated getting out of the relationship she had. Helen describes, with some regret, how important it has been for her to be out of relationships altogether in order to avoid getting into more bad ones.

J. I had an unhealthy relationship when I first entered the Sanctuary. I think I probably wasn't in the process of fully grieving yet but in the process of trying to get to some recovery path and still somehow grieve the childhood I didn't have. I moved through that relationship and that person did not react very well to my becoming healthier.

H. I stopped talking to my parents. That was the biggest change. I haven't talked to them in over eight years. I have had to avoid getting into relationships while I try to figure out how a functional relationship works. So in the past six and a half years I have only dated for a year. I am avoiding relationships until I feel I am not so impaired, until I can figure out what I want and need. I guess my relationships with men before I got into therapy weren't productive but at least I knew how to relate on a dysfunctional level, so I could relate to them. Now I wish sometimes I could still because at least I could be relating to somebody.

Giving up the fantasy of restoration

Inside every adult abused as a child, there is a child hoping to be rescued, actively fantasizing about how different things will be someday. Continuing the symptomatic self-destructive behavior is a disguised way of holding on, of waiting for the rescue that never comes. Grieving for the losses of the past means giving up the fantasy that amends will be made, that the loveless parents will turn into loving ones, that innocence will be retrieved – the fantasy of restoration. Jodie describes that process of holding on, toying with the fantasy, and letting go, seeing in her sister an earlier version of herself. Samantha talks about the process of allowing herself to be overwhelmed by the grief as a fundamental part of being able to let go of the fantasy that her parents would ever be there for her and how critical her present therapeutic relationship was in helping her let go of that continuing engagement with them through her own self-harming behavior.

J. I find myself wavering once in a while about still wanting it to be, or wishing it had been, different. But overall, no, I have let it go. I can see my sister going through the same process. She hasn't been in therapy yet and she is still at the point of saying "wouldn't it be nice to move back to [the Midwest] where my parents are and stay in a little house in the back" – still looking to them for certain things that they are never going to be able to give.

S. We were talked about discharge for Monday. On Friday I got hysterical crying – I could not stop. The nurses started to panic. But my doctor told them to leave me alone, that it was something I needed to do. I was wailing. I was realizing that no matter what I do, my parents are not going to come through. I remembered when I had been anorexic at [another hospital]. The social worker who was working with me called my parents to try to get them involved and I heard them on the speakerphone saying not to bother them until the situation was grave. Through this feeling of overwhelming loss I felt in the hospital, I finally gave up on my parents. I thought of my mom's mom who had killed herself. The next day in the community, I felt like shit, I didn't want any help. My doctor challenged me and said that if I wanted to be like my parents, she didn't want any part of it, that as long as I keep hurting myself I am like my parents. That was the last time I did anything to hurt myself.

Working with the nonverbal

It may not be possible to resolve grief, particularly longstanding, unresolved, traumatic grief, through the use of verbal abilities alone. From what we now understand about the way the brain processes overwhelming experience, we need art, enactment, story and ritual to help us safely integrate the verbal and nonverbal aspects of our experience. As Samantha described earlier, the work she did using video therapy was vital to her progress and here Jodie touches on the importance of her artwork in surfacing feelings and making the entire experience available for verbal integration.

> **J.** It starts with just feelings and emotions and I do a lot of artwork as well. The trauma happened before I was verbal. It started just with putting a lot on paper with colors and shapes and then I became able to write the words. But it started just as dictating what was happening in my life and looking at it as an outside observer, as if I were a director or something. Finally I became integrated so I could talk as it was happening to me. But I still think in colors a lot. I think it will make me a better artist and a more integrated person.

The vital nature of social support

Social support throughout the grieving process is vital to the course of normal bereavement. Just as vital is the restoration of social support for the victims of grief that has been disenfranchised and stigmatized. Jodie talks about how vital it was for her to get validation of the work she was engaged in during the most deadened part of her grieving experience.

> **J.** The worst thing is not to got get validation that you are doing anything. I remember one day when my doctor showed me a graph that I was actually at the peak of doing the work and for someone like me that meant all the difference in the world. It was awful, feeling so down, to think that I was stuck for that long and not doing any work after all the work I had done. I felt like I was in the valley. There would be nothing worse than throwing more medicine at someone like that because you just feel like you aren't getting anywhere, like "Oh my God, I am back at the beginning and I am never going to get out of all this".

Making meaning

We now understand how vital it is for trauma survivors to make meaning out of their experience[42]. But making meaning out of an abusive childhood is a difficult task. Samantha survived with her integrity as a human being intact because she was intelligent and she had a vivid fantasy life in which people behaved differently and she modeled herself after the people that she did not know, but that she saw. Jodie is actively wrestling with her own sense of spirituality and her relationship with a higher power and with forgiveness.

---

[42] Janoff-Bulman, *Shattered Assumptions*

S. I can't make sense out of it. There were senseless acts of violence abuse, neglect, but they also crossed the line into making bad things happen. They created violence when it didn't have to happen. I want to make sense out of it. I think a lot of people lose their will to survive. All the time this was going on I knew I was different from the other kids. I knew it wasn't happening to other people. I knew our family was different, that people could not understand me because I was different. I created a life in my head that was a fantasy. The only way I could get to sleep was a fantasy of other families in my head, other brothers and sisters from other people I saw but could never approach. I created all kinds of scenarios like that. I dreamed it could be different. I was always aware of people and what they did. I always knew what was going on around me. I never miss a trick, I guess it is what you call hypervigilance. I would watch what other people did and the decisions they made, people who were passionate about things in their lives, their work, other things and that is what keeps me going. I want to have that kind of passion about things. Being a part of something deeper than routine and ritual. I have some ideas about educating people about misconceptions, misperceptions about people who are victimized and people who are trying to help. So many doctors told me you will never get better, you have this or that disease. I have the opportunity to contribute something other people can't - art, writing. There are times I don't use it for healing but just for fun, just to express myself.

J. Somehow I have actually only recently come to terms with an idea of God or spirituality. For the first time this weekend I looked up at the stars and thanked God for my family and at least the best they thought they could do at the time. I was raised Catholic, but I am not Catholic now, mostly because of issues with the Catholic Church. I have looked at many different things trying to find an organized religion that I can relate to and haven't really found anything yet. So I was just kind of thanking the universe, or the idea of God, unformed as yet. I guess I was thanking my parents despite all of their flaws that they still have now. They have finally managed to come together as a unit, far away from us, and have managed to make a go of it somehow. My father has been broken, he has not been able to find a job for four or five years. He's got migraines every day, but though this is awful to say, he is much more easy to be around, I can relate to him as a person now. My Mom is now the main breadwinner of the family so things have completely switched and she is finding it in her power somehow, although of course, she won't talk about it. She is still the meek person but she is finding some kind of self-confidence. It is interesting to see. My sister is turning into an interesting young woman, very caring, and my brother is as well and I was just thanking God for that.

J. It still doesn't make any sense to me. I still don't understand how anyone could do that to a child. I can understand how things can go through the generations and how my Mom and Dad had their own awful childhoods but at some point someone has to be accountable for it, somebody has to stop it. And I haven't really made sense of that yet.

Making sense of the intergenerational nature of abuse

Part of the struggle to make some meaning out of the abusive past is about the struggle to understand how, if not why, this could have happened. The automatic question that arises in some point on the road to recovery, is "what happened to my parents that they could have so mistreated me?" Jodie has learned that her abuser also had abused her mother, who suffered from childhood amnesia as well. Helen attributes much of her family pathology to her great-grandmother, an active participant in the Klu Klux Klan.

J. My abuser was my Mom's stepfather who also did things to her that I am just finding out. She doesn't remember a lot of her childhood but she remembers when she first got engaged to my Dad that there was a lot of alcohol in the family and her stepfather exposed himself to her when she was just getting engaged. Her mother found out and wanted to get her out of the house.

H. I was able to figure out something about why my parents behaved the way they did. My father was always putting me down for going to college, considered me selfish for going to college. He did that because he didn't want his children to succeed because they would see he was a failure. He gave the impression that failure was a badge of honor. If I got too successful I might figure out that he didn't really want it that way, that it was just a show he was putting on. My mother called me stupid because she was so incompetent. I met my father's mother and she was very abusive. My mother is a harder story but I know enough of the family history to know there was a lot of dysfunction. My great grandmother was in the women's auxiliary of the Klu Klux Klan. I heard stories about her. She used to go to lynchings, and kept momentos of them. When you have that in your history it is going to affect you. She was a terrible woman.

Moving on

As the grieving process progresses, the darkness begins to lift and survivors become involved in the process of moving on that is represented by the "F" in S.E.L.F. - "Future". Here Samantha compares her own progress to the absence of any change in her siblings while recognizing that there is always going to be pain. She can talk about how hard it is, and has been.

S. I think I have an uncanny sense of perception about people and integrity about people. When I see it I am drawn to it. I lost a lot but I really can't say what my life would have been like without it. All I know is that it is getting better, I look at my brothers and sisters but they are still addicted and not learning to feel and they are not where I am. As hard as it is, it is exciting self-discovery.

S. People don't get the grieving thing. There are always anniversaries, always reminders. No matter how far I get in my life I am always going to feel a heartache, a loss for the things I never even knew were available or couldn't get to because I was so sick. A lot of grieving for me, is that I never thought it would be this hard, I never realized how much work is involved in taking responsibility for myself, how much I have to struggle just to let people know how I really am. I never expected anything to be this hard. That is the kind of thing I would like to give to people for a week, just to know how difficult it is. To keep moving forward and to have them get it.

Transforming the pain

Ultimately, we hope that adult survivors of childhood abuse and neglect will be able to transform their pain into something of value to themselves and others, what Judy Herman has called a "survivor mission"[43]. Helen talks about how she believes that good has already come from bad in that she is proud of some characteristics that she has developed that she attributes to her abusive past. Jodie shares her creative aspirations and how her wish is to be able to change the world for children as a result of working through her own painful experiences.

H. I think there is always something to be said for every experience. I don't have a sense of entitlement that I know some people have and I am glad I don't and that comes from not having very much. I don't have the sense of materialism that other people have. I think that the insight you get from going through that experience and then evaluating the experience in therapy gives you insight about human nature I wouldn't otherwise have and gives me in the ability to apply it to other situations. I can deal with harsh situations better than the average person.

J. I can feel that I am on the verge of turning my experiences into something positive. For the first time I feel like I am grieving as an integrated person and it feels like there might be positive energy coming out of that. I remember talking to my therapists in the beginning about anger and grief and asking them why I couldn't turn it all into something positive right away, why can't I just take a shortcut? But you have to go through the intermediate shit before you can do that. I can feel I am on the verge of finally doing that. I think in terms of my creativity. I think it has affected my creativity. And I think in terms of what I want to do and being able to change the world – that sounds too idealistic – but to affect children's lives in a positive way. I don't think I could have done it in the same way if I hadn't gone through it myself.

---

[43] Herman, *Trauma and Recovery*

Conclusion

Grief is one of the natural outcomes of human attachment. Predictably then, anything that interferes with the course of attachment produces the potential for loss and bereavement. The more trauma the person has experienced, the more likely it is that traumatic and complicated grieving will be involved. Individually and socially we are relatively comfortable with supporting the mourning process when someone has literally died. But the losses attendant upon child abuse and neglect are not usually about literal death, although actual death – particularly traumatic death - of an attachment figure can compound and complicate other losses. Instead, the losses that adults must recapitulate and work through in order to recover, are long delayed, sometimes tangible, but at other times, metaphorical, spiritual, or moral losses. In this chapter I have reviewed those losses utilizing the testimony of several adult survivors who volunteered to share their experiences. Finding a new life path always means shedding the old, and the recovery process involves loss as well if the survivor is to move past the fragmentation of childhood trauma – is to get "beyond the beveled mirror" and heal.

References

Adam, K. S. "Suicidal Behavior and Attachment: A Developmental Model." In *Attachment in Adults: Clinical and Developmental Perspectives.*, edited by M. B. Sperling and W. H. Berman, 275-98. New York: The Guilford Press, 1994.

Allen, I. M. "Ptsd among African Americans." In *Ethnocultural Aspects of Posttraumatic Stress Disorder: Issues, Research, and Clinical Applications*, edited by A. Marsella, M. J. Friedman, E. Gerrity and R. M. Scurfield. Washington, D. C.: American Psychological Association, 1996.

Anderson, E. "Living Hard by the Code of the Streets." *Philadelphia Inquirer*, May 15 1994, C7.

Baer, J.. "As Bullets Fly, Bodies Drop, Where's Street?" *Philadelphia Daily News*, August 14, citing statistics from Philadelphia Police Department 2006.

Bazelon Center for Mental Health Law. *Disintegrating Systems: The State of States' Public Mental Health Systems*: Bazelon Center for Mental Health Law, 2001.

———. "Get It Together: How to Integrate Physical and Mental Health Care for People with Serious Mental Disorders." Washington, D.C.: Bazelon Center for Mental Health Law, 2004.

Becker, M.G., J.S. Hall, C. M. Ursic, S. Jain, and D. Calhoun. "Caught in the Crossfire: The Effects of a Peer-Based Intervention Program for Violently Injured Youth." *Journal of Adolescent Health* 34, no. 3 (2004): 177-83.

Berman, L. H. "The Effects of Living with Violence. ." *Journal of the American Academy of Psychoanalysis* 20, no. 4 (1992): 671-5.

Bills, L. J. , and S. L. Bloom. "From Chaos to Sanctuary: Trauma-Based Treatment for Women in a State Hospital Systems." In *Women's Health Services: A Public Health Perspective*, edited by Bruce Labotsky Levin, Andrea K. Blanch and Ann Jennings. Thousand Oaks, CA: Sage Publications, 1998.

Bloom, S. L. *Creating Sanctuary: Toward the Evolution of Sane Societies*. New York: Routledge, 1997.

———. "The Sanctuary Model of Organizational Change for Children'S Residential Treatment." *Therapeutic Community: The International Journal for Therapeutic and Supportive Organizations* 26, no. 1 (2005): 65-81.

Bloom, S. L., J. F. Foderaro, and R. A. Ryan. *S.E.L.F.: A Trauma-Informed, Psychoeducational Group Curriculum*: Available at www.sanctuaryweb.com, 2006.

Bloom, Sandra, and Michael Reichert. *Bearing Witness : Violence and Collective Responsibility*. Binghamton NY: Haworth Press, 1998.

"Blueprint for a Safer Philadelphia." http://www.phillyblueprint.com/index.cfm?page=Documentary.   Accessed March 10, 2007. Philadelphia: MEE Productions Inc., 2007.

Boss, P. *Loss. Trauma, and Resilience: Therapeutic Work with Ambiguous Loss*. New York: W. W. Norton, 2006.

Bowlby, J. *Attachment and Loss, Volume Iii: Loss, Sadness and Depression.*, 1980.

———. "Developmental Psychiatry Comes of Age." *American Journal of Psychiatry,145:1-10.* 145 (1988): 1-10.

———. "Grief and Mourning in Infancy and Early Childhood." *The Psychoanalytic Study of the Child* 15 (1960): 9-52.

———. "Pathological Mourning and Childhood Mourning." *Journal of the American Psychoanalytic Association* 11 (1963): 500-41.

Breslau, N., and G. C. Davis. "Posttraumatic Stress Disorder in an Urban Population of Young Adults: Risk Factors for Chronicity." *American Journal of Psychiatry* 149, no. 5 (1992): 671-75.

Breslau, N., G. C. Davis, P. Andreski, and E. Peterson. "Traumatic Events and Posttraumatic Stress Disorder in an Urban Population of Young Adults." *Arch Gen Psychiatry* 48, no. 3 (1991): 216-22.

Brooks-Gunn, J., and G. J. Duncan. "The Effects of Poverty on Children." *Future Child* 7, no. 2 (1997): 55-71.

Bureau of Justice Statistics. "Prisoners in 2004." Washington, D.C.: U. S. Department of Justice, 2005.

Canada, G. *Fist Stick Knife Gun: A Personal History of Violence in America.* Boston: Beacon Press, 1995.

Centers for Disease Control and Prevention. "Web-Based Injury Statistics Query and Reporting System (Wisqars) [Online]." (2006) [cited 06 Feb 8]. Available from: URL: www.cdc.gov/ncipc/wisqars.: National Center for Injury Prevention and Control, 2006.

Cicchetti, D., and M. Lynch. "Failures in the Expectable Environment and Their Impact on Individual Development: The Case of Child Maltreatment." In *Developmental Psychopathology, Volume 2: Risk, Disorder, and Adaptation,* edited by D. Cicchetti and D. J. Cohen. New York: Wiley, 1995.

"The Clinical Supervisor. Vol. 18, No. 2. Publication: New York : Haworth Press, Year: 1999 Description: 210, 19 P. ; 22 Cm."

Cooper, W. *Behold a Pale Horse.* Sedona, AZ: Light Publishing, 1991.

Doka, K. *Living with Grief after Sudden Loss.* Philadelphia: Taylor & Francis, 1996.

Doka, K., and J. Davidson. *Living with Grief: Who We Are, How We Grieve.* Washington, D.C.: Brunner/Mazel, 1998.

Edwards, Valerie J, Robert F Anda, Vincent J Felitti, and Shanta R Dube. "Adverse Childhood Experiences and Health-Related Quality of Life as an Adult." In *Health Consequences of Abuse in the Family: A Clinical Guide for Evidence-Based Practice,* edited by Kathleen A Kendall-Tackett, 81-94. Washington: American Psychological Association, 2004.

Ellason, J. W., and C. A. Ross. "Childhood Trauma and Psychiatric Symptoms." *Psychol Rep* 80, no. 2 (1997): 447-50.

Engel, G. L. "A Challenge for Medical Research." *Psychosomatic Medicine,* 23 (1961): 18-22.

Felitti, V. J., R. F. Anda, D. Nordenberg, D. F. Williamson, A. M. Spitz, V. Edwards, M. P. Koss, and J. S. Marks. "Relationship of Childhood Abuse and Household Dysfunction to Many of the Leading Causes of Death in Adults. The Adverse Childhood Experiences (Ace) Study." *Am J Prev Med* 14, no. 4 (1998): 245-58.

Figley, C. R., B. E. Bride, and N. Mazza. *Death and Trauma: The Traumatology of Grieving.* New York: Brunner/Mazel, 1999.

Figley, CR. *Traumatology of Grieving: Conceptual, Theoretical and Treatment Foundations.* New York: Brunner/Mazel, 1999.

Foderaro, JF. "Creating a Nonviolent Environment: Keeping Sanctuary Safe." In *In Violence: A Public Health Menace and a Public Health Approach,* edited by SL Bloom, 57-82. London: Karnac Books, 2001.

Fonagy, P., M. Steele, H. Steele, T. Leight, R. Kennedy, G. Mattoon, and M. Target. "Attachment, the Reflective Self, and Borderline States: The Predictive Specificity of the Adult Attachment Interview and Pathological Emotional Development." In *Attachment Theory: Social, Developmental, and Clinical Perspectives*, edited by S Goldberg, R. Muir and J. Kerr, 233-78. Hillsdale, NJ: The Analytic Press, 1995.

Garrett, P., N. Ng'andu, and J. Ferron. "Poverty Experiences of Young Children and the Quality of Their Home." *Child Development* 65 (1994): 331-45.

Goffman, E. *Stigma: Notes on the Management of Spoiled Identity.* New York: Simon & Schuster, 1963.

Grady, K. T. "Posttraumatic Stress Disorder and Comorbidity: Recognizing the Many Faces of Ptsd." *Journal of Clinical Psychiatry,* 58, no. Supplement 9 (1997): 12-15.

Greenspan, M. *Healing through the Dark Emotions: The Wisdom of Grief, Fear and Despair.* Boston: Shambhala, 2004.

Haile, E. S., J. Lowy, and D. Pennington. " Lethal Lou's: Profile of a Rogue Gun Dealer - Lou's Loan of Upper Darby, Pennsylvania. ." Washington, D.C.: Brady Center to Prevent Gun Violence, 2006.

Hardy, K. V., ed. *African American Experience and the Healing of Relationships in Family Therapy: Exploring the Field's Past, Present and Possible.* Edited by D. Denborough: Dulwich Centre Publications http://www.dulwichcentre.comau/kenhardyarticle.html, 2001.

Hardy, K. V., and T. A. Laszyloffy. *Teens Who Hurt: Clinical Interventions to Break the Cycle of Adolescent Violence.* New York: The Guilford Press, 2005.

Henry, K., and J.G. Homes. "Childhood Revisited: The Intimate Relationships of Individuals from Divorced and Conflict-Ridden Families." In *Ttachment Theory and Close Relationships*, edited by J. A. Simpson and W.S. Rholes, 280-316. New York: Guilford Press, 1998.

Herman, JL. *Trauma and Recovery.* New York: Basic Books, 1992.

Jacobs, S. *Traumatic Grief: Diagnosis, Treatment and Prevention.* New York: Brunner/Mazel, 1999.

James, B. *Handbook for Treatment of Attachment Trauma Problems in Children.* New York: Lexington Books, 1994.

Janoff-Bulman, R. *Shattered Assumptions: Towards a New Psychology of Trauma.* New York: Free Press, 1992.

Kaiser Daily Health Policy Report. "15,000 Children Incarcerated Because of Lack of Mental Health Treatment in 2003." *Kaisernetwork.org*, July 8 2004.

———. *15,000 Children Incarcerated Because of Lack of Mental Health Treatment in 2003, http://www.Kaisernetwork.Org/Daily_Reports/Rep_Index.Cfm?Dr_Id=2460* 6, *July 8* 2004 [cited.

Karen, R. *Becoming Attached: First Relationships and How They Shape Our Capacity to Love*. New York: Oxford University Press, 1994.

Kessler, R. C., A. Sonnega, E. Bromet, M. Hughes, and C. B. Nelson. "Posttraumatic Stress Disorder in the National Comorbidity Survey." *Arch Gen Psychiatry* 52, no. 12 (1995): 1048-60.

Khan, M. M. R. "The Concept of Cumulative Trauma." *Psychoanalytic Study of the Child* 18 (1963): 286-306.

Koss, M. P., P. G. Koss, and W. J. Woodruff. "Deleterious Effects of Criminal Victimization on Women's Health and Medical Utilization." *Arch Intern Med* 151, no. 2 (1991): 342-7.

Krystal, H. *Integration and Self Healing: Affect, Trauma, Alexithymia*. Hillsdale, NJ: Analytic Press, 1988.

Kupers, T. A. "Mental Health in Men's Prisons." In *Prison Masculinities*, edited by D. Sabo, T. A. Kupers and W. London, 192-97. Philadelphia: Temple University Press, 2001.

Leserman, J., Z. Li, D. A. Drossman, T. C. Toomey, G. Nachman, and L. Glogau. "Impact of Sexual and Physical Abuse Dimensions on Health Status: Development of an Abuse Severity Measure." *Psychosom Med* 59, no. 2 (1997): 152-60.

Liotti, G. "Disorganization of Attachment as a Model for Understanding Dissociative Pathology." In *Attachment Disorganization*, edited by J. Solomon and C. George. New York: The Guilford Press, 1999.

———. "Disorganized/Disoriented Attachment in the Psychotherapy of the Dissociative Disorders." In *Attachment Theory: Social, Developmental, and Clinical Perspectives.*, edited by S. Goldberg, R. Muir and J. Kerr, 343-65. Hillsdale, NJ: The Analytic Press, 1995.

Lyons, J. S., D. R. Baerger, J. E. Quigley, and E. Griffin. "Mental Health Service Needs of Juvenile Offenders: A Comparison of Detention, Incarceration, and Treatment Settings." *Children's Services: Social Policy, Research, and Practice* 4 (2001): 69-85.

Main, M., and E. Hess. "Parents' Unresolved Traumatic Experiences Are Related to Infant Disorganized Attachment Status: Is Frightened and/or Frightening Parental Behavior the Linking Mechanism?." In *Attachment in the Preschool Years: Theory, Research, and Intervention*, edited by M.T. Greenberg, D. Cicchetti and EM. Cummings, 161-82. Chicago: University of Chicago Press, 1990.

Mayberry, R. M., F. Mili, and E. Ofili. "Racial and Ethnic Differences in Access to Medical Care." *Medical Care Research and Review* 57, no. Suppl1 (2000): 108-45.

Miller, L. "Young Lives Lost." *The Philadelphia Tribune* 2006, www.phila-tribune.com/channel/inthenews/092606/behindbards3.asp, accessed March 9, 2007.

Moran, R. "Living, Dying in Phila.'S 'Iraq' - a Mother Is Shot to Death, and a Community Is Torn." *Philadelphia Inquirer*, July 20 2006, A01.

National Center for Health Statistics. *Health, United States, 2006, with Chartbook of Trends in the Health of Americans.* Hyattsville, MD: Centers for Disease Control and Prevention, 2006.

Ochberg, F. M. *Post-Traumatic Therapy and Victims of Violence.* New York: Brunner/Mazel, 1988.

Perry, B. D., and M. Szalavitz. *The Boy Who Was Raised as a Dog: What Traumatized Children Can Teach Us About Loss, Love, and Healing.* New York: Basic Books, 2006.

Poussaint, Alvin F., and Amy Alexander. *Lay My Burden Down: Unraveling Suicide and the Mental Health Crisis among African-Americans.* Boston: Beacon Press, 2000.

President's New Freedom Commission on Mental Health. *Interim Report* 2002 [cited September 17 2005].

Prevention, Centers for Disease Control and. "Web-Based Injury Statistics Query and Reporting System (Wisqars) [Online]." (2006) [cited 06 Feb 8]. Available from: URL: www.cdc.gov/ncipc/wisqars.: National Center for Injury Prevention and Control, 2006.

Putnam, F. W., and P. K. Trickett. "Child Sexual Abuse: A Model of Chronic Trauma." *Psychiatry* 56, no. 1 (1993): 82-95.

Rando, T. A. *Treatment of Complicated Mourning.* Champaign, IL: Research Press, 1993.

Rich, J. A., and C. M. Grey. "Pathways to Recurrent Trauma among Young Black Men: Traumatic Stress, Substance Use, and the "Code of the Street"." *American Journal of Public Health* 95, no. 5 (2005): 815-24.

Rich, J. A., and M. Ro. *A Poor Man;S Plight: Uncovering the Disparity in Men's Health.* Vol. 30. Battle Creek, MO: W. K. Kellogg Foundation, 2002.

Rich, J. A., and L. M. Sullivan. "Correlates of Violence Assault among Young Male Primary Care Patients." *Journal of Health Care for the Poor and Underserved* 12, no. 1 (2001): 103-12.

Rivard, J.C., S. L. Bloom, D. McCorkle, and R. Abramovitz. "Preliminary Results of a Study Examining the Implementation and Effects of a Trauma Recovery Framework for Youths in Residential Treatment." *Therapeutic Community: The International Journal for Therapeutic and Supportive Organizations* 26, no. 1 (2005): 83-96.

Roberts, N., and P. Noller. "The Associations between Adult Attachment and Couple Violence: The Roles of Communication Patterns and Relationships

Satisfaction." In *Attachment Theory and Close Relationships*, edited by J. A. Simpson and W. S. Rholes, 317-51. New York: The Guildford Press, 1998.

Roth, S., E. Newman, D. Pelcovitz, B. van der Kolk, and F. S. Mandel. "Complex Ptsd in Victims Exposed to Sexual and Physical Abuse: Results from the Dsm-Iv Field Trial for Posttraumatic Stress Disorder." *J Trauma Stress* 10, no. 4 (1997): 539-55.

Sampson, R. J., and J. H. Laub. "Urban Poverty and the Family Context of Delinquency: A New Look at Structure and Process in a Classic Study." *Child Development* 65 (1994): 523-40.

Simon, C. "Bringing the War Home." *Psychotherapy Networker* January/February (2007): 32-33.

Sims, D. W., B. A. Bivins, F. N. Obeid, H. M. Horst, V. J. Sorensen, and J. J. Fath. "Urban Trauma: A Chronic Recurrent Disease." *J Trauma* 29, no. 7 (1989): 940-6; discussion 46-7.

Smalley, S. "Hub's Rise in Deadly Violence Reflects Disturbing Us Change." *Boston Globe*, March 9 2007.

Smedley, B.D., A. Y. Stith, and A.R. Nelson. "Unequal Treatment: Confronting Racial and Ethnic Disparities in Health Care." Washington, D.C.: Institute of Medicine, 2002.

Solomon, S., and R. T. Davidson. "Trauma: Prevalence; Impairment; Service Use; and Cost." *Journal of Clinical Psychiatry* 58 (Suppl 9) (1997): 511.

Sprang, G., and J. McNeil. *The Many Faces of Bereavement: The Nature and Treatment of Natural, Traumatic and Stigmatized Grief*. New York: Brunner/Mazel, 1995.

Staub, E. "Cutural-Societal Roots of Violence: The Examples of Genocidal Violence and of Contemporary Youth Violence in the United States." *American Psychologist* 51, no. 2 (1996): 117-32.

Teplin, L. A., K. M. Abram, G. M. McClelland, M. K. Duncan, and A. A. Mericle. "Psychiatric Disorders in Youth in Juvenile Detention." *Archives of General Psychiatry* 59 (2002): 1133-43.

Tolan, P. H. , and D. Henry. "Patterns of Psychopathology among Urban Poor Children: Comorbidity and Aggression Effects." *Journal of Consulting and Clinical Psychology* 64, no. 5 (1996): 1094-99.

Tuakli-Williams, J., and J. Carrillo. "The Impact of Psychosocial Stressors on African-American and Latino Preschoolers." *Journal of the National Medical Association* 87, no. 7 (1995): 473-78.

United States Public Health Service Office of the Surgeon General. "Mental Health: Culture, Race, and Ethnicity: A Supplement to Mental Health: A Report of the Surgeon General." Rockville, MD: Department of Health and Human Services, U.S. Public Health Service, 2001.

Vaidya, Y. "What's Behind a New Wave of Crime." *The Pennsylvania Gazette* 2007, http://www.upenn.edu/gazette/0107/gaz06.html, January -February,Accessed March 10, 2007.

Van der Kolk, B. "The Body Keeps the Score: Approaches to the Psychobiology of Posttraumatic Stress Disorder." In *Traumatic Stress: The Effects of Overwhelming Experience on Mind, Body and Society.*, edited by Van der Kolk B., L. Weisaeth and McFarlane A. C., 214-41. New York: Guilford, 1996.

Van der Kolk, B. A., P. Brown, and O. Van der Hart. "Pierre Janet on Post-Traumatic Stress." *Journal of Traumatic Stress* 2 (1989): 365-78.

Walker, E. A., A. Gelfand, W. J. Katon, M. P. Koss, M. Von Korff, D. Bernstein, and J. Russo. "Adult Health Status of Women with Histories of Childhood Abuse and Neglect." *Am J Med* 107, no. 4 (1999): 332-9.

Weil, J. L. *Early Deprivation of Empathic Care.* Madison: International Universities Press, 1992.

Weischselbaum, S. " Weischselbaum, a Quest to Save Youth at Risk. Philadelphia Daily News, January 2, 2007." *Philadelphia Daily News*, January 2 2007, www.philly.com/mld/philly/entertainment/family_guide/16364558.htm, accessed March 9, 2007.

———. "Youth-Crime System Broken." *Philadelphia Daily News* 2007, www.philly.com/mld/philly/entertainment/family_guide/16857074.htm, accessed March 9, 2007.

West, M. A., and S. Keller. "Psychotherapy Strategies for Insecure Attachment in Personality Disorders." In *Attachment in Adults: Clinical and Developmental Perspectives.*, edited by M. B. Sperling and W. H. Berman, 313-30. New York: Guilford Press, 1994.

Zinner, E. S., and M. B. Williams. "Summary and Incorporation: A Reference Frame for Community Recovery and Restoration." In *When a Community Weeps: Case Studies in Group Survivorship*, edited by E. S. Zinner and M. B. Williams, 237-64. Philadelphia: Brunner/Mazel, 1999.

Zinner, ES, and MB Williams. *When a Community Weeps: Case Studies in Group Survivorship.* New York: Brunner/Mazel, 1999.

Zulueta, de F. *From Pain to Violence, the Roots of Human Destructiveness.* London: Whurr, 1993.

CHAPTER TWO

UNTANGLING INTANGIBLE LOSS IN THE LIVES OF TRAUMATIZED CHILDREN AND ADOLESCENTS

KENNETH V. HARDY, PH.D.

Eighteen years old Tara sat stoically in my office appearing to stare off into a far away unnamed place. Her often soft-spoken voice was much lower than usual, appearing slightly above a whisper. As she sat motionless and emotionless, she spoke to me in a way that was reminiscent of the speech of someone speaking while heavily sedated with medication. It was Tara's body sitting in my office, it was Tara's voice speaking, and it was Tara's words methodically slipping through her lips yet her mind, body, and words all seemed disconnected from each other. It was September 12, 2007, the sixth year anniversary of the terrorists' attacks on the World Trade Center in New York, New York. Tara's father Seymour worked on the 40th floor of Tower 2 and along with many others died when it collapsed to the ground. Seymour's remains have never been recovered although his wedding ring bearing the initials 'T&S' for his wife and Tara's mother, "Teresa and Seymour" was recovered from the rubble of "Ground Zero" eights months following the attacks.

Tara has been in and out of therapy since confronted with the death of her father. Over the past several years, she has had good moments as well as moments of deep disfiguring despair. She has been a model student academically at times, only to have her achievements overshadowed by multiple school suspensions for drug use; She has been active and influential mentor to her younger siblings later having her image tarnished by several arrests and an adjudication for shoplifting; she has been an emotionally present daughter, actively participating in the family and she has been a distant, disaffected, and disconnected member of the family who at times has been a virtual stranger. Needless to say, Tara's life has been a tumultuous roller coaster ride. The anniversary 'celebrations' acknowledging the events of September 11th, 2001 do little to help stabilize Tara's life. In fact the anniversary celebrations have been devastating for her. As she has mentioned several times in therapy, "every

September I have to watch my Mom relive the entire ordeal over and over again...it is heartbreaking to see her sadness and to know that there is nothing that I or anyone can do to make things better for her... we can never get away from it....the images, the memories, the waiting, and more waiting." Although she was quite ambivalent about it, Tara's thought her mother's remarriage would help.

Teresa remarried in 2003 but was divorced two years later. Teresa and husband Henry, according to Tara, had a loving but conflictual relationship that unfortunately often involved the children (Tara's brother Seth, Henry's daughter Maya, and Tara). Tara believed that Henry was jealous of her mother's relationship with she and Seth, and he often accused Teresa of mistreating (his daughter) Maya. After a protracted period of intense conflict, Henry (and Maya) moved out of the household until the divorce between he and Teresa was finalized in 2003. Tara admitted that she was very happy when Henry moved out although she missed Maya for whom she was a big sister, surrogate mother, and mentor. While Tara was happy that Henry was out of their lives, she noted that she did worry about what the change would mean for her mother, who now had lost two husbands in six years.

Children and Loss

As demonstrated by the aforementioned vignette, Tara's life, from a very early age, was inundated with loss. Although loss was pervasive in her life it was seldom at the forefront of discussions regarding "what's wrong with Tara?" Beneath the clinical hypotheses about her "oppositional and defiant" 'conduct disordered' 'addictive personality disordered' behavior was little to no examination of the losses that she had endured during the very formative stages of her young life. Although central to much of her underlying disturbing and inexplicable behavior, the vast losses that characterized her life was seldom a point of serious inquiry. If it were not for the death of her father and all of the publicity surrounding September 11th, it is conceivable that this loss probably would have only received scant attention particularly as it related to many of her underlying struggles. The more egregious Tara's acting out behavior became, the more invisible the significant impact of losses in her life became to all who endeavored to help her.

Unfortunately, Tara's story is all too common for many children and adolescents. Regardless of race, class, gender, or sexual orientation, loss is a salient issue in the lives of most children and adolescents today. The contemporary world of young people is inundated with their exposure to loss. The everyday lives of most children and adolescents are severely affected by loss. Whether the loss is experienced directly, as in Tara's case, or vicariously as in the case of children who experience it through watching or hearing on television about young children, often girls, who have been abducted.

The internet and cable television have increased children and adolescents' exposure to violence, tragedy, and trauma in ways that did not exist just ten years ago. Whether it is watching thousands of displaced children and families scramble for their lives during the aftermath of Hurricane Katrina, grief stricken families trying to recover from the horrors of the September 11th Terrorists attacks, or crowds of school age children desperately seeking shelter following yet another random mass murder school shooting—children's exposure to violence, tragedy, trauma, and ultimately loss is inescapable. Even beyond the world of television and the entertainment industry, countless numbers of children today, especially those in urban settings are exposed almost daily to loss associated with violence and/or socio-cultural oppression. It is increasingly difficult to even find elementary school age students who have not experienced a direct loss attributable to violence or don't know of someone who has.

Despite the prevalence of loss in the lives of children and adolescents, it is seldom acknowledged or addressed. Teachers, parents, and surprisingly enough, many mental health professionals find it challenging to engage children and adolescents into meaningful and transformative discourse about loss. The reasons why children and adolescents' losses are often greeted with silence are varied and complicated. Some of the critical reasons why loss is often unacknowledged and unaddressed with young people are as follows:

It is better not to bring it up: The altruism rationale—Many adults believe that if children don't voice concerns regarding a loss that "it is better to not bring it up." As one father who was a licensed Clinical Psychologist once asserted in therapy: ' I never bring up his mother's death (referring to his teenage son, Martin) because he seems to be handling it well and I don't want to make things worse." I have also had recently divorced parents to echo the exact same words in offering an explanation why they never initiate a discussion about divorce and loss. This rationale often masks some of the other reasons why conversations about loss are often avoided with children and adolescents. For example, many adults avoid conversations about loss because they often trigger their unresolved and unaddressed loss related issues.

Loss is too painful to talk about: The Unconscious rationale—Talking about loss often evokes very strong emotional reactions, especially if a loss has not been properly addressed, grieved, or resolved. Living with loss (McGoldrick, 2004) is a way of life that affects everyone. When a significant loss has not been acknowledged, properly grieved, or given appropriate time to heal, the emotional underpinning of the experience remains raw and sensitive like an unhealed physical wound. The only way that pain and re-injury can be circumvented is to avoid the wound coming in contact with anything that is capable of reopening it. Loss and the underlying emotional pain attached to it often works the same way. When one has not adequately dealt with the emotional pain associated with a loss, initiating conversations or bearing witness to the pain of someone else's loss becomes an excruciatingly painful and difficult feat to accomplish. Since adults, especially those of us who are teachers, parents, and/or therapists, are expected to be the pillars of emotional strength and support for young children and adolescents, giving way to the vulnerability of one's unresolved loss in the presence of youth who are hurting is not only difficult but potentially threatening as well. Rather than embrace the emotional intensity that a heart-to heart conversation about loss would engender, unconscious avoidance is easier. When loss is too painful to talk about it may be unconsciously avoided either by not talking about it or by failing to see it. Either way the result is the same: avoidance of engagement.

Children are Strong: The Resilience Rationale—There are times when adults' failure to constructively address issues of loss with children and adolescents is precipitated by either an over estimation of young people's capacity for resilience or an under estimation of the emotional and psychological impact of trauma on their lives. Wolin and Wolin (1993) have written prolifically about the resilience of children and adolescents. Children adapting to and overcoming incredible adverse life circumstances have been very well documented in the literature. Thus, the point here is not to debate whether children are resilient or not. Instead, the issue is one of degree. The anticipated resilience of children should not be a license to avoid having painful and difficult conversations with children about matters that matter. Loss matters. Consider the following event that occurred at a High School in a large Mid-Western city following a school shooting:

'Shootings Are Nothing New'

I, along with my School Base Consultation Team, was retained by The Mid-Western City Schools Board of Education in response to a school shooting that resulted in several fatalities with a host of other students seriously injured. One of the first things we noticed upon our arrival at the school was the hardened, dark red, almost black-like blood lodged between the cracks in the tile floor. The site of the blood prompted one of my colleagues to ask: "Is that blood"? The school social worker replied: "yes, it's from the shooting…we have had blood splattered everywhere….it has been a challenge to get to it all…everytime we think we have completely sanitized the place we find blood remnants in places where we least expected to find it. I then asked Mr. Godby, the Principal, if classes or school had been suspended in light of the crisis. He turned to me, looking at me with utter amazement, disdain, and incredulousness. He chose his words carefully as he replied: "Dr Hardy………(long Pause)……….I don't know what your circumstance is in New York…..but her at Waterside High…these kids are accustomed to shootings, blood, and death…they live with it everyday…they don't have to come to school to witness violence……..they live with it everyday, it's their lives…the last thing they need to do is miss more days of school…no… we did not close the school…these kids are accustomed to this, they are resilient."

It may well be that Mr. Godby's assertion about his students was absolutely accurate. Maybe the majority of the youth in the school was unfazed and unaffected by the shootings. However, I would caution against misinterpreting their lack of expression with the absence of effect. The youth enrolled at Waterford High School, although seemingly unaffected by the complexities of their socio-cultural conditions, appeared traumatized by their over-exposure to violence and loss. While my colleagues and I were sure that their life circumstances had prepared them for the harshness of their life circumstances, we were equally sure that their resilience did not negate the need for them to address and grieve their losses.

In addition to over-estimating their resilience, it was quite evident that Mr. Godby and other school personnel had also under-estimated the emotional and psychological impact that violence has had on these children's lives. Many of the students talked very emotionally about the ways in which they felt unsafe, powerless, and anxious about "what might go down next." The loss of "safety", "empowerment", and "certainty" are all losses, yet Mr. Godby and school officials seemed oblivious to this fact.

Losses are Physical: The Tangible Loss Rationale—In U.S. society it is commonplace for a higher premium to be placed on *physical* rather than on *metaphysical* phenomena. Physical health is usually regarded more seriously and significantly than is mental health, for example. Similarly, 'physical abuse' is usually considered more seriously than 'mental abuse.' The fact that *the metaphysical* is much harder to see and measure, typically calls it into question. The same type of thinking seems to pervade our ideology with regard to loss. When any type of loss is considered, it is usually conceived physically. For example, when Mr. Godby, the Principal at Waterford High School spoke of loss associated with the shooting, he invariably referred to physical losses. He mentioned, for instance, the boys who were involved in the melee, the innocent passerby who was shot and will probably lose a finger, and the shattered glass to the cabinet where the Boy's Basketball State Championship trophy was stored. He consistently spoke knowledgeably and conscientiously about the gravity of losses that the school had sustained—all physical. He did not, for example, acknowledge the students' loss of safety as a loss. Nor did he give any indication that he considered the students' loss of 'the familiar,' that is, life as they knew it before the shootings as a loss. All of the losses that the students were most troubled by were intangible losses—those that could not be concretized or quickly measured. When the definition of what constitutes a loss is narrowly defined as a physical phenomenon only, it becomes difficult to acknowledge other manifestations of loss—especially intangible ones. Acknowledging intangible loss in the lives of traumatized children and adolescents is essential to working effectively with them.

Given the widespread occurrences of loss in the lives of traumatized children and adolescents, it is imperative for teachers, therapists, parents and other adults working with young people to make every conceivable effort to sharpen their loss detection devices and enhance their skills for addressing it. A re-conceptualization of our notions regarding loss, children's resilience, and the role of unresolved loss is critical to better position ourselves to work effectively with a growing number of young people whose lives have been ravaged by trauma and loss.

Tangible and Intangible

Hardy and Laszloffy (2005) identified loss as one of four critical aggravating factors associated with youth violence. Their work with aggressive and violent youth has centered around two types of loss: tangible and intangible.

Tangible Loss—refers to any loss that is concrete. Typically, it is relatively easy to detect and ultimately measure. The loss of a love one, a sweater, or a limb would all be example of tangible losses.

Intangible Loss—refers to the emotional psychological loss that is usually attached to a tangible loss. These losses are much more difficult to detect because they are typically metaphysical. Although difficult to detect, intangible loss can have a very debilitating effect on children and adolescents' lives and well-being.

Intangible Loss

Intangible loss is invisible to the naked eye. It is often experienced but seldom acknowledged. Because it is difficult to detect, it is also difficult to treat clinically. Hence, it usually festers and gradually eats away at the well-being of children and adolescents like a slow moving but progressive untreated cancer.

Intangible loss is connected to children and adolescents' existential being. When undetected, it assaults the soul, crushes the spirit, and erodes one's sense of meaning and purpose. The students at Waterford High School whom I referred to earlier in this Chapter were a case in point. As they reported, and I alluded to earlier, many of them admittedly were simply waiting for the next shooting. They spoke with a kind of hopeless despair and disillusionment that things could ever be better. Their sense of safety and innocence had been deeply eroded. Unfortunately, it is doubtful that the intangible loss with which they suffered would ever actually be addressed in a meaningful way. Despite the School Based Consultation team's repeated efforts to bring these issues to the attention of the school personnel, they remained (perhaps out of necessity) primarily focused on the tangible losses.

Intangible loss, like loss in general, has a very high rate of incidence among children and adolescents. It is more widespread than what is commonly acknowledged but is often obscured by egregious acting out behavior and/or a preponderance of tangible losses. Tara, with whom this Chapter opened, was also struggling mightily with intangible loss that was buried beneath her acting out behavior and a huge tangible loss. She unwittingly described her intangible loss in the following way during one of our sessions:

"You Know Doc, I have finally gotten to a place where I can accept that my Daddy isn't coming home. For a countless number of nights I went through the painful and disappointing motions of running to the kitchen window every time I heard a car door slam...or when someone unexpectedly opened the screen door to the front door. Each time something like this happened I allowed myself to feel hopeful and excited...only to again be disappointed. You probably can't imagine what it is like to run to the phone...to see a phone number that I didn't recognize appear on the caller I.D. and immediately assume that: oh, it could be Daddy calling from someone else's phone. I feel stupid....I have done this hundreds of time only to be disappointed. So...I can now accept that he is gone and will never be back. What I can't seem to accept.....(she pauses and begins to cry)..is that he will never see me in my prom dress...that he won't be there to give me away at my wedding....this, I don't know that I will ever be able to accept."

As Tara's words would suggest, she has reached a place of peace, resignation, and fragile resolution regarding her father death. After periods of denial, she has finally come to terms with both the finality and certainty of the reality that she is and will be fatherless. Yet, what troubles her most is the disruption that has occurred to her sense of idealism, future orientation, hope and dreams. Her core struggle at this point is not with the physical (tangible) loss of her father but instead with what it all means. In other words, what does it mean to live life without the father that you assumed would always be an integral part of your life? The death of Tara's father, when and how it happened has left her searching for (new) meaning and purpose in her life. She is for all intense purposes, psychologically homeless.

Psychological homelessness is a state of existential yearning. It is often inextricably tied to experiences with trauma and intangible loss. It is a type of homelessness that has little to do with the artifacts that we often associate with home: heat, hot water, or a concrete physical structure. Instead psychological homelessness refers to a kind of spiritual, existential waywardness that is precipitated by loss, especially that which is intangible. It is the type of loss that dismantles the safety, security, predictability, and familiarity of everyday life as we imagined it. Psychological homelessness crushes the spirit and often punctures one's sense of hope and optimism. It is invisible as are many of the locations of its assault. It one sense, it is the epitome of intangible loss.

In Tara's case, as is the case with so many young people who have experienced trauma, she has a home (in the classical sense of the term), stable objects in her life, and family members who love her. Yet in spite of all she has, she continues to search for that elusive 'something else.' She has a sense of yearning for that which is experienced but can never be measured concretely. She is looking for home….the hope, optimism, and dreams that she had about life with a father who has gone all too soon.

Tara has received a great deal of therapy, although most of it has been geared towards either helping her modify her acting out behaviors or addressing her tangible losses. The powerful intangible losses that shape her approach to her "new" life" remain unnamed, and ultimately unaddressed. Effectively, untangling intangible loss is a major challenge to overcome when working with traumatized children and adolescents.

The Challenges of Untangling Intangible Loss

Efforts to effectively detect intangible loss are often unsuccessful because it is often masked by other more distracting emotional, psychological, and/or behavioral problems. Aggression and violence, exaggerated non-compliant behavior, and the overwhelming presence of despair, despondency, and/or withdrawal type behaviors are but few of the common behavioral difficulties that obscure an accurate assessment and detection of intangible loss.

Aggressive and Violent Behavior—Intangible loss is not only difficult for others to identify but it can be equally challenging for youth experiencing it to acknowledge and embrace it. Aggressive and violent behavior often makes it possible for young people to avoid coping with the emotional impact of loss. Intangible loss often leaves children and adolescents with a deeply intense set of emotions that are often experienced but seldom acknowledged or expressed. Both aggressive and violent behaviors require an expenditure of energy and can be quite cathartic for children and adolescents who (unconsciously) want to ignore the pain and agony of grappling with underlying serious loss issues. The following case of is illustrative of this point.

✓ *It Makes Me Want To Kill Somebody*

Sixteen years old Tarique sat in my office completely overcome with anger and rage, and I also suspected despair and anguish as well. His despair and anguish were a bit harder to get to because they seemed to be buried beneath the surface of his profanity-laced accounts of what just happened to his main dawg, Lamar. Tarique and Lamar have been best friends since they were in elementary school together. Their families are friends and Lamar and Tarique often had "sleep overs" at each others' homes when they were younger. Unfortunately, Lamar was recently murdered leaving a Convenience Store in their neighborhood hours after he and Tarique had been together. Tarique believes the shooting of his best friend was retaliatory stemming from a basketball game played earlier during the day of murder. According to Tarique, Lamar, a very gifted basketball player, "was schoolin' this dude who thought he had game but couldn't touch "Mar's" game…he was fuc^&# scorchin' the dude….his game was on and every mother F^*& body started yellin' 'give he ball to Mar.' The more the crowd got into the game…the more it seemed to fire Mar up…he was hot…I don't think he missed more that three shots the entire game…The dude stickin' him felt totally DISSED….Mar played him like a Mother F*^% ~@ deck of cards!" Tarique believes that it was the player from the game or someone connected to him who murdered Lamar. He is convinced that the Police will never solve the case because "they don't give a fu*^ about killings in the hood." Despite my numerous attempts to talk with Tarique about the loss of Lamar and what it means to him, he remains angrily focused on getting revenge. Although I believe that Tarique is devastated by the loss of a childhood friend and the lack of fairness, justice, and safety that characterizes his life, he speaks only of revenge. With tears in his eyes and voice elevating by the second, he screams at me stating…"You don't get it Doc…nobody gives a damn about feelings…nobody gives a shit about some half black, half Puerto Rican dude being smoked on the streets…nobody cares, man…NOBODY…you want me to sit here and talk..talk for what?….Is talkin' gonna bring Mar back….is it going to stop my ass from being smoked next?…What do you want me to say…it's a fuckin jungle out there….you have to watch your back…you can't trust nobody especially not the cops…..You want me to talk Doc?….ok, I'll talk…what about this…."I believe in an eye for eye…you reap what you sow…what comes around goes around….do unto others and you would have them do unto you….what happened to Mar, it makes me wanna kill somebody…how bout that for feelings, Doc?"

Tarique's case is a very difficult one. His anger and rage regarding the senseless and untimely death of his beloved best friend is understandable. The more he had his enraged and tyrannical outbursts, the more evident it was to me how his life was inundated with loss, much of it entangled with intangible loss. Tarique's rage and despair was just as attributable to the intangible loss in his life as it were to the loss of Lamar. In fact, the intangible losses—the assaults to his sense of dignity and respect, disruptions to his sense of safety and security, and the reshaping of life as he knew it and imagined it to be—are interspersed throughout his rants of rage and insatiable desire for revenge. Unfortunately, his robust language of rage and revenge dwarfed these significant aspects of his life and emotional state. Not only were his intangible losses difficult for others to see, they were equally as difficult for Tarique to acknowledge as well. His overt and unrelenting expression of anger, rage, and the desire for revenge masked his deeper struggles with intangible loss.

Exaggerated Non-Compliant Behavior—*The presence of intangible loss can also be obscured by exaggerated non-compliant and acting out behaviors. The term "exaggerated" is used here to differentiate extreme egregious non-compliant behavior from that which is often benign and normative for children and adolescents. For example, I am referring to the difference between a child who may on a rare and inconsistent basis defy a parent's request by eating the chocolate chip cookies in their lunch before eating their vegetables, in contrast to a child who on a consistent basis defies parental rules and expectations regarding serious substantive matters such as stealing, etc.*

Tara's behavior was a textbook example of Exaggerated Non-Compliant and Acting Out Behavior. She has been arrested several times for theft, under-aged drinking, and curfew violations. Unlike Tarique, Tara's behavior often appeared self-destructive and self-sabotaging, a difference that is common for males and females. Boys tend to externalize their anger and rage, while girls often internalize. In either case, whether overly aggressive behavior that is externalized or exaggerated self-directed, self sabotaging acting out, non-compliant behavior, the underlying and critical dynamic is the same: the intangible loss that undergirds the behavior is unacknowledged.

Tara's stealing, for example, has belied logic and has appeared very bizarre. She has been arrested numerous times for stealing non-essential petty items such as lipstick, nail polish, and a Sharpie Pen. Her behavior has baffled her mother, stepfather, teachers, and the several school social workers because she continually steals items that she could easily afford financially or that her mother would glad give to her. Virtually everyone around Tara, both professional and lay people alike posit that "something very troubling is bothering Tara." Unfortunately, seldom has the hypotheses regarding "what is wrong with Tara" extended beyond notions of her as a 'troubled (sometimes bad) girl who lost her father in the terrorists attacks on the World Trade Center who probably needs more discipline and sense of direction.' Tara's loss of hope, innocence, idealism and future orientation, remain hidden, and unaddressed. As in the case with Tarique and so many other young people like them, it is doubtful that even Tara can explain why she does what she does. For her to suggest this to most people in her life would be tantamount to admitting that she was either dishonest and manipulative or lacking the capacity for critical introspection.

Inexplicable Despair, Sullen, and Withdrawn Behavior—Just as stealing and other forms of exaggerated acting out behaviors can mask intangible loss so can despair, sullen, and withdrawn behaviors. Since all of these affective expressions are typically associated with depression, loss is often considered a plausible hypothesis. While loss, unlike with the other aforementioned behaviors, is often considered to be intertwined with despair, sullen, and withdrawn behaviors, it is usually tangible loss that is foremost in our thinking. When children and adolescents are demonstrably sullen, withdrawn, or overcome with despair, tangible losses are almost always immediately explored. This is often a fortuitous move since intangible loss is virtually always connected to tangible loss. The problem, however, is that the exploration for underlying loss usually stops with the identification of a tangible loss. Tara's case is an excellent illustration of the difficulties inherent with this approach.

Following what Tara feared was the death of her father in 2001, she spent several months crying, feeling sad, hoping against the odds and barricaded in her home with her mother and brother. She went to school sparingly and when she did attend more regularly, she made a concerted effort to avoid contact with her old friends and classmates. Everyone in her world knew that she was attempting to deal with an imaginable loss. Those who loved and admired her wished her well but never quite knew exactly what to say. Teachers, friends, and relatives all stumbled over their words as they searched for the right words to console her. Privately, they all probably knew that there were no such words that could soothe the pain of losing a father, especially at such a young age. In spite of the seemingly futility of it all, everyone around Tara continued to reach out to her. For months, anguish and despair kidnapped the bright beaming smiling face that once belonged to Tara. It was obvious to everyone around her that she was grief-stricken and lifeless as she went through the motions of her life in zombie-like fashion. Friends, immediate and extended family, as well as a number of community based organizations made sure that Tara was constantly surrounded by people who loved and cared about her. In one sense, they kept her alive.

Once the visible markers of Tara's despondency subsided, the support around her began to slowly dissipate. Gradually, according to Tara's mother, "she began to smile again tho' she at times had a faraway look in her eyes....on the outside she looked fine...but somehow she seemed shut down on the inside." As Tara began to adjust to her new life, many were convinced that the worse was over and that she was on the long road to recovery. She began to mingle with her friends again and do all of the typical things that teenagers do. For all practical purposes, she seemed as "over it" as anyone could expect her to be.

Thanks to a committed group of friends, family, and therapists, Tara received a down pouring of love and support. While her loss was consistently acknowledged, it was always the assumption that the totality of it was relegated to the physical loss of her father. The death of her father and the gravity of her emotions in response to it almost made it impossible to imagine that there could be any other loss related issues for her to deal with at the time. Yet, intangible loss was omnipresent throughout her life. In the presence of an overpowering tangible loss, such as the death of a parent, it is exceedingly difficult to identify and honor loss that can neither be seen nor measured. Even though it cannot be measured, intangible loss is pervasive and can take on many different forms.

Types of Intangible Loss

The following types of intangible loss are common for traumatized children and adolescents to experience: Loss of hope; Loss of Innocence; Loss of Dignity; and Loss of Safety.

Loss of Hope erodes one's sense of liveliness. It calls into question one's desire to live or that there is anything for which to live. It destroys one's ability to "believe." It leads to a dispirited state where despair and disillusionment become the norm.

Loss of Innocence is born out of a loss of hope and is concomitantly the by-product of the loss of hope. When there is a loss of innocence, life becomes soiled and stripped of goodwill. In the face of the loss of innocence, life becomes a place characterized by mistrust, an erosion of altruistic spirit, and faith in others. For example, young children who have been exploited, abused, and neglected usually suffer from a loss of innocence. Girls who have been molested, especially by a family member, are often maligned by the loss of innocence.

   Loss of Dignity is a major silent assassin for poor children regardless of racial background and Children and Adolescents of Color without regard to social class. Dignity is essential to our sense of being as humans. The loss of dignity strips one's of respect and positive self worth. When children and adolescents have memberships in groups that are marginalized or devalued by the broader society, they are forced to live lives void of dignity. For many young people, it is the loss of dignity that makes their untimely deaths desirable. After all, when dignity is destroyed or lost it contributes to the spiritual death of the soul.

   Loss of Safety destroys traumatized children and adolescents sense of security and predictability. It severely compromises one's ability to manage both emotional and physical vulnerability. The loss of safety heightens (emotional and physical) fear and reduces risk taking.

   Each of the aforementioned intangible losses is inextricably tied together. They feed off of one another and rarely exist in isolation. Understanding and untangling intangible loss are critical steps to take towards working effectively with traumatized children and adolescents.

Summary

   The lives of traumatized children and adolescents are inundated with loss. There are two types of loss that comprise the everyday life experiences of traumatized children and adolescents: tangible and intangible.

   Tangible loss refers to any loss that is physical and/or can be concretely measured. Intangible loss, on the other hand, refers to any loss whose major properties are metaphysical. While loss is difficult to detect and work with effectively, intangible loss is particularly difficult to discern because it is often buried beneath the surface.

   There are four types of intangible losses that are commonplace among traumatized children and adolescents: the loss of hope, innocence, dignity, and safety.

References

Hardy, K. V., and Laszloffy, T. A. *Teens Who Hurt: Clinical Interventions to Break the Cycle of Adolescent Violence.* New York: Guilford Press, 2005.

Walsh F., & McGoldrick, M. *Living Beyond Loss: Death in the family* (2nd). New York: Norton, 2004.

Wolin, S., & Wolin, S. *The resilient self: How survivors of troubled families rise above adversity.* New York: Villiard Books (Random House), 1993.

CHAPTER THREE

WALKING TOGETHER:
A CHILD THERAPIST'S JOURNEY THROUGH LOSS

KATHRYN KEHOE-BIGGS, L.C.S.W., PhD

The Meaning of Loss

As humans we need to attach meaning to events based on our experiences. Without a system of some kind there is an overwhelming feeling of chaos. For children, this type of predictability depends on a sense of shared meaning which is generally passed from one generation to the next. Any significant disturbance in this process can constitute a disruptive loss. Some losses are good and promote positive change, development, and movement toward independence. In fact, each developmental phase is marked by a slow, moving away from the primary caregiver and toward independence. With the first bite of solid food an infant looses the closeness which accompanies breast feeding. When that child crawls, she is held less often. There is the loss of security and comfort when a child falls while walking away from the caregiver. In a healthy relationship the hope is that this child can hold a positive image of the caregiver within and take that image on her journey toward independence. But what about the losses that inhibit this inner strength so vital to healthy human development? All over the world children are exposed to violence, death and a variety of traumas which emotionally and cognitively impact their perception of themselves and the world. Early relationships and experiences teach children the meaning of information. If this time period is riddled with violence and death, then sensory function, memory and language are all affected. These childhood experiences create a mental framework used throughout development and form a lens through which the child views the present, past and future[1]

Unfortunately, for many children unpredictability and chaos become the norm. Community violence, death or maltreatment provides a context which

---

[1] Crittenden, *Language and Psychopathology;* Perry et al, *Childhood trauma;* van der Kolk, *The body keeps the score*

enables the children to feel as if their actions have meaning and purpose. Crittenden studied the coping styles of abused children and found that often they do not recognize situations where coping mechanisms are not required and as a result will never try other strategies[2]. When these children are removed from the abusive situations they experience loss. It is the loss of the familiar and the predictable, even if what was familiar was physically and emotionally unhealthy. There is a need to maintain the norm and recreate this chaos even when placed in a nurturing living situation. While living in an unpredictable, violent or maltreating environment some children develop the belief that they are 'bad'. In an attempt to protect other's from their 'badness', these children tend to distance themselves from others. Previously, this behavior was an adaptive mechanism needed for survival; however, outside of that environment these same behaviors are no longer productive, they inhibit positive interactions that could work toward changing the mental frameworks which evolved from maltreatment. Problematic behavior in school or at home is often the result, as well as the child being labeled as having an innate psychological pathology. However, when examined closely within the context of the child's previous life experiences these 'problematic' or 'pathological' behaviors can also be viewed as resilient methods for coping with unsolvable problems.

Once removed from a maltreating situation there is a loss followed by mourning. This type of mourning may be difficult for others to understand especially when the child's new living situation provides the security, comfort and structure which is so desperately needed. Remember, this child is grieving over the loss of what she has always known and is struggling to create and use new tools in a different environment. Healing occurs through repeatedly encountering relationships and experiences which do not include violence, death, rejection, maltreatment or loss. Unfortunately, many of these children are caught in a bind. They need closeness to heal, but they are afraid their internal 'badness' will hurt others. They are viewing their new environment through a lens formed during their earlier life experiences. Van der Kolk presents the idea that traumatized people often perceive their environment as threatening because they develop reflexive responses called "defensive reactions"[3]. Defensive reactions are subjective and are affected by the context of the current situation and the past trauma. As a result, many victims of trauma are unable to learn from experience because they continue to perceive themselves as traumatized over and over again[4]. The challenge then becomes helping the traumatized child recognize a positive, nurturing relationship when this type of experience is not the norm. It is through these positive interactions that the slow and

---

[2] Crittenden, *The Treatment of Anxious Attachment in Infancy and Early Childhood*
[3] Van der Kolk, *The body keeps the score.*
[4] Ibid

painstaking process of building up self-worth occurs. The goal is for the child to feel worthy of being in a nurturing relationship and then help her develop tools to maintain that relationship. These positive experiences allow the child to truly see her previous life story as a loss; a loss of innocence, safety, structure and security, and then mourn the loss of the story she wishes she could tell and deserved to have.

When a maltreating parent dies a child is not only faced with the task of mourning the parent, but she must also mourn the loss of the dream that an abuser may change. This hope dies when the person dies. There are no more second chances. The wish which may have nurtured and sustained the child for many years suddenly becomes irrelevant and emptiness emerges. This emptiness symbolizes the loss of innocence. There is the realization that dreams frequently do not come true and that there will be no happy ending to this particular life chapter. Healing occurs through the slow and painful realization that this chapter does not have to define the rest of the child's life. This process takes a lot of hard painful work for both the child and helping professional.

The Mourning Process

Losses come in all shapes and sizes. Whether a child is removed from a maltreating home or loses a loving and caring parent to cancer or an accident there is the common experience of struggling to create a new sense of 'normal'. Anger, regret and memories (both good and bad) are all a part of this struggle. Mourning and grief take time. There is no way to skip over or rush through the feelings of pain, sadness, anger, loneliness or frustration. These feelings need to be felt sooner or later. Unfortunately, in a culture of instant messaging, fast food and quick fixes, the importance and growth which can occur as a result of struggling through the process of grief often goes unrecognized. In our fast-paced world, society does not allow the proper time and space to grieve. Grief can not be hopped over or squeezed under, grief must be experienced For example, a fifty year old woman came to see me for support after the death of her eighty- five year old mother. She described her mother as a very controlling and needy person who had difficulty expressing her feelings. After some time, this woman became frustrated with herself. She could not seem to 'get past' her mother's death. It was eventually revealed that when she was a young child her father died while she was away at summer camp. No one informed her of his death until she returned and at that time all the services were over. Nothing was ever discussed again, until she sought professional help for her mother's death.. As a child she was tuned-in to the unspoken message from her mother that this death and death in general should not be talked about or processed. During her time with me, she revisited the choices she made in her life and the way she related to others, including her mother. She began to fill in the pieces of her life with a new respect and understanding for the grief she was never allowed to feel. She realized how much she had missed. Finally, forty years after his death, she began to mourn the loss of her father for the first time.

The way families understand or deal with loss and death is usually passed from one generation to the next. Children do not necessarily have to be told of these norms. Instead, they become a part of the shared meaning which makes each family unique. It is when a member steps outside of the family's boundaries and witnesses alternative ways of being that these norms are questioned. Children have less opportunity to do this because of their dependence on the family unit and the security and meaning the family culture provides. Helping professionals who work with children should be cautious and respectful when addressing these familial norms. A child's need for and attachment to their family is very strong and these norms which appear unhealthy may be vital to maintaining this connection. Exposing the family to alternative ways of addressing loss and death should be done with a respect for cultural and familial norms. Action becomes the focus. As Van Waning states, *"Talking about it is not enough; the [therapist] must join in the action"*[5]. It is through the actual experiencing of an open, understanding, nurturing relationship with the therapist that the child feels empowered to explore. These sessions may be the child's first exposure to a different type of adult-child relationship which is completely focused on the child's individual needs.

The grieving child

Children, especially those experiencing a significant loss, tend to be very in-tune with the unconscious and unspoken thoughts and feelings of their adult caretakers and frequently use non-verbal, action oriented communication[6]. As a result, these children tend to be highly sensitive to the emotional atmosphere surrounding them and may delay their own grieving until they are certain the adults in their lives are able to tolerate their feelings. There is an attempt to maintain any remaining stability. Numbness and the feeling of 'going through the motions' may also occur. During these times caretakers or other adults may believe the child is doing just fine and adjusting well to a new life. This could be true, but during times of overwhelming stress or strain there

---

[5] Van Waning, *To be the best or not to be, that is the question,* p550
[6] Ablon, *Where work is play with mortal stakes*; Beebe, *A dyadic systems view of communication*; Hauge, *Reconstruction in an Analysis of a Child*; Lanyado, *Variations on the Theme of Transference & Counter-Transference in the Treatment of a Ten Year Old Boy*; van der Kolk, *The body keeps the score.*

may also be a shutting down and an inability to process information[7]. While the child's behavior looks 'good', there is frequently a sense that she is not truly present and her actions lack authenticity. For example, the commonly referred to 'honeymoon period' is often used, when a child is removed from a maltreating home and put into a new placement. It is when the day to day stressors of living evolve and the reality of the loss emerges that the real work begins and the child's feelings, thoughts and behavior become more authentic. At this time, the child may fluctuate between participating in normal developmental tasks and expressing their grief in short, intense spurts. Regression to an early stage of development and reckless or acting out behavior may occur. Young children will often collect, horde, make piles and bring things "back together" in their play. However, they may also tear up, knock down and bury things to express their sense of abandonment and disruption[8].

Without attachment there is no loss

Attachment theory describes the special bond between infant and caregiver as based on the human biological need to survive[9]. The need to attach is as primary as the need for food and warmth. Bowlby calls this need 'Primary Object Clinging'[10]. Modern researchers and theorists use this idea in their quest to understand the impact of loss and trauma on human development. Beebe's and Lachmann's research links early mother-infant relationship to self and internal maternal representations[11] They believe this early relationship provides the cognitive foundation for organizing and perceiving relationships and experiences. Early experiences create mental frameworks used throughout development. Attachment figures teach children the meaning of information, and if that figure is lost or abuse or maltreatment occurs, sensory function, memory and language are all effected[12].

The unique aspects of grief are significantly impacted by these early relationships. While some of the common grief responses are discussed in the section above, the mourning process is unique for each individual. Loss is perceived, felt and understood based on these "mental frameworks" which may appear innate, but are actually formulated very early in life. A child whose early attachments were nurturing and stable will experience a significant loss in a

---

[7] Perry, *Childhood trauma.*
[8] Cameron, *Understanding and Supporting a Child or Teen Coping with a Death.*
[9] Bowlby, *The nature of a child's tie to his mother*
[10] Ibid
[11] Beebe et al, *A Dyadic Systems View of Communication*
[12] Crittenden, *Language and Psychopathology;* Perry et al, *Childhood trauma;* van der Kolk, *The body keeps the score*

much different way than a child with a history of deprivation. During times of stress these positive internal maternal representations are the source of strength and internal self worth. When someone important dies or is otherwise lost it is normal to experience feelings of sadness, abandonment, fear, regret, guilt and loneliness. The child's ability to formulate relationships and gain support from others is significantly impacted by previous loving and nurturing care giving. This internal stability does not remove the intense pain associated with death or significant loss, but it does impact how this pain is managed and perceived. In addition to the child's early attachments, the child's connection to and relationship with the person who is lost also makes their experience unique. This separates their experience from others who may also be mourning.

This chapter uses Jay's story of trauma, loss and grief to explore the impact of death, abuse and maltreatment on human development and a child's ability to connected and maintain connections with other people. Helping Jay carry his load becomes something that brings us together and moves our relationship forward In the process, the untold parts of Jay's story unfold.

Jay

Loss can be equated with a lack of meaning or purpose. Perception of the self and the environment is altered by this loss. As a result, the structure of daily life is disrupted. What used to 'feel normal' no longer 'makes sense'. As a result, the predictability of life is compromised, which impacts ones sense of security and safety. The desire to maintain what is familiar is in conflict with the need to adapt and change. Jay's seven years of existence was marked by this conflict, which perpetuated his cycle of loss and grief. This is the story of my struggle, as a therapist, alongside Jay as he tries to work against the tide of his history and create a new life story.

Jay's early years

Jay's mother used cocaine and contracted an untreated venereal disease during her pregnancy. As a result of his mother's abuse and neglect, Jay was removed from his home at the age of one. He spent six months in foster care until he went to live with his father, a recovering heroin user who had AIDS. Jay's father remained drug free and showed him love and affection; however, his illness progressed and eventually he entered hospice care. During this time, Jay's paternal aunt, Helen, gradually became his caretaker and a big part of his life. When Jay was four years old his father died. Jay was truly present during his father's illness and death. He watched as his father slowly died.

When he came to see me at six years old, the memories of his father's death were fresh in his mind. He had a remarkable memory and could articulate the smallest details of his life history. However, he told his story with little emotion. It seemed as if he were talking about a character in a book or a movie. Children who have experienced repeated trauma often use dissociation as a defense against and an escape from overwhelming feelings. Slowly, this defense becomes a part of how the child experiences the world[13]. It was evident that Jay had great affection for his father and was significantly impacted by his death. However, he seemed disconnected from those feelings.

At the time of his father's death Jay's cognitive ability to understand death was limited by his age. At the age of four, death is often viewed from an egocentric perspective, with children believing their own actions may have somehow magically caused the death. In addition, during this developmental time period death is commonly perceived as temporary. It is between the ages of five and seven that children generally begin to understand that death is irreversible. Therefore, when Jay began his relationship with me at age six he was just beginning to understand and feel the permanency of his father's death, yet his ability to express those feelings was limited.

After his father's death, Jay's mother illegally took him out of state for seven months. Jay was removed from her care again when she broke his arm in two places and subsequently was charged with abuse and neglect. As a result, Jay was placed in one foster home for a few weeks and then moved to another for his remaining nine months in foster care. While he was in foster care, Aunt Helen visited Jay weekly and finally attained guardianship when Jay was five years old. Jay is now eight and still lives with his Aunt Helen who provides a loving and stable home. Helen hopes to adopt Jay; however, Jay's mother was granted supervised visits with the hopes of regaining custody. Jay has expressed conflicting feelings about his future with his mother.

The prospect of Jay returning to his mother invokes in me a tremendous amount of anxiety and anger. I have never met Jay's mother, but I have hateful feelings toward her because of her brutal actions. I question her ability to care for Jay and his younger sibling. Krell and Okin lists reactions commonly experienced by child therapists toward parents of abused and neglected children; such as disgust, fury, anger and a desire for retaliation[14] The challenge becomes owning, managing and preventing those feelings from limiting Jay's subjective expression of his feelings toward his mother. If Jay does feel anger, disappointment or rage toward his mother these feelings should come from within him and not from my projections. Anastasopoulos and

---

[13] Perry, *Childhood trauma*
[14] Krell and Okin, *Countertransference Issues in Child Abuse and Neglect Cases*

Tsiantis and Ryan discuss the "savior complex", in which the therapist fantasizes that they are caring for the child in a way that the child's parents never could[15] This process can lead to disillusionment and over-identification with the child or anger when the child expresses anger toward the therapist[16]. Feeling anger and outrage toward an abusing parent is normal and this is why boundaries are very important. It is not my job to 'save' Jay from his pain or become a substitute parent. Instead, I need to walk next to him and be available to carry some of his pain, allowing him time to become stronger. I then must eventually give it back when he is ready. For me, seeing a child in pain is a heart wrenching and difficult task, but a task is exactly what it is. I need to make a conscious effort to stop myself from quickly moving in and working toward taking his pain away. My job is to withstand the pain with Jay; to take it away would be self-serving.

A developmental perspective

Knowing at what developmental time period Jay's major losses and traumas took place is an important piece of his life story. His story of trauma and loss begins at birth. Jay seems to be fixated in this early stage of development where words are not used and instead the unspoken connection between caretaker and child is the primary means of communication. It is as if he is seeking out a type of intuitive and unspoken understanding which he missed long ago. In many respects, Jay wants to experience what he lost when he was born- the feeling of being held and understood. This is an experience every infant needs and deserves. Of course I am unable to fully meet these types of needs, and frequently feel as if I am failing him. But, slowly our relationship becomes about my willingness to struggle along side of him instead of my ability to meet his demands and insatiable needs.

Children frequently become fixated in the period of development in which a trauma or loss took place[17] It is important to examine the tasks and goals of that time period or periods along with the tasks and goals of the child's current stage of development. This examination is framed by the question: Is a fixation in an earlier stage of development impacting the child's mastery of current developmental tasks? Since Jay's trauma and losses began during the

---

[15] Anastasopoulos & Tsiantis *Countertransference in Psychoanalytic Psychotherapy with Children and Adolescents;* Ryan, *The chronically traumatized child.*
[16] Gartner, *Countertransference Issues in the Psychotherapy of Adolescents*
[17] Balint, *Changing Therapeutic Aims and Techniques in Psychoanalysis*; Fairbairn, *A Revised Psychopathology of the Psychoses of Psychoneuroses*; Kernberg, *Borderline Conditions and Pathological Narcissism*; Lanyado, *Variations on the Theme of Transference & Counter-Transference in the Treatment of a Ten Year Old Boy.*

early pre-verbal stage of development, words are frequently unavailable when he tries to communicate the feelings or thoughts associated with his losses. Due to this primitive communication style and way of relating, Jay is having difficulties negotiating the social tasks of his current developmental stage- early latency. Winnocott explains that latency is a stage where school plays a substitute for home[18] Erikson categorizes the six to eleven year old child as focusing on producing and acquiring skills. These skills provide preparation for adult roles. The potential problems in this period are feelings of inadequacy and inferiority[19]. Jay has few friends and commonly describes feeling victimized and ridiculed or is accused of doing the same to his peers. His most difficult times during the school day are the less structured periods such as lunch time and physical education where freedom of movement requires him to cooperate and interact with his peers. Jay has the desire to relate to others, but his behavior often results in his rejection and isolation. It is my job to provide Jay with a nurturing place where he feels safe enough to create and try out new tools for relating to others. In many ways I must act as an "organizer" of Jay's personality[20], with our relationship providing the security and understanding which he was denied earlier in his life. The hope is that at some point Jay will internalize this positive relationship and bring it with him as he ventures out into the world.

Our journey together begins

Jay's story of loss begins with his human relationships; and this is where the healing process starts. Feelings, ideas and actions evolve from significant relationships. When this familiar context no longer exists emptiness emerges. The mourning process involves the slow and painstaking creation of a new understanding of 'normal', including the formation of new relationships which provide new meaning and purpose. However, the multiple losses and extensive abuse which permeate Jay's history impact how he perceives and experiences his environment. The challenge becomes to provide Jay with a new relationship which he perceives as supportive, when he continually attempts to recreate his story of loss and rejection within these relationships. My genuine struggle to understand Jay's experience knowing that I will continually disappoint becomes a big part of the healing process.

---

[18] Winnicott, *The Maturation Processes and the Facilitating Environment.*
[19] Erikson, *Childhood and society*
[20] Maenchen, *On the Technique of Child Analysis in Relation to Stages of Development,* p.200

Jay tells me his story

Jay often requests extra sessions which I continually must reject. Generally, Jay displays minimal reaction when I attempt to verbally explore his feelings regarding my inability to meet his demands. He does not seem willing or able to verbally express negative feelings toward me. However there are times when he acts out his anger. For example, after denying his request to extend the length of our session, Jay opened the door to my office for me and allowed me to leave the room in front of him. He then proceeded to lock himself in the room. Through the door I attempted to verbally express what his actions displayed. Jay laughed taking pleasure in his act. He stated; "I will not open the door until you tell me the password". I didn't know the password. A panic started to swell inside of me. What if he went through my purse or my files? What if he hurt himself or stayed in there for hours? I had no control. Others started to look at me, waiting to see if I could 'handle' the situation. I was sure they thought I didn't know what I was doing. At this moment I had a choice. I could become overwhelmed by my own feelings or I could try to use them to understand Jay's experience. My response was, "you know the password and it is up to you to tell me what it is." After a few moments, Jay opened the door. This exchange through a locked door showed Jay that within our relationship it is his choice to 'let me in' or 'keep me out.' Either choice is acceptable and does not result in rejection or the destruction of our relationship. Prior to locking himself in the room, Jay felt powerless and 'shut out'. I would not allow him to stay longer than our hour session. The boundaries I set up did not meet his insatiable needs. As I stood on the opposite side of the door, I felt powerless and 'shut out'. This of course is how Jay feels most of the time. He was communicating through invoking his feelings in me. It was up to me to manage, understand and use my own feelings to understand Jay's struggle. He was telling me his story.

This experience presented an opportunity to explain to Jay that it is my job to understand and his job to reveal, but it is up to him to set the pace. Jay's actions did not change the length or frequency of our session, but there was a communication of need and an attempt to understand, culminating in the survival of our relationship. He trusted our relationship enough to tell me about his feelings of anger, powerlessness, frustration and inadequacy in his own way. Kernberg believed that countertransference — the therapist's own thoughts, feelings and experiences— helps the therapist feel what the patient is feeling[21]. He stressed that this process results in an increase in awareness and helpfulness. He also warns therapists to be vigilant in their use of countertransference to

---

[21] Kernberg, *Notes on countertransference,* p.40.

enhance rather than hinder treatment. While standing outside a locked door, Jay allowed me to have a small peek inside is his world. In locking me out, Jay may have been attempting to invoke in me his feelings of frustration, fear, inadequacy, loneliness, powerlessness and anger. At that moment I needed to listen to my countertransference to hear what Jay had to say.

The above scenario emphasizes the importance of non-verbal, action oriented exchange. The therapist who is aware of her own "non-verbal system" will understand the meaning behind feelings and actions such as yawning, hunger and clock-watching[22]. The range of non-verbal communication is extensive because of the many ways it can be conveyed. The indirectness involved with non-verbal communication presents a challenge to the therapist who is striving to discover and understand the child's inner world[23]. At times it may feel as if there is a "flood of information" when the "entire body becomes an organ for communication"[24] Following Jay's lead and communication style is overwhelming at times, but I have no choice. It is the only way his inner world can emerge. This process works against the overly directive interactions, which can often emerge between an adult and a child. In this instance, the adult therapist uses their power and authority to promote the use of words, the adult form of communication, allowing the therapist to feel more comfortable at the expense of the healing process. Anthony cautions against the use of only words in response to a child's non-verbal play; "Children often show surprising sensitivity to what is expected of them by adults. If they sense that the [adult] is ill at ease....they will switch to verbal communication[25] Jay has the control. I want to know about his inner world and he is the only one who holds the key. I must respect this important aspect of our relationship. This may be the only time in his life where he can experience this kind of control. How Jay uses this control and the way he relates to me is where the healing starts. Building the type of relationship where Jay can tell me or act out his inner world takes time and a willingness to struggle along with him.

Leading up to this event, Jay often had difficulty viewing me as multidimensional. I was all 'good'. He impulsively hugged me when he came into each session. He seemed to have difficulty seeing 'bad' at the same as 'good' in someone he loved. When he knocked over my player attempting to 'kill' him after I beat him at a board game, he rejected my interpretation that he was angry at me for winning. His response was, "You could never do anything to make me angry...you are too nice." When he locked me out of my office, he stated, "I was only playing around." However, the process of verbalizing the

---

[22] Anthony, *Nonverbal and Verbal Systems of Communication*, p. 312
[23] Ibid
[24] Ibid, p.312
[25] Ibid, p.308

feelings behind his actions slowly created an atmosphere of tolerance. Jay's presentation of 'locking me out' as a 'funny joke' and 'killing my player as 'just playing around' enabled him to express his feelings while maintaining my 'good' status. It is my hope that the survival of our relationship will result in altering Jay's belief in the destructive quality of his 'badness'. The goal is for Jay to slowly relate to me as a whole person. The completion of this process may never fully take place, but the healing occurs through our struggle together, side by side. I have to be comfortable with not knowing the end to Jay's story. All I can hope for is that our relationship will make a small positive change in his view of himself and others.

Neurobiological impact of loss and trauma

Jay's behavior and character is often labeled as pathological, but at an earlier time when loss and trauma were a part of his everyday life, these behaviors served an important purpose. Perry and his colleagues measured the heart rate of young children who experienced acute trauma[26] This study made a connection between the type of adaptive response utilized by children during the traumatic situation and the symptoms that were apparent six months later. The results of his study found that traumatized children commonly utilized the adaptive responses present in the original trauma — a mixture of dissociative and hyperarousal responses[27]. Other research has uncovered neuronal and hormonal changes in traumatized people and explored how these changes impact functioning[28]. Jay's behavior placed within a neurobiological context could be labeled as adaptive coping mechanisms which aided in his emotional and physical protection. An abused child develops coping mechanisms in reaction to an external threat[29]. For example, Jay is very perceptive of others unspoken thoughts and feelings and is hyper vigilant regarding exterior threats. His teachers and other students often call him 'paranoid'. However this 'paranoia' served Jay well when faced with an unpredictable and at times violent environment. Jay is frequently disconnected from his feelings and presents as flat or apathetic. Again, this type of disconnection may have been emotionally protective when he felt overwhelmed and unable to cope. Unfortunately, many of Jay's coping mechanisms are now stifling his development and isolating him from others. One of the first steps toward giving children like Jay the tools to function is a willingness to understand the purpose their current behavior once served. This understanding will only emerge if the

---

[26] Perry, *Childhood trauma*
[27] Ibid
[28] Van der Kolk, *The body keeps the score*
[29] Perry, *Childhood trauma*

adult is able to be an active participant in the acting out of the child's story of loss. Perry and his colleagues discuss the effects of trauma on brain functioning, " The single most significant most distinguishing feature of all nervous tissue is that they are designed to change in response to external signals" [30]. The only way to change Jay's cognitive mechanisms is to change his external experiences. When Jay locked me out of my room he was acting out his story, but the story did not end in the usual way. I did not reject or abandon him. Our relationship survived and continued. It is through these painful reenactments that Jay slowly realizes that there is the possibility of a different ending than what he has grown accustomed to.

Through Jay's Eyes

Jay's view of himself as 'bad' or 'unworthy' dominates all his relationships. Jay is currently in second grade and is experiencing emotional, behavioral and relational problems. His IQ of 130 allows him to achieve academically, but he frequently uses his intellect to distance himself from his peers and challenge authority. Within our relationship Jay has difficulty differentiating his feelings and actions from mine. He continually strives to figure out who he should be or what he should do to attain my approval and acceptance. It often appears as if he is performing a dramatic role, instead of being himself and he continually asks whether I 'like him'. Winnicott talks about the development of the 'False' self as beginning during infancy when the caretaker's needs are continually substituted for the needs of the infant[31]. Slowly, the infant becomes compliant. In childhood, this compliance can look like apathy. For example, Jay shows little affect in reaction to both positive and negative situations. He generally describes the traumatic events of his life in a very ordinary manner and expresses minimal joy when discussing happier things, such as going to an amusement park. He states he is 'happy', 'sad', or 'angry', but his statements lack conviction. Bringing toys he likes or a story he wrote in class into the session is his attempt to make a connection. It is as if he wants to be close, while at the same time fearing the consequences of getting attached. As a result, there is an avoidant, disconnected quality to his interactions. Feelings are painful and there is a sense of hopelessness that the pain will never be alleviated. It appears easier for him to not feel and instead present a dramatization of the person he believes I want him to be. Jay's intense need to be held corresponds with his fear of abandonment and his own 'badness'. In our relationship, Jay continually fluctuates between attachment

---

[30] Perry, *Childhood trauma*, p. 272.
[31] Winnicott, *The Maturation Processes and the Facilitating Environment.*

and avoidance. He will impulsively hug me at the beginning of the session and lock me out of the room at the end. Underlying aggression can emerge during moments of anxiety and frustration. When working with children like Jay, the goal is to provide an environment where a feeling of safety can emerge based on the acceptance of the child's ever changing and seemingly contradictory need for closeness and distance.

Trauma and loss create a lens through which Jay views himself and the world. I will never fully understand his perspective, but it is the process of my struggle to understand that is important. For example, while painting a picture Jay spontaneously painted a small line on his face. He looked at me with hesitation. He then asked, "Can I paint my face?" His faced looked surprised when I said yes. He proceeded to paint his entire face. The result was a 'scary' looking Jay with red paint on his neck which he called blood. He looked in the mirror and admired his 'scary' and 'bloody' exterior and stated "I wish I could stay this way. I don't like the real Jay." His perception of himself as' bad' or 'undesirable' is influenced by his abuse, loss and abandonment. His use of symbolic play to tell me his story may have been the best way for him to express feelings which originated in a preverbal stage of development. While much of this session was spent cleaning up paint, it only took a few moments of play for him to tell me his story. When he asked me if he could paint his face, the 'adult' in me wanted to say no. The paint was messy; it could get on his clothes and my clothes resulting in his teacher or his aunt becoming annoyed; however, I had to give Jay the control and let him tell me his story in his own way. If I didn't, I would have had a neater room, but no story. Anthony states, " The child …sits constantly in what has been termed a 'sessile' position [like Whistler's mother] and the child patient circles around him, near or far, in a sort of therapeutic solar system"[32]. Jay and I together are creating a culture within the treatment room where a delicate balance between structure and freedom has emerged. Initially, Jay tested the limits of his freedom and control, for example, when he locked me out of my office. However, over time our struggles together have created a sense of peace and comfort. After two years of working together, Jay will be moving to his mother's out of state and the loss of his current school, our relationship, and the security of living with his aunt is looming in the distance. In the face of all these losses he is moving toward me and others instead of away. He gave me a small green manatee figure which he bought with his own money, and stated "I know green is your favorite color and manatees are your favorite animal." This small gesture displayed that he had learned a way to connect with others and used it to show the value he placed on our

---

[32] Anthony, *Nonverbal and Verbal Systems of Communication*, p. 317

relationship. However, whether Jay will be able to fight against the cycle of loss and gain the tools needed to stop the cycle of loss remains to be answered.

Discussion

It was my job to remind Jay of how young he actually was when he was expected to cope with violence, death and loss. I had to say out loud to Jay that his life was unfair and unjust, I was sorry for his losses and how sad it was that his innocence was taken away. Jay seemed surprised by my words, as if it was the first time he had heard such a statement. The death of his father and removal from his mother were very tangible losses. But he also lost a big piece of his infancy and early childhood — the sense of security, warmth and attachment which every child needs and deserves. He is now only eight and is being asked if he wants to move back with his mother. Once again he is being robbed of his childhood. Jay deserved and deserves better and he has a right to feel angry. It was my job to remind Jay that he was and still is a child with a child's cognitive and emotional capabilities, even though he was and is exposed to adult-like stressors. Reminding children that they are children may seem simplistic, but it can be very comforting to a child who has lost so much. Jay frequently spoke about feelings of envy when he witnessed other children worrying or becoming angered by minor 'childish' events. This envy is a symbol of his loss of innocence and his desire to connect with his peers who seem so far away.

The challenges we both face

Currently, Jay is caught in a cycle of loss and rejection which he is partly responsible for perpetuating. His behavior invokes feelings of anger and frustration in others, which frequently result in the loss of that relationship. These experiences validate his view of himself as 'bad' and 'destructive' and others as rejecting. My job is to tolerate his anger, fear and sadness, use the feelings invoked in me to try to understand Jay's experience and finally have him experience a close relationship that does not end in loss or rejection. If our relationship can make even a small change in the way Jay views himself and others, he will be one step closer to breaking the cycle of loss. But even these small steps forward are generally combined with steps backward. The journey never really ends. As helping professionals, our task is to truly enter into the child's journey for better or for worse, for as long as that child is in our care, knowing that we may never know how the story ends or if our struggles have had any sizable impact.

This type of active participation can provoke anger, frustration and hopelessness within the person trying to help. These feeling are not necessarily a sign of failure. It is normal to feel negative hateful feelings when bombarded with the rage of an angry child[33]. The child's reenactment of past experiences and feelings are part of the treatment process. The child may be invoking in you their own feelings of hate, anger, frustration and loneliness. In these cases, the adult is required to understand and use their own feelings to connect with the child. Having these negative feelings is not wrong. Instead, it is the way these feelings are managed, understood and used to help the child heal which is important.

The child's unpredictability, narcissism and highly charged emotions can be overwhelming to the therapist[34]. Their use of action instead of words is often intimidating to a highly verbal adult. Unfortunately, there is a societal myth, which perpetuates the false sweetness and purity associated with adult feelings toward children. This can stifle the therapist's recognition of these angry or negative feelings. Marshall states; "formidable defenses are erected against destructive thoughts, impulses and feelings toward children"[35]. This societal taboo can inhibit the discussion of negative feelings experienced by those working with children. Many believe that there is too much emotion evoked in child treatment and as a result clinicians and theorists are apprehensive about discussing the issue[36]. Open communication among those working with this population is a necessary first step toward managing, understanding and using these feelings toward a meaningful purpose.

To empathize with a child

The proper use of negative feelings as a tool for understanding and healing is a form of empathy and the main idea put forth in this chapter. My struggle to empathize with Jay will hopefully enable him to gain the tools to empathize with others. Empathy is needed to truly connect with others and this connection is the only way to begin to mend the hole created by loss. Jay's early losses and traumas were the result of his mother's inability to empathize with her baby resulting in maltreatment. To empathize means to share in the

---

[33] Winnicott, *Hate in the counter-transference*
[34] Bornstein, *Emotional Barriers in the Understanding and Treatment of Young Children*; Gabel & Bemporad, *Variations in Countertransference Reactions in Psychotherapy with Children*
[35] Marshall, *Countertransference in the Psychotherapy of Children and Adolescents*, p.413
[36] Gabel & Bemporad, *Variations in Countertransference Reactions in Psychotherapy with Children;* Kohrman, *Technique of child analysis*

feelings of another person (Greenson, 1960). It has been defined as, "the inner experience of sharing in and comprehending the momentary psychological state of another person"[37] and "a mode of perceiving by vicarious experiencing (in a limited way) the psychological state of another person. Literally, it means 'feeling into' another person, as contrasted with sympathy, which means 'feeling with' [38]. The ability to empathize is associated with the preverbal mother- infant relationship. It is "preconscious, silent and automatic"[39]. To fully and completely empathize with another person is impossible.

While working with Jay a shift needed to occur from me feeling *about* him to me feeling *with* him[40]. I was required to take in his anger and hold it while at the same time remain whole and separate. I frequently did not meet this challenge. The goal is to strive for this type of experience knowing you will not be fully successful. The hope is that the pain experienced throughout this struggle will result in healing and eventually some form of peace.

An adult's ability to truly empathize with a child is a beautiful and rare quality. Olden authored one of the few articles, which closely examines this phenomenon[41] She lists the attributes which facilitate the unique ability to feel as a child feels:

> The people who can adjust to the child's world, who can not only work but live with children are those who have preserved some infantile traits: a certain amount of passivity, which makes possible their admirable patience; some remnants of the belief in magic, which accounts for the lack of over anxiousness...some casualness about destruction and disorder[42].

This type of empathy requires a balance between feeling as a child feels, and having the adult senses of reality and responsibility. Working and consistently being with children is a demanding task, which requires the adult to develop a comfort level with re-feeling and reliving the emotions of their own childhood. It is vital to know your ability to tolerate and contain these powerful emotions. Traumatized and bereaved children frequently develop an adaptive hyper-vigilance to other's affect and mood. They may hold a mirror up and show us who we are, and we need to be ready if that happens. Before starting to work with this population self-exploration should occur. It is important to examine your own feelings and familial history regarding death, abuse, neglect and other pertinent childhood experiences which could impact your relationship

---

[37] Schafer, *Generative Empathy in the Treatment Situation,* p.345.
[38] Moore & Fine, *Psychoanalytic terms and concepts,* p.67
[39] Ibid
[40] Beres & Arlow, *Fantasy and Identification in Empathy*
[41] Olden, *On Adult Empathy with Children*
[42] Ibid, p. 124-125

with the child. Remember, this relationship should be based on the child's needs and not your own. The ultimate goal, while impossible to fully achieve, is for every action, comment or unspoken message to be child based. This is why it is vital for the helper to attend to their own needs outside of the child's sessions. As adults in the lives of children who are frequently voiceless in our society, we are obligated to protect these children not only from maltreatment outside the session, but also from using them to heal our own emotional wounds. A therapist's most "powerful weapon" is stopping treatment in response to the child's hostility. Prior to helping children who have experienced significant losses, it is important for the adult to understand their ability to tolerate and contain the emotions of a traumatized child. Terminating the treatment relationship based on the child's 'badness' merely perpetuates the cycle of loss and their view of themselves as toxic.

Using empathy as a tool for healing

Empathy is the struggle to understand; knowing that this struggle may open up doors we wish could be kept shut. Understanding ourselves is vital to having empathy for others. Jay's time with me was a short chapter in his quest to understand himself. He displayed signs of being able to empathize with me and others toward the end of our time together. Empathy cannot be taught. It evolves over time from within, after exposure to others who are empathetic. If the ability to empathize is present, a therapist can be taught how to use it effectively[43]. Healing begins with the genuine struggle to understand an experience which will inevitably be outside of our ability to grasp. Children who have suffered multiple losses or traumas often fear closeness, which creates distance and an obstacle to being understood. This presents a considerable challenge to the adult who is struggling to empathize. A willingness to walk next to a child, to tolerate and hold onto the type of pain which we cannot and should not attempt to take away, displays a respect for the child's experience. In child treatment, the therapist is called upon to be more 'real'[44]. What does it feel like for a child to watch a parent wither away from a disease? How is a child's self and world view impacted by the loss of safety and structure which occurs in an abusive or neglectful home? These are questions we may never be able to adequately answer. Lanyado describes her treatment of a ten year old child who had suffered maltreatment and multiple losses: " It would be accurate

---

[43] Ibid
[44] Marshall, *Countertransference in the Psychotherapy of Children and Adolescents*

to describe him as being someone who has struggle to carry a load for a long while, and suddenly sees a place where he can put it down"[45].

Conclusion

Jay moved away and is now living with his mother in another state. I will never see him again. Will loss continue to permeate his life? Will he ever be able to maintain a committed relationship with an adult? Will he ever truly fall in love with someone who is good to him and for him? I will never know the answers to these questions. This is one of the main difficulties in trying to find ways to help children who have suffered trauma and loss. Children grow up and move on. Some may return and provide us with insights, but more often when a childhood is riddled with loss there is a protective need to disconnect. This may be why clinical and empirical literature discussing child treatment and in particular the treatment of traumatized children is significantly lacking compared with adult focused literature[46]. Jay's story is so valuable and I am honored to be able to share it with others because it offers a glimpse inside the world of a child who ordinarily has no voice. Children depend on adults to be their mouthpiece. Listening and then telling these kinds of stories is one way to develop methods which will help children like Jay. It is in the close, scrutinizing examination of our journey together, that the many small steps taken toward a new type of story are revealed. Thank you Jay.

References

Ablon, S. L. "Where Work Is Play for Mortal Stakes: The Good Hour in Child Analysis." *Psychoanalytic Study of the Child* 55, no. 113-123, 2000.

Anastasopoulos, D , and J Tsiantis. *Countertransference in Psychoanalytic Psychotherapy with Children and Adolescents*. Madison, CT: International Universities Press, Inc., 1996.

Anthony, E. J. "Nonverbal and Verbal Systems of Communication: A Study of Complementarity. ." *PsychoAnalytic Study of the Child* 32, no. 307-325, 1977.

---

[45] Lanyado, *Variations on the Theme of Transference & Counter-Transference in the Treatment of a Ten Year Old Boy,* p.87

[46] Brandell, *Countertransference in the Psychotherapy of Children and Adolescents;* Fantuzzo et al, *Community-Based Resilient Peer Treatment of Withdrawn Maltreated Preschool Children*; Gabel & Bemporad, *Variations in Countertransference Reactions in Psychotherapy with Children*; Marshall, *Countertransference in the Psychotherapy of Children and Adolescents*

Balint, M. "Changing Therapeutic Aims and Techniques in Psychoanalysis." *International Journal of Psychoanalysis* 31, no. 117-124,1950.

Beebe, B., J. Jaffe, and F Lachmann. "A Dyadic Systems View of Communication." In *Relational Perspectives in Psychoanalysis*, edited by N. Skolnick and S. Warshaw. Hillsdale, NJ: The Analytic Press, 1992.

Beres, D., and J.A. Arlow. "Fantasy and Identification in Empathy." *Psychoanalytic Quarterly* 43: 26-50, 1974

Bornstein, B. "Emotional Barriers in the Understanding and Treatment of Young Children." *American Journal of Orthopsychiatry* 18, no. 691-697, 1948.

Bowlby, J. "The Nature of a Child's Tie to His Mother." *International Journal of Psychoanalysis* 30: 350-73, 1958.

Brandell, J. R. Countertransference in the Psychotherapy of Children and Adolescents. Northvale, N. J.: Aronson, Inc, 1992.

Cameron, J. B. *Understanding and Supporting a Child or Teen Coping with a Death*. Tuckahoe, NY: The Bereavement Center of Westchester, 2006.

Crittenden, P. M. "Language and Psychopathology: An Attachment Perspective." In *Language, Learning, and Behavioral Disorders: Developmental, Biological, and Clinical Perspectives*, edited by J. Beitchman and N Cohen, 59-77. New York: Cambridge University Press, 1996.

———. "The Treatment of Anxious Attachment in Infancy and Early Childhood." *Development and Psychopathology* 2 (1992): 575-602.

Erikson, Erik H. *Childhood and Society, 35th Anniversary Edition*. New York: W. W. Norton, 1985 (1950).

Fairbairn, D. W. "A Revised Psychopathology of the Psychoses of Psychoneuroses." *International Journal of Psychoanalysis* 22 (1941): 250-79.

Fantuzzo, J., B. Sutton-Smith, M. Atkins, R. Meyers, H. Stevenson, K Coolahan, A Weiss, and P Manz. "Community-Based Resilient Peer Treatment of Withdrawn Maltreated Preschool Children." *Journal of Consulting and Clinical Psychology* 6 (1996): 1377-86.

Gabel, S. , and J. Bemporard. "Variations in Countertransference Reactions in Psychotherapy with Children." *American Journal of Psychotherapy* 48, no. 1 (1994): 111-19.

Gartner, A. "Countertransference Issues in the Psychotherapy of Adolescents." *Journal of Child and Adolescent Psychotherapy* 2 (1985): 187-96.

Hauge, K. "Reconstruction in an Analysis of a Child." *The Scandinavian Psychoanalytic Review* 20, no. 160-177 (1997).

Kernberg, O. F. "Borderline Conditions and Pathological Narcissism." New York: Jason Aronson, 1975.

————. "Notes on Countertransference." *Journal of the American Psychoanalytic Association* 13, no. 1 (1965): 38-56.

Kohrman, R., H. Fineberg, R. Gelman, and S Weiss. "Technique of Child Analysis: Problems of Countertransference." *International Journal of Psychoanalysis* 52 (1971): 487-97.

Krell, H.L. , and R.L. Okin. "Countertransference Issues in Child Abuse and Neglect Cases." *American Journal of Forensic Psychiatry* 5, no. 1 (1984): 7-16.

Lanyado, M. "Variations on the Theme of Transference & Counter-Transference in the Treatment of a Ten Year Old Boy." *Journal of Child Psychotherapy* 15, no. 2 (1989): 85-101.

Maenchen, A. "On the Technique of Child Analysis in Relation to Stages of Development." *Psychoanalytic Study of the Child* 25, no. 175-208 (1970).

Marshall, R. "Countertransference in the Psychotherapy of Children and Adolescents. " *Contemporary Psychoanalysis* 15 (1979): 595-639.

Moore, B.E., and B.D. Fine. *Psychoanalytic Terms and Concepts.* New Haven: Yale University Press., 1990.

Olden, C. "On Adult Empathy with Children." *Psychoanalytic Study of the Child* 8, no. 111-126 (1956).

Perry, B.D., RA Pollard, Blakely TL, WL Baker, and D Vigilante. "Childhood Trauma, the Neurobiology of Adaptation and "Use-Dependent" Development of the Brain. How " States" Become "Traits"." *Infant Mental Health Journal* 16, no. 271-291 (1995).

Ryan, K. "The Chronically Traumatized Child." *Child and Adolescent Social Work Journal* 13, no. 4 (1996): 287-310.

Schafer, R. "Generative Empathy in the Treatment Situation." *Psychoanalytic Quarterly* 28, no. 34-373 (1959).

Van der Kolk, B. "The Body Keeps the Score: Memory and the Evolving Psychobiology of Posttraumatic Stress." *Harvard Review of Psychiatry* 1 (1994): 253-65.

Van Waning, A. "To Be the Best or Not to Be, That Is the Question...' on Enactment, Play and Acting Out." *International Journal of Psychoanalysis* 72, no. 539-551 (1991).

Winnicott, D. W. "Hate in the Counter-Transference." *International Journal of Psychoanalysis* 30, no. 69-74 (1949).

————. *The Maturation Processes and the Facilitating Environment.* Madison, CT: International Universities Press, 1963.

CHAPTER FOUR

RESPONDING TO TRAUMA, VIOLENCE AND BEREAVEMENT OVERLOAD IN THE LIVES OF YOUNG AFRICAN AMERICAN MEN: TRAUMA-INFORMED APPROACHES TO HEALTH CARE

THEODORE J. CORBIN, M.D. AND JOHN A. RICH, M.D., M.P.H.

Introduction

We begin this chapter by discussing some of the devastating results of living in America's urban war zones – the inner cities – and the toll this takes particularly on young black men. Currently, most victims of youth violence are young men of color. Black men, however, are sorely underrepresented among providers of care, especially physicians and this under representation deepens the sense of mistrust in young men who already believe that the deck is stacked against them. We have a special interest in this issue because both authors of this chapter are African-American physicians. For us, the war that is being waged at home – so slowly but insidiously destructive – is like a slow rolling disaster with no end in site.

We have both been involved in trying to intervene in the lives of trauma survivors at two key points of contact: medical emergency rooms and primary care clinics. In this chapter we describe two programmatic efforts within the healthcare system to provide a higher level of care for young men in inner city who are victims of violence and who are largely African-American.

The Thomas Jefferson University Hospital Community Violence Prevention Program represents a coalition of providers focused on emergency department-based interventions that have the potential to address trauma and loss more effectively for an urban population. The Young Men's Health Clinic at Boston City Hospital is a primary care based intervention that is designed to provide holistic health care for young man who aged out of adolescent care and who are utilizing adult health care.

We conclude the chapter by discussing some of the key lessons learned in implementing these programs. We believe that it is possible to transform existing health care services by providing a trauma-informed healing perspective that will benefit not only the young men who are seen themselves but also the communities that they come from. It is our hope that by addressing the past and on-going traumatic and bereavement experiences of these young men, that we may make them better able to avoid passing their trauma along to their children.

Living in a War Zone

The streets of Philadelphia, one of the nation's largest cities, have become an urban war zone. In one particularly brutal neighborhood, the word "Iraq" is spray painted on vacant buildings[44]. In a seven month period in 2006, 1, 192 people were shot, 242 of them were killed and 142 of these shooting victims were children and teenagers[45]. In the same period, victims of gun violence in Philadelphia equaled 54% of all American military deaths in Iraq[46]. Homicides claimed 406 victims in Philadelphia in 2006 – the deadliest toll since 1997's 418[47]. Over the past two years, the murder rate among people age 18 to 24 is 30% higher than the rate for all victims and overall they make up a third of all homicides in Philadelphia[48]. Since 2004, 102 children seventeen years old or younger, have been murdered in Philadelphia[49]. Some 88% of all victims in all age categories are male[50].

These numbers, however, only represent the most graphic exposure to violence. What lies hidden behind the statistics of victimization is the enormity of "co-victimization" – every witness to violence, every family member or friend that loses a loved one, is also victimized. And in the process of this devastation, entire communities are affected. As noticed by those who have studied collective trauma,

> Competency in coping can be overwhelmed and weakened in groups that have experienced an accumulation of losses and are still dealing with unresolved past

---

[44] **Moran**, *Living, dying in Phila.'s 'Iraq' - A mother is shot to death, and a community is torn.*
[45] **Baer**, *As bullets fly, bodies drop, where's Street?*
[46]**Haile, Lowy and Pennington**. *Lethal Lou's: Profile of a Rogue Gun Dealer – Lou's Loan of Upper Darby, Pennsylvania.*
[47] **Weischselbaum**, *A Quest to save youth at risk.*
[48] **Ibid**
[49] **Ibid**
[50] **Ibid**

traumas. Bereavement overload, often observed in individuals who have suffered many losses within a circumscribed period of time, can numb a community and interfere with efforts to respond to a current crisis[51].

Being Young, Black and Male

Young African-American men in particular are often victims of violence. National data show that African-American men are more likely to report that they have been victimized through violence. Homicide is the leading cause of death for African-American males between the ages of 15 and 34. In addition, African-American males have the highest rate of so-called legal intervention homicide, or death at the hands of law enforcement officials, also known as "suicide by cop"[52]. As Geoffrey Canada has noted, *"It takes years of preparation to be willing to commit murder, to be willing to kill or die for a corner, a color, or a leather jacket. Many of the children of America are conditioned early to kill and more frighteningly, to die, for what to an outsider might seem a trivial cause"[53]*.

And what lies behind violent victimization is the impact of chronic, grinding, unrelenting chronic sources of stress and loss. As a group, young black men in the inner city experience trauma and loss throughout their lives. The chronic, institutional stresses of poverty and racism are examples of social forces that can be termed traumatogenic in that they breed interpersonal traumatic acts[54]. Young black men historically have been victims of trauma through discrimination, lack of access to jobs, high rates of imprisonment and brutalization at the hands of the police. Difficult life conditions give rise to a constellation of cultural circumstances which make the transmission of interpersonal violence normative[55]. Poverty has been found to have a primary influence on how well parents manage family life[56]. Family poverty inhibits parental processes of family control, for example, increasing the likelihood of childhood acting out[57]. In discussing the causes of the rising violence in Philadelphia among youth, Richard Gelles, Dean of the School of Social Policy and Practice at the University of Pennsylvania, suggested that one cause of the

---

[51] Zinner and Williams, *Summary and Incorporation: A Reference Frame for Community Recovery and Restoration*
[52] Poussaint and Alexander, *Lay My Burden Down*
[53] Canada, *Fist Stick Knife Gun*
[54] Bloom and Reichert, *Bearing Witness*
[55] Staub, *Cultural-societal roots of violence.*
[56] Garrett et al, *Poverty Experiences of Young Children and the Quality of Their Home*
[57] Sampson and Laub, *Urban Poverty and the Family Context of Delinquency: A New Look at Structure and Process in a Classic Study.*

rise in youth violence could be the welfare reforms of 1996 – which he helped to write. The city:

> may be at the front end of a wave because Philadelphia set a 24 month limit for welfare benefits while the rest of the country set a 60-month limit....We turned a blind eye to the fact that many of them [welfare recipients] were single parents. It's not a bad idea putting people to work – except that if you're going to put moms to work, it's *really* a good idea to have daycare and it's *really* a good idea to have healthcare. We didn't do that. We created a situation where there's nobody home" and without anyone to watch over them, children are being raised by the streets[58].

Because of a high rate of violence among African-American men, many have lost friends or family members to violence or to imprisonment. Many young men have grown up without fathers, and as a result they cannot access the advice, role modeling and mentorship that they would expect. Further, they are deprived of the future economic benefits of having two wage earners in the home and this has a marked effect on their economic security.

Under such conditions, it is not surprising that unchecked aggression is more frequently exhibited in children from poverty families[59]. Other at-risk factors for violence are also associated with economic and race stressors. The "single common pathway to high-risk adolescent behavior" has been found to be early academic failure[60]. Yet a child's chances for success in school has been found to be powerfully affected by early childhood experiences of poverty[61]. Anderson has vividly documented the manner in which the

> inclination to violence springs from the circumstances of life among the ghetto poor - the lack of jobs that pay a living wage, the stigma of race, the fallout from rampant drug use and drug trafficking, and the resulting alienation and lack of hope for the future"[62].

Most significantly, the cumulative effect of violence in the home and on the streets impairs the establishment of interpersonal trust, a central outcome of the human attachment process that ideally endows citizens with a sense of investment in their community[63]. The constant background of violence for

---

[58] Vaidya, *What's Behind a New Wave of Crime*

[59] Tolan and Henry, *Patterns of Psychopathology among Urban Poor Children: Comorbidity and Aggression Effects.*

[60] Tuakli-Williams and Carrillo, *The Impact of Psychosocial Stressors on African American and Latino Preschoolers*

[61] Brooks-Gunn, *The Effects of Poverty on Children*

[62] Anderson, *Living hard by the code of the streets*

[63] Bloom and Reichert, Bearing Witness

poor urban youth creates, by contrast, a "culture of disengagement"[64]. At this point in the culture, with black males threatened from a convergence of powerful trends, the manner in which a child internalizes the content of negative messages through distorting self-image provides an additional explanation for the culture of violence swirling through urban communities.

Post-Traumatic Stress and African American Youth

It then follows from the catastrophic levels of violence that young black men have high rates of trauma exposure. Yet the medical and mental health literature has not documented clearly the rates of acute stress and post-traumatic stress that occur in these young men, in part because of the problem of definition. Geoffrey Canada has pointed out that, *"for the handgun generation there is no post-traumatic stress syndrome because there is no 'post'. We need a new term to describe what happens to people who never get out from under war conditions, maybe 'continuous traumatic stress syndrome' "*[65]. Breslau and colleagues have documented high rates of post-traumatic stress among inner-city youth[66].

Research findings on the incidence of posttraumatic stress disorder in the African American community are, however disturbing. In the early 1990s, researchers surveyed 7-18 year olds who were participating in a summer program near Washington, D.C. Twenty-two percent of the children reported symptoms of PTSD. The researchers also reported that 70% of the children were victims of violence and of those studied, 85% had witnessed at least one violent attach and over 43% had witnessed a murder. In the study, the greater the exposure to violence, the greater the likelihood of PTSD symptoms[67]. Also in the early 1990's, another study screened over a thousand children in the Chicago area and found that 75% of the boys and 70% of the girls had seen someone get shot, stabbed, robbed, or killed and linked these experiences to deterioration in cognitive performance and both behavioral and emotional dysfunction[68].

More recently, Rich and Grey documented that 2/3 African-American males hospitalized for violent injury fulfilled criteria for post-traumatic stress disorder when surveyed a month or more after their injuries[69]. Even those men

---

[64] Berman, The effects of living with violence

[65] Canada, Fist, Stick, Knife, Gun

[66] Breslau, Andreski and Peterson, Traumatic Events and Posttraumatic Stress Disorder in an Urban Population of Young Adults.; Breslau and Davis, Posttraumatic Stress Disorder in an Urban Population of Young Adults

[67] Allen, PTSD Among African Americans, p. 215-216.

[68] Ibid, p.216

[69] Rich and Grey, Pathways to recurrent trauma among young black men

who did not meet full criteria for PTSD showed evidence of hypervigilance on the PTSD Symptom Scale. While these studies alone do not paint a full picture, it follows that young black men having experienced trauma and loss in so many areas of their lives would show the short-term and long-term effects of trauma.

Several studies show that victims of violence are more likely to be re-victimized[70]. Rich and Grey, using qualitative methods suggested the trauma that results from violent injury sets in motion a cascade that makes another episode of violence more likely to happen[71]. They found that young men who live in the inner city and who do not trust the police may feel the need to arm themselves after they have been injured believing that they will protect themselves. They also found that these young men believe that if they fail to retaliate when they are victimized, others in their community will see them as week and will seek to victimize them as well. While these ideas are prevalent in the community among victims of violence, they are exacerbated by active symptoms of post-traumatic stress that lead them to over-interpret any signs of danger as a real clear threat to their safety.

And are these young victims likely to receive adequate mental health treatment? An abundance of reports highlight the present dysfunction of the mental health system as a whole. According to multiple reports looking at the present state of the mental health system, separate health, mental health and substance abuse service delivery systems and funding sources, differences among clinicians in practice orientation and training, and various consumer concerns are just some of the barriers that must be overcome to deliver effective integrated care. According to the President's New Freedom Commission on Mental Health,

> The mental health services system defies easy description.... Taken as a whole, the system is supposed to function in a coordinated manner; it is supposed to deliver the best possible treatments, services, and supports-but it often falls short"[72]. As the Bazelon Center for Mental Health Law points out, "Fragmented care remains the norm for individuals with serious mental disorders. The delivery systems for mental health, substance abuse and physical health care are separate, often with different financing arrangements and policy-setting"[73]

And as multiple investigators have pointed out, the services for young people are in even worse disarray than those for adults, with children stuck for days and even months in emergency rooms waiting residential programs[74].

---

[70] Sims et al, Urban trauma: a chronic recurrent disease
[71] Ibid
[72] President's New Freedom Commisiion, Interim Report
[73] Bazelon Center, Get It Together
[74] Bazelon, Disintegrating Systems

This is particularly a problem for underserved children and young adults. Unfortunately, the mental health system has not kept pace with the diverse needs of racial and ethnic minorities, often under-serving or inappropriately serving them. Specifically, the system has neglected to incorporate respect or understanding of the histories, traditions, beliefs, languages, and value systems of culturally diverse groups. Misunderstanding and misinterpreting behaviors have led to tragic consequences, including inappropriately placing minorities in the criminal and juvenile justice systems. For example, these populations: are less likely to have access to available mental health services, are less likely to receive needed mental health care, often receive poorer quality care, and are significantly under-represented in mental health research. However, additional barriers prevent racial and ethnic minorities from seeking services, including: mistrust and fear of treatment; different cultural ideas about illnesses and health; differences in help-seeking behaviors, language, and communication patterns; racism; varying rates of being uninsured; and discrimination by individuals and institutions[75].

Young African American Men Incarcerated

African-American men also have rates of incarceration, probation and parole that are much higher than white men. For every 100,000 Black juveniles living in the United States, more than 750 are in custody in a juvenile facility[76]. One in three Black men ages 20-29 has either been in prison or is on parole[77]. African Americans currently constitute 12% of the national population but 44% of the prison population, which means 5% of Black America is behind bars. Even worse, 10.1% of all black men between the ages of 18 and 29 are in prison[78].

In the Philadelphia prison system current figures show that 70% of the incarcerated population is Black[79]. The number of juveniles arrested for murder and gun possession in 2006 was twice the figure for 2002[80]. One out of every 15 Philadelphia residents is under court supervision – a total of about 97,000 people, 5700 of whom are under 18[81] In 2006, 646 kids were arrested for illegally carrying a gun compared with 319 in 2002. And 26 juveniles were

---

[75] United States Public Health Service, *Mental Health: Culture, Race, and Ethnicity*
[76] Miller, *Young lives lost.*
[77] Ibid
[78] Bureau of Justice Statistics, *Prisoners in 2004.*
[79] Ibid
[80] Weichselbaum *Youth-crime system broken.*
[81] Ibid

charged with murder in 2006, up from 13 in 2002[82]. According to a report studying the causes of the violence problems in Philadelphia, handguns are easy to come by and are often used to settle disputes, both big and small; youth believe they have an almost non-existent support system of adults and feel they live in a city with limited messages of recovery for those who have "fallen" and limited access to meaningful assistance to get their lives on the right track[83]. As Alvin Poussaint and Amy Alexander point out in their study on the mental health crisis among African-Americans:

> The young black male who takes up a firearm and engages an opponent in a confrontation… has made a decision to put his life on the line. Consciously or not, such a youth sees violence carried out in the name of "respect" as an acceptable way of dying. Often faced with the message that their lives are not valued in American society, young blacks many internalize their despair – or externalize it. The hard-living man or woman[84]

Adding to this problem, health and mental health services delivered within correctional facilities are often inadequate to deal with the stress and trauma that these young men have experienced and the conditions of imprisonment may themselves be traumatic[85]. Reports have demonstrated that children entering juvenile detention facilities, particularly those with mental illnesses are unlikely to get adequate treatment. According to a report requested by Senators Waxman and Collins, about 15,000 children with mental illnesses were improperly incarcerated in detention centers in 2003 because of a lack of access to treatment, and 7% of all children in detention centers remain incarcerated because of a lack of access to treatment. In addition, the report found that 117 detention centers incarcerated children with mental illnesses younger than age 11. The report also found that 66% of detention centers said they incarcerated children with mental illnesses "because there was no place else for them to go," Some witnesses who testified at the hearing said that children with mental illnesses often are incarcerated in detention centers because their parents do not have access to treatment in schools or lack health coverage for such treatment[86].

According to the President's New Freedom Commission, at least 7% of all incarcerated people have a current serious mental illness; the proportion with a less serious form of mental illness is substantially higher. People with serious

---

[82] Ibid
[83] *Blueprint for a Safer Philadelphia, Focus Group Research Summary*
[84] Poussaint, *Lay My Burden Down,* p. 14
[85] Kupers, *Mental health in men's prisons*
[86] Kaiser Daily Health Policy Report. "15,000 Children Incarcerated Because of Lack of Mental Health Treatment in 2003"

mental illnesses who come into contact with the criminal justice system are often: poor, uninsured, disproportionately members of minority groups, homeless, and living with co-occurring substance abuse and mental disorders. They are likely to continually recycle through the mental health, substance abuse, and criminal justice systems.

> As a shrinking public health care system limits access to services, many poor and racial or ethnic minority youth with serious emotional disorders fall through the cracks into the juvenile justice system. When they are put in jail, people with mental illnesses frequently do not receive appropriate mental health services. Many lose their eligibility for income supports and health insurance benefits that they need to re-enter and re-integrate into the community after they are discharged[87].

More than 106,000 teens are in custody in juvenile justice facilities across the country[88]. Recent research shows a high prevalence of mental disorders in children within the juvenile justice system. A large-scale, four-year, Chicago–based study found that 66% of boys and nearly 75% of girls in juvenile detention have at least one psychiatric disorder. About 50% of these youth abused or were addicted to drugs and more than 40% had either oppositional defiant or conduct disorders. The study also found high rates of depression and dysthymia: 17% of boys; 26% of detained girls[89]. As youth progressed further into the formal juvenile justice system, rates of mental disorder also increased: 46% of youth on probation met criteria for a serious emotional disorder compared to 67% of youth in a correctional setting[90].

Rape is known to be widespread in men's prisons and often leads to post-traumatic stress disorder which is not usually classified by the correction's department as a "major mental illness". As one author points out, *the male prisoner faces overwhelming obstacles to talking through the trauma or prison rape*[91]. Under such circumstances, when young men enter the correctional system, the possibility that they will have any opportunity to work through their previous traumatic experiences and traumatic losses is remote. For young men who have perpetrated violence or been prosecuted for any crime, there is little regard or empathy for the losses that they have experienced throughout their lives that may be significant contributors to their present dysfunctional behavior.

---

[87] President's New Freedom Commission, *Achieving the Promise,* p. 32
[88] Ibid
[89] Teplin et al, *Psychiatric disorders in youth in juvenile detention*
[90] Lyons et al, *Mental Health Service Needs of Juvenile Offenders*
[91] Ibid, p.194.

Health Disparities and Unequal Medical Care

Black men overall also have worse health than their white counterparts. Black men live on at an average of five years less than white men and die at a higher rate from heart disease, stroke, AIDS, and violence[92]. This results in many young African-American men and older African-American men having to bid farewell to friends and family members who have died prematurely or who suffer with chronic illness. There is also substantial data that shows that people of color receive worse health care in the healthcare system[93]. A body of research shows that black patients receive dramatically different care than whites for such diverse conditions as heart disease, stroke, cancer, diabetes, renal transplant, HIV/AIDS, immunizations and asthma. Similar disparities in mental health care have also been uncovered[94]. Poor health, due not only to different rates of disease but also to poorer medical care, leads to loss of economic resources through disability. Even more importantly, the prospect of a foreshortened life expectancy often limits the horizon of possibilities of people who live in the inner city, particularly in neighborhoods of color.

Among blacks, depression and symptoms of post-traumatic stress syndrome resulting from regular exposure to violence may also constitute a mental illness that neither they nor clinicians would readily recognize or acknowledge. And it is not far-fetched to argue that many of the pathologies currently bedeviling many in the black community – including high rates of drug and alcohol abuse, health-threatening diets, and violence – are fatalistic life-threatening behaviors that can be viewed as long-term or slow-motion suicide. Individuals experiencing poor health due to overeating, alcohol abuse, or drug abuse often go unchallenged by relatives if they keep up the appearance of "normalcy", holding down a job or at least keeping their addiction under wraps. The fact that African-Americans suffer from cirrhosis of the liver, heart ailments, sexually transmitted diseases, and obesity-related illnesses in disproportionately higher numbers that whites may be evidence that some African-Americans turn to food, drugs, alcohol, or even sexual activity as a form of medication to ameliorate stresses resulting from racism, discrimination, and other social pressures [95].

Young Men on Bereavement Overload

Every act of violence drags grief along with it. One expert on complicated mourning highlights seven high-risk factors that predispose

---

[92] National Center for Health Statistics, *Health, United States, 2006*
[93] Smedley et al, *Unequal treatment*
[94] Mayberry, *Racial and ethnic differences in access to medical care.*
[95] Poussaint and Alexander, *Lay My Burden Down,* p.126.

individuals to complicated mourning. These include: sudden, unexpected death especially when traumatic, violent, mutilating or random; death from an overly lengthy illness; loss of a child; the mourner's perception of the death as preventable; a premorbid relationship with the deceased that was markedly angry or ambivalent, or dependent; prior or concurrent mourner liabilities such as other losses, stresses or mental health problems; and the mourner's lack of social support. All of these factors result in greater numbers of people experiencing complicated mourning[96]. These are characteristics typical of acts of violence that have become normative in the lives of so many urban youth.

The most obvious losses are those associated with homicide. For the friends and family members of homicide victims, the mourning process may be a slow and arduous one and are sometimes considered as "high risk" deaths, meaning the loss contains elements that put people at risk for complicated mourning, requiring treatment for both PTSD and unresolved loss. As one worker in the field has suggested,

> a caregiver can expect to observe more intense and more prolonged reactions and will witness a greater incidence of symptoms of post-traumatic stress, victimization, and compulsive inquiry in subjects adjusting to unnatural vs. natural dying[97].

> Reactions of family survivors of homicide victims are likely to differ from other forms of bereavement in the depth of horror, rage, and vengefulness; the persistence of anxiety and phobic reactions; and the impediments to the adjustment process posed by continuing involvement with the criminal justice system[98].

It is easy to understand how the homicide of one youth can create a seemingly endless cycle of retaliation that involves entire families and entire communities.

Traumatic injury causes problems for the injured party and for those who are witnesses to it. The injured person suffers the loss of whatever bodily function is involved, but may also suffer sustained loss from the impairment in emotional and cognitive function that often accompany post-traumatic stress symptoms. These losses are likely to be "disenfranchised" when expressions of loss are seen as unmanly, or uncool, or unacceptable because they were brought on by intentional acts[99].

---

[96] Rando, *Treatment of Complicated Mourning,*
[97] Rynearson, as quoted in Randon, *Treatment of Complicated Mourning,* p.538
[98] Rando, *Treatment of Complicated Mourning,* p.539
[99] Doka, *Living With Grief*

Imprisonment represents a wide variety of losses for those who are incarcerated and for others left behind, beyond the most obvious loss of freedom of movement. For those left behind, the imprisoned family member represents an ambiguous loss, where although not physically present the person remains psychologically present[100].

Loss can compound loss over the course of a lifetime and the resulting numbing, alienation, inability to manage affective arousal, disturbed attachment patterns, oversensitivity, over-reactivity, rigid and compulsive behavior, inability to express feelings, inability to establish or maintain intimacy, tendency to engage in self-defeating and self-destructive behaviors, unmanageable anger, and a preoccupation for revenge are a prescription for the continuing escalation of violence and community disintegration[101]. As a society, we have a fundamental moral obligation to help young people find there way out of this trap in any way we can. Interventions at the point of contact in medical settings offer opportunities to provide information, social support, and resources that could make a difference in the lives of young men already at risk.

Emergency Department Based interventions: Building a Trauma-informed Approach

According to the Centers for Disease Control, in 2004, more than 750,000 young people ages 10 to 24 were treated in emergency departments for injuries sustained due to violence[102]. The *2001 Surgeon General's Report on Youth Violence* stated that addressing youth violence must start with identification of those that are at highest risk[103]. The report named emergency departments as the ideal place to identify such high risk individuals, and start the healing process. Yet, in general, trauma centers have not adopted this recommendation.

Given that these young men do not have easy access to insurance or to a healthcare provider, they often present to the emergency department for episodic care. This care is related not only to their injuries but to the psychological aftereffects of their trauma. Even though this is well known among emergency medicine providers and health care systems, few of these systems are truly equipped to provide trauma-informed services for this population. It is impossible to calculate the cost of such an oversight but to the

---

[100] Boss, *Loss, Trauma and Resilience.*
[101] Rando, *Treatment of Complicated Mourning*
[102] Centers for Disease Control
[103] Satcher, *Youth Violence*

degree that it leads to recurrent violence, and untreated post-traumatic stress, this oversight is tragic and costly.

A trauma-informed approach considers the suffering and pain that people have experienced over the course of their lives and recognizes that trauma feeds the cycle of violence and recurrent loss. As Sandra Bloom, a nationally known expert in trauma states, "hurt people hurt people"[104]. Emergency department-based trauma-informed interventions, seek to use the healing process as an opportunity to help youth understand the effects of trauma and change their responses to the stimuli in their environment.

Emergency Department Provider Narrative

I had spent the night tending to patients from all walks of life with complaints from a simple cut on the hand to major heart attacks that had to go to the catheterization laboratory for speedy life saving intervention. Near the end of my long 8-hour shift, the alert system rang out in the emergency department: "combative male injury, blunt object to head, vital signs stable, patient is awake and alert, patient is bleeding from head, have security on standby....repeat, combative male injury from blunt object to head, awake and alert have security on hand."

The charge nurse turned and asked me, "Should I call the trauma team?"

I responded, "Not yet. Let's stabilize him and assess his injuries. Then we will go from there." I asked the charge nurse to ready the emergency department trauma team at the trauma bay. Then I told my senior resident to get set up in the trauma bay. I glanced around the department to ensure that things are on auto-pilot when the paramedics came charging through the trauma bay doors with an African-American youth shouting obscenities while lying on the stretcher. I walked briskly to the trauma stretcher and asked the paramedics what had happened.

"He was at the corner store on 12th and Walnut and someone tried to rob him. He left the store and when we got to the store there was a trail of blood that led to him about 500 feet around the corner. When we found him he was bleeding from his head. He didn't want to come, but we finally secured him on the stretcher. He wouldn't let us put a neck collar on. His vital signs are stable."

"Hello, my name is Dr. Corbin," I said to the patient as he was being transferred to the emergency department trauma stretcher. "I am going to be one of many doctors taking care of you. Just try to cooperate and things will run smoothly. What is your name?"

---

[104] Bloom and Reichert, *Bearing Witness*

"Jeffrey," he responded with a look of anger.

At this point, the normal protocol of the emergency department staff is in full gear, my senior resident is at the head of the bed, gowned up and gloved, and calling out his assessment while he evaluates the patient.

I said, "Jeffrey, please bear with us. We just want to take care of you."

He responded, "I am straight. Get the fuck off of me. I don't need y'all mothafuckers!" Jeffrey started to fight us, trying to sit up and throw punches at the staff. His head was wrapped in blood stained gauze and we were not able to assess the extent of his head injury. The emergency technicians tried to restrain him, because without knowing the extent of his injuries, we all realized that he could die if we could not get close enough to him to evaluate him. We had no idea how much of his behavior was a result of his head injury. Jeffrey continued to yell and fight as we connected him to the cardiac and blood pressure monitor.

I continued to ask him, "Jeffrey, will you please work with us? You could be hurt worse then you know."

He looked at me directly in my eyes and said softly: "Doc you got to let me go."

I told him, "You are hurt. I need to know how bad."

My resident said, "He has a really large scalp laceration." At this, Jeffrey started to fight more and began to scream profanities. His heart rate was elevated. This worried me, because I was not yet able to tell whether or not he had suffered an intracranial bleed or if he was just agitated. I progressed to the next more aggressive step.

I announced to the team, "We need to intubate him. I cannot tell what is going on and he is not cooperating. He could hurt himself more." At this point we were all following the trauma protocol. My senior resident was excited about this procedure, but I was reluctant because of the way Jeffrey looked at me. I knew that medically it was the to do and the safest way to determine the extent of his injuries. Jeffrey was sedated and paralyzed by the medication the senior resident gave him in order to perform the procedure. We were administering oxygen to him through a bag valve apparatus. According to the monitor he was getting enough oxygen. My resident then tried to intubate him, but was unable to do so.

I asked, "Do you see the vocal cords?"

He responded, "No, I just can't see them." I told him to take his time as I know this is not an easy procedure, and it is anxiety-provoking. The resident stopped and asked the technician to continue to oxygenate with the bag valve. I traded places with my resident and looked in to Jeffrey's mouth with the laryngoscope.

As soon as I did, I saw a small plastic bag lodged into the area above his vocal cords. I thought, "How could he talk without choking?" I used forceps to remove the small bag filled with a whitish substance I assumed was an illicit drug and I was able to insert the endotracheal tube without a problem. We were then able to put him on the mechanical ventilator to breathe for him, ensure proper placement of the tube and continue with our assessment. We found that he had a 10 centimeter scalp wound with a moderate amount of bleeding. His vital signs appeared stable at this point. I ordered the appropriate scans to check for any life threatening injuries. Fortunately for him, minutes later the CAT scan of his head showed that Jeffrey did not show a life threatening intracranial bleed. The police showed up asking about the status of the patient and asked if they could talk to him. I knew I was not obstructing justice in any way when I tell them that the patient is not able to talk because he is intubated and that we have not finished our evaluation of him.

Clearly, what I found in Jeffrey's mouth was an illegal substance, but I am obligated to care for his medical problems as the first priority. Now I know why Jeffrey said that I had to let him go. "He needs drug rehabilitation," I think to myself, "no he needs direction. He needs direction and drug treatment."

I looked at the registry and found that he had been in our emergency department before for a previous injury and multiple other complaints. In reviewing the chart, I found that Jeffrey had a long history of exposure to violence going back to childhood. It became clear to me that this young African American man had been affected by the impact trauma has had on his life. Sadly, I recognized that nothing else would be done for him after we cleared him medically. I could have argued with the psychiatry department to admit him, but because I see he is deemed a "self-pay" which equals uninsured, and because he is a substance abuser, the likelihood of him being admitted was extremely low.

I questioned myself, "Where do I refer this young man? Is he going to follow up with the suggestions that I make for him? Does he even want to follow up? Clearly he is suffering from the impact of his environment and situation, but how does he get redirection?" Jeffrey finally left the emergency room, still alive but just as much at risk for a violent early death as when he entered.

The scenario depicted above is not an unusual one. In Philadelphia, and across the country, emergency providers are confronted with young victims of violence who present with complex stories and complex needs. While the young man above was involved in the illicit drug economy, he also came in with significant trauma and a history of substantial violence in the past. Emergency providers are daily faced with men, women, and children with histories of similar exposure to violence. Providers would like to make a difference but often lack the time and resources to do so.

Jefferson Community Violence Prevention Program

It was in response to frustration over patients like Jeffrey that the Jefferson Community Violence Prevention Program at Thomas Jefferson University Hospital (TJUH) was developed as part of a larger initiative known as the Health Care Collaborative. This violence prevention initiative at TJUH began in 1997 through a three-year grant from the William Penn Foundation. The grant was designed to identify young victims of violence who were seen and discharged from the emergency department to provide follow-up referral services that would improve these patients' quality of life and prevent return visits to the emergency department for reinjury or death. Identification of young violence victims was accomplished through medical staff referrals to Jefferson's Department of Pastoral Care and Education.

The program was developed in response to concern about increased youth violence in Philadelphia. It envisioned the opportunity to collaborate with other area programs in creating a network of services offering community-based resources for employment, education and personal counseling to at-risk young people. When victims of violence between the ages of 14 and 25 were admitted to the trauma service or seen in the emergency department, a coordinated attempt was made to develop trust and rapport that would extend beyond the hospital stay, and offer support for the future. The program included:

Identification

Jefferson's Emergency Department medical staff was trained in the risk-assessment protocol developed for this project. Overall, the staff demonstrated a high level of acceptance and willingness to use the protocol to help identify, screen and assess youths they treated in the ED after incidents of violence. To assist in identification, two full-time social workers were hired and trained in the risk-assessment protocol as well. These social workers, stationed in the ED ten hours a day and seven days a week, provided real-time screening at the bedside and referral to Pastoral Care for community follow-up. They were helpful in capturing walk-in patients with less critical injuries who still would benefit from bedside counseling and referral. All staff members received training quarterly and were encouraged to attend violence prevention seminars offered off-campus as well. Monitoring of emergency patients for victims of violence was done by the social workers from noon until midnight, our peak time for trauma cases. From midnight to noon, the ED physicians, nurses and technicians paged pastoral care staff, who evaluated patients in the department. Every morning, the Project Director conducted computer surveillance of the previous 24 hours of emergency department activity to ensure that all youths eligible for the project were captured.

Screening and Intervention

Youths who were screened would be stratified into low, moderate and high-risk categories according to safety factors in the youths' lives at the time. High risk was defined by the extent of the injury plus more than two specific or contributing risk factors, such as a plan for retaliation and a history of drug abuse or violence. Moderate risk was more than one specific or contributing high-risk factor. Low risk was a violent event without a previous history of violence, drug use or plans for retaliation. High-risk youths were referred to a community health worker and community resources. Moderate-risk youths were referred to the community liaison for interviews and further interventions as needed. Low-risk youths were referred to the Pastoral Care resident. Emergency Department staff conducted brief screenings of youth at the bedside, and continued to do so for the duration of the project. Assessments of high, moderate or low risks were determined then. Youths at high risk of further injury to themselves or others were referred to the on-call Pastoral Care resident, who saw patients in the ED and contacted the community liaison. The hiring of two community health workers that were assigned only to this project was a vital link between youths and community referral. The community health worker program provided caring adults who were able to de-escalate conflicts, establish a rapport, and move youths towards more constructive thought processes surrounding the event.

Assessment

A member of the emergency department staff or a Pastoral Care resident screened youths at the bedside using the violence risk assessment form. Risk stratification, as described in the preceding paragraph, was determined then. After the level of risk was determined, patients were referred to the community liaison, a community health worker, or the Pastoral Care resident. The community liaison and PAAN (Philadelphia Anti-Drug, Anti-violence Network) mentors met with the project director weekly. Information gathered at these meetings helped in further evaluation and planning of the patients and the program.

Linking Youth to Interventions

High-risk youths were referred to community health workers for one-on-one community follow-up, moderate-risk youths to the community liaison and/or pastoral care resident, and low-risk youths to the pastoral care resident. Cases were closed in situations where we were unable to contact a youth, a significant relationship was developed between a youth and a referring agency, or a youth dropped out of the program.

Unique Project Elements

Jefferson's Violence Prevention Project was unique in that we utilized faith-based staff as a core ingredient of our front line emergency department assessors. Chaplains were present in the hospital 24 hours a day, seven days a week, and were automatically paged to all trauma codes in the ED. These chaplains were available to both the patient and the family at a time of crisis. Community follow-up was carried out by our full-time pastor and community liaison, who followed youths from the Hospital through transition into the community. The full-time pastor/community liaison's strength was her ability to connect with young people and develop personal relationships via routine visits with families and patients in their homes as the core of follow-up. For patients who were walk-ins, we had two, full-time social workers, who are paid employees of Jefferson's Emergency Department, stationed in the Department from noon until midnight, seven days a week. The social workers worked very closely with the ED staff and with the youths and their families.

Despite demonstrated successes in connecting young victims to community services and widespread acceptance from the Emergency Department providers, the Foundation ended its support of the program in 2003. The Foundation chose to change its funding focus toward children in the first 5 years of life. We remain grateful to the Foundation for the years of support that it provided. Still, the demise of this program demonstrates the tenuous status of health care based programs that focus on preventing violence. Since health care coverage fails to reimburse for community-based services needed to keep these young people safe, such programs are dependent on external, so-called "soft" funding for their survival. Nonetheless, the JCVPP stands as a potential model for emergency department intervention for violence and trauma. Efforts are ongoing to resurrect the program at Jefferson and at other hospitals in the Philadelphia area.

Primary Care Approaches to Young Black Men

Meet David

David is a 21-year-old African American man who comes to the clinic for follow-up after he sustained a mild gunshot wound to his upper left arm for which he was hospitalized for less than 24 hours about two weeks ago. He was scheduled for follow-up in the clinic because while he was in the hospital he was discovered to have mild hypertension. When he arrives at to the clinic the nurse notices that he appears anxious and jumpy. Once in the examining room, he reports that he has been having nightmares and flashbacks for which he uses three to four marijuana filled cigars per day. The patient also says that he feels numb and finds himself unable to feel love or fear when he is in situations where those emotions are appropriate.

When I ask what happened, he is at first reticent. He tells me that he never told the story to anyone before for fear that he would have to testify against the assailants. However the patient reports that he was at home when two men in masks invaded his home and held him and a friend at gun point. While holding a gun to his head, they repeatedly threatened to kill him.

While he is afraid that these men will target him again, he is also afraid to tell the police since he believes that they will force him to testify against the assailants. He believes that this cooperation with the police will make him a target. He has been staying with an aunt who lives several blocks away from the home where he was assaulted. He rarely leaves her house because he is afraid to ride the buses or trains. He would like to move away, to stay with relatives in North Carolina, but he cannot afford to travel. He also has a 2-year old son who lives with his girlfriend. He is also reluctant to leave his son. Because of his fear of leaving the house, he cannot look for jobs.

Young Men's Health Clinic

In 1993, providers at the Boston City Hospital in Boston, Massachusetts founded the Young Men's Health Clinic. The clinic came about because doctors working in primary care noticed that they were few young men between the ages of 18 and 29 seeking regular primary care in the clinic. Rather, at this urban inner city Hospital serving the largely African-American areas of Roxbury Dorchester and Mattapan, young men sought care only for acute illness. Hospital statistics showed that most of these patients were seen in the emergency department, sexually transmitted disease clinic, dermatology, orthopedics, or surgical clinic. For orthopedic and surgical clinic, many of these patients were there for follow-up care after a violent injury.

In speaking with health care providers in these various settings, the primary care physicians learned that these providers did not know where to refer these men for further care. In general, these providers were well-meaning, but unaware that African-American men suffer from particular chronic diseases at a higher rate and might need referral for longitudinal care.

Initially, the clinic was designed to provide general primary care ranging from routine physicals, episodic treatment of mild medical conditions, screening for hypertension, high cholesterol and diabetes, as well as education about self-examination for testicular cancer, healthy eating and exercise. The initial strategy of the clinic was to invite referrals from clinics throughout the hospital system of young men who were too old to be seen in the adolescent clinic and had no usual source of care. The idea of the clinic was feasible only because Massachusetts had an uncompensated care pool it that reimbursed hospitals for the care of uninsured patients. This was particular important since 80% of the patient seeking care in the clinic had no insurance.

Not far into the course of the clinic, it became clear that while medical issues were important, many of the young man presented with some emotional distress. To better understand what experiences our patients brought to the clinic, we surveyed all new patients over two year period. We found that 34.4% of patients had been shot, stabbed or both at some point in their lives. Overall 45% of patients said that they had been victims of a violent assault (defined as having been shot, stabbed, shot at or beaten up in the past.) Forty-three percent of those with histories of violent injury had experienced more than one type of violent assault[105].

In addition, many of our patients had experienced other traumatic experiences. Fifty-one percent said that they had seen someone shot or stabbed in the past; 25% reported that they did not feel safe; 14% reported carrying a weapon; 59% reported that they had been arrested in the past; 30% reported that they were incarcerated for more than one day; and 44% reported having been harassed by the police.

We went further to compare those young men who were victims to those who had not been victims. We found marked differences between those who reported past victimization and those who did not. Specifically victims had fewer years of education, were more likely have children and were more likely to be African-American. Victims were also more likely to report such traumatic experiences as having been harassed by the police, not feeling safe, having been arrested, having witnessed past violence, carrying a weapon and having been incarcerated. They were also much more likely to the report past use of heroin,

---

[105] Rich and Sullivan, *Correlates of violence assault among young male primary care patients*

cocaine, marijuana or cigarettes. A multiple logistic regression showed that a combined index of their traumatic experiences accounted for much of the difference between the victims and non-victims. Those men who reported having been incarcerated, carrying a weapon or having witnessed violence were significantly more likely to report that they had also been victims of violent assault. This evaluation proves that victims of trauma also have a disproportionate burden of other health and social problems. These data reinforced what we felt in our clinical encounters: exposure to trauma is a potent risk factor that is associated with other behaviors that relate to violence.

Many of these young men reported anxiety, difficulty sleeping, and use of large amounts of marijuana and alcohol. On further probing, it also became apparent that many of these young men had experienced some level of trauma in their lives. The traumas that they talked about included being mistreated by the police, sexual abuse as children, witnessing the physical or sexual abuse of their mothers, witnessing violence, loss of friends and family to violent injury and extreme feelings of anger toward fathers who were all too often not with the family. Quickly, we began to make referral to the mental health resources within the system. However this proved to be ineffective. Young man had to wait long periods of time for appointments. When they were seen in the clinic, many young men reported that they only went for one appointment because they found the psychiatric providers to be judgmental and unfamiliar with their needs and circumstances. One young patient reported to his doctor that after his initial visit, he not gone back to the psychiatric clinic. When the provider questioned why, the patient said "I told the psychiatrist that I used to be something of a hoodlum and the psychiatrist asked 'what's that?'" Anecdotes like this one helped up to realize that many of the resources available at that time were not culturally competent and were not well-suited to the extreme social context in which these young man grew up.

In response to this, we worked with the primary care clinic to identify and hire a psychologist with expertise in trauma and with particular interest in holistic treatments like meditation and stress management techniques. This provider saw patient in the same clinic space, with flexible hours that coincided with clinic hours. During the clinic, if a patient needed to be seen urgently for a crisis, often the psychologist was available. In addition, because of the perceived need to treat post-traumatic stress symptoms rapidly, the psychologist allowed the primary care physicians to overbook his schedule if the patient had experienced extreme trauma. This innovation, in response to a recognized need among young black men, made us able to meet the needs of young patients who otherwise would have been alienated from healthcare.

Over time, the providers in the clinic recognized another need. Patients who came to the clinic were unfamiliar with the general workings of the clinic and could be intimidated by the staff there. The providers recruited a health outreach worker, who had been trained in a special program designed to prepare young men of color to be health educators, and have him work in the clinic. This health educator counseled each patient, first greeting him in the waiting room and providing him with information about male reproductive health, condoms, and the functions of the clinic. In addition, the health educator would orient the patient to mental health resources that were available.

In describing resources, the health educator found it useful to use the analogy of living in a war zone. In health educator would describe to the patients that many of their symptoms were like those seen in people returning from war. With that introduction, many of young men were able to discuss the ways in which their own existence felt to them like being in a war. By representing the mental health services as treatment for stress and trauma, the young patients found it much more acceptable to see the psychologist.

The Young Men's Health Clinic continues to serve the needs of young men in Boston. In Boston, since 2004, rates of aggravated assault have increased 23% and homicide has increased 32%[106]. Similar increases are being seen in many cities in the US. This re-emergence of violence combined with increasing numbers of young men re-entering communities after periods of incarceration has meant that the clinic continues to see many young men with dramatic manifestations of trauma. There are challenges that come with trying to provide preventive and behavioral health services in an environment where health care institutions are facing increasing pressure to focus on services that are more generously reimbursed. Still, institutions that have a mission to provide care to the poor and underserved resonate with the conclusions of the Kellogg Foundation-sponsored monograph, *Poor Man's Plight: Uncovering the Disparity in Men's Health* in which the hope is expressed that *"a coordinated response to the health issues facing men of color will help us to reclaim a lost potential for health and productivity and contribute much to our health as a community*[107].

Lessons Learned

A shared trauma-informed framework

Drawing upon the benefits of hindsight, if we were to create similar programs today we would have incorporated a trauma informed framework from the beginning. By placing trauma squarely on the radar screen right

---

[106] Smalley, *Hub's rise in deadly violence reflects disturbing U.S. change*
[107] Rich and Ro, *A poor man's plight*

alongside the emergency and primary care needs, a trauma informed framework would have shaped the programs from the beginning. To accomplish this, we would make sure that every staff member was fully versed in the ways in which post-traumatic stress and unresolved loss can present in medical care settings. A trauma-informed approach could be more easily reinforced in the health care setting if we were to use a whole-system, trauma-informed approach to the staff as well as the clients. An overarching framework like that described by the Sanctuary Model is a powerful way to bring together an entire institution to deal with the issue of youth violence[108]. Although both of the efforts described in this chapter experienced some success, we believe they would have been measurably more effective had they been embraced by larger institutional change. Because the Sanctuary Model values such as committing to a culture of nonviolence and a culture of open communication were not explicitly shared, these efforts were sometimes viewed as fringe efforts to deal with an equally fringe population. To be most successful entire institutions must embrace not only the importance of addressing youth violence but address it from a trauma-informed perspective. Such a perspective would transform not only the way is provided to injured patients but to the larger institution as well.

The Sanctuary Model could inform not only the intervention for the patient but also the way in which providers would agree to relate to each other and relate to patients. The cultural dictates and strong principles embodied in the acronym SELF, would help providers identify the needs of traumatized patients and identify the best resources needed[109]. It would follow that if an institution embraced addressing youth violence from a trauma-informed perspective then appointed personnel would be responsible for making sure that the best outcomes were achieved. In the programs described above, there were limited number of personnel who supported the programs and most were viewed as pursuing their own passions. Therefore, additional staff was not hired and additional resources did not necessarily follow. This was due in part to the fact that many of the services that we provided to patients (such as mentoring, community health workers, referral and follow-up) are not directly reimbursable. Consequently, there is little incentive for health care institutions to put them in place.

Better assessment and screening

Each of the programs described above did an early assessment that helped to better understand the problems that patients brought to the emergency

---

[108] Bloom, *The Sanctuary Model of Organizational Change*
[109] Bloom, *S.E.L.F.: A Trauma-Informed Psychoeducational Curriculum*

department and to the primary care clinic. However, these instruments were developed as needs assessments to better understand how to provide services. Better screening instruments that include an assessment of the patient's history of trauma and resulting symptoms would be of great benefit to providers. A sound trauma informed assessment would stimulate a human dialogue between providers and patients that would help both to understand how the patient's past trauma would affect their health. For example, such a history would allow better referral to preventive mental health services and supportive community resources. Looking forward, a strong user-friendly instrument that could be used both in an emergent setting and also in primary care would benefit and speed evaluation of these patients. This is especially important when providers are themselves are under pressure to see more patients in less time.

Dedicated staff

In each case, a designated program coordinator who was charged with the responsibility of coordinating the care of the patient, gathering critical data and engaging the entire department in the work of youth violence would be a valuable and necessary component of any such future projects. This staff member would be responsible for a global assessment prior to the patient seeing the physician. In emergency departments, an injury prevention coordinator, much like the staff person currently in place at Alameda County General Hospital, would help to understand the needs of a given patient and immediately make referral to community resources[110].

Community Involvement

The realization that these patients come from underserved communities which are foreign to the most providers in the health care setting means that dramatic participation from community members is critical. This participation can take many forms, but at its best it involves community members from the beginning of the intervention through evaluating the data and the delivery of services. The emergency department program at Jefferson Hospital partnered with a community-based organization known his Philadelphia Anti-Drug, Anti-violence Network (PAAN) and this resulted in a strong community connection. Similarly, in the Young Men's Health Clinic, a trained community health educator was an integral part of the clinic. Programs that envision reproducing either these models would do well to engage community members from the beginning using a community-based participatory model where institutions and

---

[110] Becker and Hall, *Caught in the crossfire*

communities have an equal stake in making sure that youth violence decreases and that the health of young men improves.

In each setting, the presence of highly trained community members who are employed as staff and who are charged with making referrals, providing support and mentoring to the patient after discharge would be ideal. When these staff members are trained as part of the team in the Sanctuary Model there is a continuity of care that provides for the patient and will also help to immunize the staff against the secondary effects of trauma.

Institutional buy-in

Institutional buy-in from the highest levels of the institution is critical. The highest levels of leadership within the institution must have an understanding of the trauma-informed approach and investing in the success of the program. In this way, programs that are started through the passion of an individual faculty or staff member will not be viewed as fringe and marginalized but will be seen as a part of the institutional mission. Program directors and support this buy-in by collecting strong data that demonstrate the effectiveness, and if possible cost-effectiveness, of such programs.

Trauma-informed policy

At a policy level, trauma-informed services have not received the robust reimbursement that they deserve. Advocacy at the local state and federal level for reimbursement for trauma related services is critical. Coalitions consisting of the leadership of health care institutions, providers, patients affected by violence and affected communities should advocate with leaders at all levels to improve reimbursement for services that relate to trauma. In addition, policy statements that highlight a trauma-informed approach to youth violence should be developed by professional organizations, state and local health departments and public health researchers. Requirements for training and trauma-informed practice can be incorporated into requests for proposals issued by municipalities or states. In this way, trauma-informed services will become part of the culture and fabric of care provided to victims.

Finally, a lesson learned from these interventions and that can be carried into the future, is that diversity across the providers of care to victims of youth violence is critical. Historically, racism has had a negative impact on health care and mental health care delivery to African-Americans. As Poussaint and Alexander point out:

Mistrust of the medical establishment that currently contributes to poor mental health in some blacks can be linked to the long history of troubled relations between blacks and the whole American medical community... Bias and racial insensitivity continue to affect patient care at all levels of the medical and psychiatric establishment, and has seeped into the fabric of America's health care apparatus, staining the ground-level service delivery systems with which black Americans must interact[111].

There continues to be a need for greater diversity among the health care professionals that supports these important initiatives. More specifically, a staff that is well-trained in violence and trauma, will bring various perspectives and cultural sensitivities to patients and communities struggling with youth violence.

Conclusions and Recommendations

In each of the settings a key focus was to improve the health of patients most of whom are young men and many of whom are African-American. An initial focus of each of the programs was to provide either acute medical care in an emergency setting or continuity of care in a primary care setting. In each case there was a shift in focus from simply treating the medical complaint to trying to achieve a more holistic plan of care.

Each program inductively came to conclude that trauma played a large role in the lives of their patients in these settings. These impressions were confirmed by data gathered from the patients. Each setting adapted its practices in an attempt to better address the trauma these patients were experiencing. Sometimes, the adjustments served to improve the clinical setting for patients and to address some of the patient's needs.

Most importantly, it is social policy that needs to change. As educator and activist Geoffrey Canada has put it:

Part of the problem is that most current policymakers fail to address the problem of the sheer availability of guns. Young people in our inner cities know that there is a war going on' millions have been accidentally or intentionally caught up in the many small battles that make up the war on America's streets. Most young people are interested in surviving the war, but the price they pay is being prepared to kill or be killed almost every day[112].

References

Allen, I. M. "Ptsd among African Americans." In *Ethnocultural Aspects of Posttraumatic Stress Disorder: Issues, Research, and Clinical Applications,*

---

[111] Poussaint and Alexander, Lay My Burden Down, P 64 and 76
[112] Canada, *Fist, Stick Knife Gun,* p. 68

edited by A. Marsella, M. J. Friedman, E. Gerrity and R. M. Scurfield. Washington, D. C.: American Psychological Association, 1996.

Anderson, E. "Living Hard by the Code of the Streets." *Philadelphia Inquirer*, May 15 1994, C7.

Baer, J.. "As Bullets Fly, Bodies Drop, Where's Street?" *Philadelphia Daily News*, August 14, citing statistics from Philadelphia Police Department 2006.

Bazelon Center for Mental Health Law. *Disintegrating Systems: The State of States' Public Mental Health Systems*: Bazelon Center for Mental Health Law, 2001.

————. "Get It Together: How to Integrate Physical and Mental Health Care for People with Serious Mental Disorders." Washington, D.C.: Bazelon Center for Mental Health Law, 2004.

Becker, M.G., J.S. Hall, C. M. Ursic, S. Jain, and D. Calhoun. "Caught in the Crossfire: The Effects of a Peer-Based Intervention Program for Violently Injured Youth." *Journal of Adolescent Health* 34, no. 3 (2004): 177-83.

Berman, L. H. "The Effects of Living with Violence. " *Journal of the American Academy of Psychoanalysis* 20, no. 4 (1992): 671-5.

Bloom, S. L. "The Sanctuary Model of Organizational Change for Children'S Residential Treatment." *Therapeutic Community: The International Journal for Therapeutic and Supportive Organizations* 26, no. 1 (2005): 65-81.

Bloom, S. L., J. F. Foderaro, and R. A. Ryan. *S.E.L.F.: A Trauma-Informed, Psychoeducational Group Curriculum*: Available at www.sanctuaryweb.com, 2006.

Bloom, Sandra, and Michael Reichert. *Bearing Witness : Violence and Collective Responsibility*. Binghamton NY: Haworth Press, 1998.

"Blueprint for a Safer Philadelphia." http://www.phillyblueprint.com/index.cfm?page=Documentary.   Accessed March 10, 2007. Philadelphia: MEE Productions Inc., 2007.

Boss, P. *Loss. Trauma, and Resilience: Therapeutic Work with Ambiguous Loss*. New York: W. W. Norton, 2006.

Breslau, N., and G. C. Davis. "Posttraumatic Stress Disorder in an Urban Population of Young Adults: Risk Factors for Chronicity." *American Journal of Psychiatry* 149, no. 5 (1992): 671-75.

Breslau, N., G. C. Davis, P. Andreski, and E. Peterson. "Traumatic Events and Posttraumatic Stress Disorder in an Urban Population of Young Adults." *Arch Gen Psychiatry* 48, no. 3 (1991): 216-22.

Brooks-Gunn, J., and G. J. Duncan. "The Effects of Poverty on Children." *Future Child* 7, no. 2 (1997): 55-71.

Bureau of Justice Statistics. "Prisoners in 2004." Washington, D.C.: U. S. Department of Justice, 2005.

Canada, G. *Fist Stick Knife Gun: A Personal History of Violence in America.*
   Boston: Beacon Press, 1995.
Centers for Disease Control and Prevention. "Web-Based Injury Statistics Query
   and Reporting System (Wisqars) [Online]." (2006) [cited 06 Feb 8].
   Available from: URL: www.cdc.gov/ncipc/wisqars.: National Center for
   Injury Prevention and Control, 2006.
Cooper, W. *Behold a Pale Horse.* Sedona, AZ: Light Publishing, 1991.
Doka, K., and J. Davidson. *Living with Grief: Who We Are, How We Grieve.*
   Washington, D.C.: Brunner/Mazel, 1998.
Garrett, P., N. Ng'andu, and J. Ferron. "Poverty Experiences of Young Children
   and the Quality of Their Home." *Child Development* 65 (1994): 331-45.
Haile, E. S., J. Lowy, and D. Pennington. " Lethal Lou's: Profile of a Rogue Gun
   Dealer - Lou's Loan of Upper Darby, Pennsylvania. ." Washington, D.C.:
   Brady Center to Prevent Gun Violence, 2006.
Kaiser Daily Health Policy Report. "15,000 Children Incarcerated Because of
   Lack of Mental Health Treatment in 2003." *Kaisernetwork.org*, July 8 2004.
———. *15,000 Children Incarcerated Because of Lack of Mental Health
   Treatment in 2003,*
   *Http://Www.Kaisernetwork.Org/Daily_Reports/Rep_Index.Cfm?Dr_Id=246
   06, July 8*, 2004.
Kupers, T. A. "Mental Health in Men's Prisons." In *Prison Masculinities*, edited
   by D. Sabo, T. A. Kupers and W. London, 192-97. Philadelphia: Temple
   University Press, 2001.
Lyons, J. S., D. R. Baerger, J. E. Quigley, and E. Griffin. "Mental Health
   Service Needs of Juvenile Offenders: A Comparison of Detention,
   Incarceration, and Treatment Settings." *Children's Services: Social Policy,
   Research, and Practice* 4 (2001): 69-85.
Mayberry, R. M., F. Mili, and E. Ofili. "Racial and Ethnic Differences in Access
   to Medical Care." *Medical Care Research and Review* 57, no. Suppl1
   (2000): 108-45.
Miller, L. "Young Lives Lost." *The Philadelphia Tribune* 2006, www.phila-
   tribue.com/channel/inthenews/092606/behindbards3.asp, accessed March 9,
   2007.
Moran, R. "Living, Dying in Phila.'S 'Iraq' - a Mother Is Shot to Death, and a
   Community Is Torn." *Philadelphia Inquirer*, July 20 2006, A01.
National Center for Health Statistics. *Health, United States, 2006, with
   Chartbook of Trends in the Health of Americans.* Hyattsville, MD: Centers
   for Disease Control and Prevention, 2006.
Poussaint, Alvin F., and Amy Alexander. *Lay My Burden Down: Unraveling
   Suicide and the Mental Health Crisis among African-Americans.* Boston:
   Beacon Press, 2000.

President's New Freedom Commission on Mental Health. *Interim Report*, 2002 [cited September 17 2005].

Prevention, Centers for Disease Control and. "Web-Based Injury Statistics Query and Reporting System (Wisqars) [Online]." (2006) [cited 06 Feb 8]. Available from: URL: www.cdc.gov/ncipc/wisqars.: National Center for Injury Prevention and Control, 2006.

Rando, T. A. *Treatment of Complicated Mourning*. Champaign, IL: Research Press, 1993.

Rich, J. A., and C. M. Grey. "Pathways to Recurrent Trauma among Young Black Men: Traumatic Stress, Substance Use, and the "Code of the Street"." *American Journal of Public Health* 95, no. 5 (2005): 815-24.

Rich, J. A., and M. Ro. *A Poor Man;S Plight: Uncovering the Disparity in Men's Health*. Vol. 30. Battle Creek, MO: W. K. Kellogg Foundation, 2002.

Rich, J. A., and L. M. Sullivan. "Correlates of Violence Assault among Young Male Primary Care Patients." *Journal of Health Care for the Poor and Underserved* 12, no. 1 (2001): 103-12.

Sampson, R. J., and J. H. Laub. "Urban Poverty and the Family Context of Delinquency: A New Look at Structure and Process in a Classic Study." *Child Development* 65 (1994): 523-40.

Sims, D. W., B. A. Bivins, F. N. Obeid, H. M. Horst, V. J. Sorensen, and J. J. Fath. "Urban Trauma: A Chronic Recurrent Disease." *J Trauma* 29, no. 7 (1989): 940-6; discussion 46-7.

Smalley, S. "Hub's Rise in Deadly Violence Reflects Disturbing Us Change." *Boston Globe*, March 9 2007.

Smedley, B.D., A. Y. Stith, and A.R. Nelson. "Unequal Treatment: Confronting Racial and Ethnic Disparities in Health Care." Washington, D.C.: Institute of Medicine, 2002.

Staub, E. "Cutural-Societal Roots of Violence: The Examples of Genocidal Violence and of Contemporary Youth Violence in the United States." *American Psychologist* 51, no. 2 (1996): 117-32.

Teplin, L. A., K. M. Abram, G. M. McClelland, M. K. Duncan, and A. A. Mericle. "Psychiatric Disorders in Youth in Juvenile Detention." *Archives of General Psychiatry* 59 (2002): 1133-43.

Tolan, P. H. , and D. Henry. "Patterns of Psychopathology among Urban Poor Children: Comorbidity and Aggression Effects." *Journal of Consulting and Clinical Psychology* 64, no. 5 (1996): 1094-99.

Tuakli-Williams, J., and J. Carrillo. "The Impact of Psychosocial Stressors on African-American and Latino Preschoolers." *Journal of the National Medical Association* 87, no. 7 (1995): 473-78.

United States Public Health Service Office of the Surgeon General. "Mental Health: Culture, Race, and Ethnicity: A Supplement to Mental Health: A

Report of the Surgeon General." Rockville, MD: Department of Health and Human Services, U.S. Public Health Service, 2001.

Vaidya, Y. "What's Behind a New Wave of Crime." *The Pennsylvania Gazette* 2007, http://www.upenn.edu/gazette/0107/gaz06.html, January - February,Accessed March 10, 2007.

Weischselbaum, S. " Weischselbaum, a Quest to Save Youth at Risk. Philadelphia Daily News, January 2, 2007." *Philadelphia Daily News*, January 2 2007, www.philly.com/mld/philly/entertainment/family_guide/16364558.htm, accessed March 9, 2007.

———. "Youth-Crime System Broken." *Philadelphia Daily News* 2007, www.philly.com/mld/philly/entertainment/family_guide/16857074.htm, accessed March 9, 2007.

Zinner, E. S., and M. B. Williams. "Summary and Incorporation: A Reference Frame for Community Recovery and Restoration." In *When a Community Weeps: Case Studies in Group Survivorship*, edited by E. S. Zinner and M. B. Williams, 237-64. Philadelphia: Brunner/Mazel, 1999.

CHAPTER FIVE

ACCEPTABLE LOSSES

VALERIE ANDERSON, M.S.W.

The loss of childhood to adulthood
The loss of girlhood to womanhood
The loss of singlehood to marriage
The loss of being childless to baby carriage
The loss of homelessness to home ownership
The loss of acquaintance to friendship
The loss of frigidity to sensuality
The loss of religion to spirituality
The loss of violence to peace
The loss of clutter to space
The loss of hatred to love
The loss of being under to rising above
The loss of fear to faith
The loss of hurriedness to a slower pace
The loss of complexity to simplicity
The loss of chaos to finding serenity
The loss of materialism to having abundance
The loss of judgment to acceptance
The loss of being lost to being found
The loss of noise to the beauty of sound
The loss of toxins to something pure
The loss of uncertainty to what you know for sure.

CHAPTER SIX

WHEN LOSS GETS LOST:
USING THE SELF MODEL TO WORK WITH LOSS
IN RESIDENTIAL CARE

DAVID MCCORKLE, L.C.S.W.
AND SARAH YANOSY SREEDHAR, L.C.S.W.

Introduction

Residential care is rooted in loss. Children who are identified by their families, school districts, state agencies, or courts as being unable to function in their homes and communities due to behavioral and mental health issues are referred to residential care for treatment. Children in residential care live in a congregate setting with other children, and are cared for by staff, receive psychiatric treatment, and reside in a therapeutic environment in order to address the issues that keep them from functioning in a home setting. Often these children have visitation with their families on weekends and attend schools affiliated with the treatment centers rather than attend in their home school districts. The mere fact that children in residential care are separated from their families of origin to live with other children and unfamiliar caregivers suggest that loss is an inherent part of residential care. Many residential treatment settings have evolved from orphanages or similar institutions created to care for children who had lost parents, families and communities. Although over time residential treatment has moved to a more clinical focus, its heritage is deeply rooted in themes of loss that continue to be a powerful force in the experience of the children who are treated in these settings.

In addition to the separation from their families, children who are placed in residential care are particularly vulnerable to issues of loss, since many carry a history of abuse or neglect which precipitated their placement. For others, some discrete event or trauma may have been a precipitant to their placement in residential care. Trauma always results in some kind of loss, whether concrete or less tangible. All children who live in residential settings have lost the sense of normalcy of living in a familiar place. Others experience a loss of safety, loss of family members, loss of innocence and loss of security. For families who are separated when a child is placed in residential care, even for those who place children voluntarily, there may be a loss of control, loss of identity, or loss of cultural traditions.

Despite the multitude of losses that are entrenched in residential treatment, we find that loss is often overlooked in the day-to-day work of caring for traumatized children. There are a number of reasons for this oversight. Often it is difficult to know where to focus on any given day in a residential treatment setting. There are issues such as physical and social safety, and other issues like family reunification, foster care placement and long term institutional or hospital care that conspire to divert the attention away from addressing loss issues with our children. The result of these daily demands raises key questions: How can residential treatment centers balance the competing priorities of our children's safety, their expressions of pain, frustration and loss of hope? How may they effectively manage staff's safety? Also, how might these institutions manage the projected pain of socially injured children, manage organizational expectations, and also address financial responsibilities? Specific demands that stem from issues relating to health care, education, recreation, creativity, psychotherapy, family therapy, medication, family reunification, and foster care placement create a complex web of potential problems that is further complicated by issues relating to placement for those without parents or foster families. Mandates about documentation, even the participation in court proceedings, contribute to a perplexing litany of issues. Obviously, within this catalog of competing priorities, it is easy to see how addressing grief and loss readily may be overlooked.

Another reason that this prevalent grief and loss in residential treatment may go overlooked is lack of recognition. Typically, caregivers focus on concrete or tangible losses, but may not identify secondary or intangible losses. What are tangible and intangible losses? Often children in residential care may have suffered the loss of family members through incarceration or endured the loss of their homes, their relationships with friends and extended family, as well as the familiarity of school or community. Some may have endured the death of a loved one, perhaps a beloved sibling or parent. These are tangible losses. There is some tangible or at least identifiable aspect of life that is lost. Intangible losses—referred to also as secondary losses are identified as those often felt by marginalized populations, those people with little power in the larger system. These intangible losses, somehow as invisible and overlooked as wallpaper, often may be more insidious and damaging. For example, many residential care prospects are children of color who come from impoverished communities; they and their families often cope with painful issues stemming from their experiences of subjugation. These social wounds—the loss of one's voice, the loss of a sense of efficacy, loss of a sense of heritage and history, a constant push from society to compromise oneself to those who are privileged—often engender extraordinary rage[1]. It is often this very rage that drives the behaviors which bring many children to residential care.

This rage also may fuel the behaviors of family members, many of whom are also people of color who have experienced trauma in addition to the subjugation and degradation of racism. A significant strain, and one often unspoken in these decisions to remove children from their homes, is that of institutional racism. Many of the children who are taken out of their communities and placed in residential care are children of color. Frequently, they are placed in agencies where the decision-makers and power-brokers are white. The implicit message that families and communities of color are incapable of caring for their own children underscores the damaging loss of family and community.

Many of the behaviors we see in the acting out children of residential treatment may be directly related to loss. Investigators have written about the cycle of violence among adolescents and the failure of acknowledging aggressive acting out as an expression of the dehumanization of loss. Losses that are "unacknowledged, not mourned and unhealed" are the fuel for the phenomena of rage. Unless the source of rage is addressed, it will continue to fuel destructive behavior. Describing this palpable rage, the authors suggest, "It is a natural and inevitable response to experiences of pain and injustice"[2]. When these losses affect children of color, the devaluation of loss also seems to simultaneously underscore the devaluation of people of color. Similarly, the same can also be said of LBGT children who are devalued simply because their sexual orientation is different from that of the mainstream population.

As one author observes, many of our youth seem perpetually angry and when hurt show anger more than hurt. *"Suppressed grief often turns into depression, anxiety or addiction. Benumbed fear can easily lead to irrational prejudice, toxic rage, and acts of violence."*[3] This anger is often *"a shield of one's vulnerability"*[4]. These researchers suggest that society unfortunately will continue to experience problems with safety and emotion management in children in residential care until these issues of loss are effectively acknowledged and treated.

---

[1] Hardy,. *African American Experience and the Healing of Relationships in Family Therapy;* Hardy and Laszyloffy Teens Who Hurt.

[2] Hardy and Laszyloffy, *Teens Who Hurt,* p.29.

[3] Greenspan, Healing through the Dark Emotions, p.xii

[4] Ibid, xiii

Rage, together with a build-up of intangible losses, may also affect organizations themselves, those facilities dedicated to helping these children. In many ways, residential treatment is viewed as a step-child in the field of mental health. Residential settings are often seen as holding cells for the most disturbed and hopeless cases, the last stop on the train before jail. Staff members who work in residential care are often poorly paid and frequently seen as babysitters rather than valid and meaningful treatment providers. Therefore, as a marginalized field, residential care remains vulnerable to the effects of these same secondary losses. The destructive cycle of trauma, coupled with issues of subjugation, seems to cut across the client, family and the organization itself, ironically the very system developed to help these children and their families. These layers of secondary loss are rarely recognized and less likely to be addressed.

Additionally, there is this daunting reality: Grief work is painful for *both* the child and the staff. Loss is so painful for our children to face; it is equally disheartening for staff members to witness. Yet, unresolved loss leads to a cycle of reenactment of past adversities in current relationships. Clients engage in a dynamic with staff or others in a way that recreates the roles of persecutor, rescuer and victim. One group of experienced clinicians refer to these reenactments as the expression of unresolved grief, of "never having to say good-by."[5]. If clients are unable to make a connection between their symptoms and their previous experiences, then they are doomed to repeat them. Sadly, people are unable to move towards a better, more meaningful future. Likewise, it has been observed that "Helpers don't want to talk about this information, so that they will frequently change the subject or minimize the pain."[6].

While the desire to minimize pain is a natural human tendency, this desire can undermine treatment. This unintended effect is unfortunately fairly evident in a multitude of examples in residential care. It is often a point of pride for an agency to know that it is giving the children both a better experience and better life than they may have had at home. It is also a point of pride for programs to be clinically astute and diagnostically savvy. Yet, it is frequently these very desires to do good work which can sometimes undermine the recognition and treatment of loss and grief with children.

---

[5] Bloom, Foderaro, and Ryan, *S.E.L.F.: A Trauma-Informed, Psychoeducational Curriculum*
[6] Ibid

This chapter explores issues of loss in residential care through case examples of children, families and a residential treatment center as a system. It focuses on the use of the Sanctuary Model, in particular the use of SELF as an effective and meaningful tool for addressing trauma and loss for children, families and entire systems.

The Sanctuary Model

The Sanctuary Model®, created by Dr. Sandra Bloom and her colleagues, represents a trauma-informed method for creating or changing an organizational culture in order to more effectively provide a cohesive context within which healing from psychological and social traumatic experience can be addressed. It is a whole system approach designed to facilitate the development of structures, processes, and behaviors on the part of staff, children and the community-as-a-whole that can counteract the biological, affective, cognitive, social, and existential wounds suffered by the children in care.

The Sanctuary Model was originally developed in a short-term, acute inpatient psychiatric setting for adults who were traumatized as children. The Model has since been adapted by residential treatment settings for children, domestic violence shelters, group homes, outpatient settings, substance abuse programs, parenting support programs and has been used in other settings as a method of organizational change.

The aims of the Sanctuary Model are to guide an organization in the development of a culture with seven dominant characteristics, all of which serve goals related a sound treatment environment:

Culture of Nonviolence – building and modeling safety skills and a commitment to higher goals

Culture of Emotional Intelligence – teaching and modeling affect management skills

Culture of Inquiry & Social Learning – building and modeling cognitive skills

Culture of Shared Governance – creating and modeling civic skills of self-control, self-discipline, and administration of healthy authority

Culture of Open Communication – overcoming barriers to healthy communication, reduce acting-out, enhancing self-protective and self-correcting skills, teaching healthy boundaries

Culture of Social Responsibility – rebuilding social connection skills, establish healthy attachment relationships

Culture of Growth and Change – restoring hope, meaning, purpose

The SELF Model

SELF is an acronym which stands for Safety, Emotion management, Loss and Future. Developed by Dr. Sandra Bloom and colleagues as part of the Sanctuary Model[7], the SELF Model (referred to in early writings by Dr. Bloom and her team as SAGE – Safety, Affect management, Grief, Emancipation – rather than SELF)

> is not a stage oriented treatment model, but rather a nonlinear method for addressing in simple words, very complex challenges. The four concepts of the model include: Safety, Emotions, Loss, and Future, representing the four fundamental domains of disruption that can occur in a person's life and within these four domains, any problem can be categorized.[8]

When we refer to the acronym as a model, we are referring to its use as a framework for organizing conversations, treatment planning, and treatment itself. Issues of safety, for example, include physical, psychological, social and moral safety. In simplest terms, physical safety means that our bodies are safe from harm; psychological safety means that we are safe with ourselves (we have self-esteem, self-protection, self-discipline, etc.). Social safety means being safe with others (having social responsibility, healthy attachments, responsible authority), and moral safety means being consistent with one's values, beliefs and conscience[9]. The second letter in the acronym stands for emotion management. Work in this area focuses on recognizing feelings and their connection to behaviors as well as managing feelings well enough that one can control behaviors rather than act feelings out in maladaptive ways. The third piece of the SELF model is loss. Work in this area involves recognizing, honoring and moving past resistance to change. It requires letting go of the past while incorporating important experiences into one's identity. The final component of the SELF model is future, finding new motivations, risking new experiences and relationships and choices and moving out of maladaptive patterns of behavior.

Because the experiences, skills, challenges and strengths that any client, family, staff person or organization presents may vary, the goals and tasks involved in the SELF process will look different for different people or groups. The model is dynamic and adaptable, providing a frame for the work to be done in healing. The model also serves as a safeguard against overlooking

---

[7] Bloom, *Creating Sanctuary: Toward the Evolution of Sane Societies*
[8] Bloom, Foderaro, and Ryan, *S.E.L.F.: A Trauma-Informed Psychoeducational Curriculum*
[9] Bloom, *Creating Sanctuary: Toward the Evolution of Sane Societies*

loss.   As loss is a critical component of the model, it becomes a focus of discussion and treatment.

Loss for Children in Residential Care

What society does to its children, so its children will do to society
– Cicero

We often find that children and families can be extremely resistant to dealing with loss. Well-intentioned staff members can be just as avoidant. At times, the wish to avoid pain, the struggle of competing priorities and the inability to recognize bereavement as an integral part of trauma treatment can result in this phenomenon of loss getting lost.   This was strikingly clear in a case of a child who witnessed the murder/suicide of her parents.

Grace

Grace was an eleven year old girl who came into residential care with pigtails and large round glasses. Her shy demeanor and simple smile belied the complexity of her circumstances. During the course of her stay, Grace was subjected to custody battles among family members who were reeling from the murder/suicide of Grace's parents, court proceedings, media attention, legal issues regarding visitation, and the involvement of multiple service agencies. Compounding this complexity was Grace's confusing presentation of symptoms: psychotic episodes, suicidality, provocative behaviors, extreme neediness, dissociation, gaps in memory, and extremely poor social interactions. The team immediately recognized the symptoms as post-traumatic stress disorder and focused on helping to stabilize her. Unfortunately, with all of these clinical issues to address, including her medications to administer and her safety to monitor, the staff had little opportunity to begin addressing this child's profound sense of loss. The staff was largely focused on keeping her safe. Staff members were unsure that the traumatized child could tolerate talking about her loss.

Grace was placed in residential care within a week of her parents' deaths, after a state agency took custody of her. Grace made some gains in her treatment, but was placed in the home of a relative several months after placement in what the treatment team felt was a premature attempt to provide normalcy and restore order to her life.   Although she had been in care for several months, she had not even begun to participate in a bereavement group, as the treatment had focused exclusively on treating overt psychiatric symptoms. The family member she was placed with felt that the best way to help this child cope with her experience was to give her a new identity. She moved the child to another state and advised the new school that Grace had lost her parents in a car accident. The desire of this family member to protect Grace from further pain instead stifled Grace's ability to process her experiences and deal with her grief. Her new identity provided an opportunity to start anew, but provided her with an altered reality, risking the possibility of invalidating her trauma and grief experience. There are numerous examples in residential care of the ease with which caring adults manage loss issues for children in ways that can unintentionally disrupt appropriate grieving. Frequently the issue of loss is placed at the bottom of the child's emotional priority lists or completely overlooked.

Acknowledging Loss

We have seen in residential settings the staff's vulnerability to overlook or avoid issues of loss. But we have also seen the unexpected ability of very troubled children to make progress around issues of loss. This was clearly demonstrated in one team's work with a young man who had been in residential care for five years. He was an extremely aggressive child who had hurt other children on several occasions.
The staff used the SELF model in their thinking and treatment planning with him.

> Gregory was a slight boy whose small size encased a well of emotion and anger. He had been in residential treatment since the age of six, having been removed from his home with his siblings after the children disclosed sexual abuse by a relative in the home. His parents were incarcerated, and although he had very limited contact with his other relatives, he had developed a strong sense of family and connection with his sisters. The team knew of his precipitous situation: one sister had been discharged to family only to move into a homeless shelter, and his other sister was at risk of leaving residential care for a more restrictive environment due to her declining functioning and dangerous behavior toward others. The staff members were also aware of Gregory's history of sexual abuse, physical abuse and extreme neglect. Despite their awareness of these losses, the staff found their attempts to talk with the child thwarted; he overtly avoided and rejected their attempts. Additionally, his use of negative behavior to avoid talking about these issues confounded effective treatment. Despite their efforts, the staff members continued to struggle with how best to address this child's loss issues, which they believed were at the core of his behavioral issues.

Most interventions focused on how to help Gregory stay safe, how to help him manage his emotions in order to keep the other children and staff around him safe, and how to work toward being able to live in a family setting in the future. Although they were not feeling particularly effective in their repeated attempts, the staff's use of the language of SELF, coupled with their creation of an emotionally intelligent environment and their awareness and openness about their own feelings, helped initiate a healthier treatment program. This environment laid the ground work for Gregory to begin to address his own grief work at his own pace. At one point, one of the direct care workers in the cottage who worked with Gregory daily lost her grandmother to an illness. She came in to work the next day, and Gregory immediately approached her. Neither she, nor any of the other staff, had shared her loss with the children, but the worker reported feeling that Gregory "just seemed to know" that something was wrong. The worker described her typical interactions with Gregory as fairly volatile, noting that she had come to expect aggression or insults from him most of the time. She was surprised when he came up to her and asked what was wrong. She shared with him that her grandmother had died, and he responded with appropriate apologies for her loss. His ability to relate to her in a compassionate way after her loss set her on a path of thinking about Gregory and the other children in a different way. The worker used her own experience of grief as a spring board for thinking about the losses of some of the children with whom she worked. She approached a teacher who worked with many of the boys in her residential unit, and suggested that they begin a loss group together. Knowing of the multiple losses that this one boy had experienced, she asked him to join the group. She and the teacher were not surprised by his refusal to participate and his denial of any losses in his life.

Several months later, this Gregory's grandmother, the woman from whom he was removed, and with whom he shared a very ambivalent relationship, died. He asked the same worker who had lost her grandmother to accompany him to the funeral. She reported to her colleagues when she returned with him that it had been an extremely emotional experience for him – and for her. His mother had been in attendance, but had not recognized him, as she had not seen him in many years. He had clung to this worker for most of the day, seeming very conflicted about connecting with the relatives who had abandoned him. That evening, the child approached the staff member who had accompanied him to the funeral. "What am I supposed to do now? I don't know how to go on. How did you do it?" he asked, referring to her coping with the recent loss of a grandparent. She told him that she was still doing it. She talked about grief as a process that she deals with every day. They began to talk about their shared losses and their experiences of losing a grandparent. The child was able to begin talking about some of his other experiences, framing them as losses. The staff and child were able to grieve together in a contained and safe way, allowing the child not only to experience being cared for, but also the experience of caring for someone in his community without being parentified or exploited, another common experience for him. This interchange prompted the child to participate in the loss group.

Creating a Context for Loss – "L" Groups

With a new awareness of the importance of addressing loss, groups were piloted in one classroom at a special education school on the campus of a residential treatment center to specifically address loss. As a way of reinforcing the groups as consistent with the SELF model, the staff and children decided to call them "L" groups. When the staff first conducted the initial "L" Group, all were anxious about "upsetting" the students. The hesitation that the adults had about how the students might respond was countered by the students' capacity for tolerating their own emotions and each other's. Even though one student was very sad when talking about his loss, he did not act out his anger. The student spoke of losing his good relationship with his mother during a disagreement. He was able to share his observation of his own process, noting a transition in his behavior: he did not trash his room as he usually did when he was upset. Another student was looking sad and was asked about his loss. He said he had lost something very important, but he did not want to talk about it. The group expressed compassion and acknowledged his loss as being important even though it was not shared with them. By the time the group went around the circle, the student who did not want to talk earlier decided to tell the group that his puppy had died last night. It was with some trepidation that group members asked him if there was a benefit to talking about his loss. He said that he would have taken his anger out on his classmates and teachers if he had not talked about it in the group. He then got help from the group in developing a safety plan for the day. Several group members told him they would respect his feelings and offered to check in with him during the day. This was extraordinary for this student who is characteristically withdrawn and tends towards acting out behaviors and for his peers who are much quicker to distance themselves from the pain of others by lashing out or teasing than by showing compassion.

It is the desire to strike a balance in treating these children that demonstrates how tenuous discussing loss may be. The fear of upsetting the children, of making their already painful lives worse often drives our staff members to avoid directly dealing with issues of loss. For example, when the loss itself is the reason for admission to a residential program, the staff, child and family may be forced to deal directly with that loss. Yet, the issue of family secrets that surround losses may compound the difficulty that some children experience when deciding whether or not to disclose information relating to loss. There are instances when children fear that they will further damage a relationship with a parent by discussing a loss or when they feel that disclosure may cause a family member to be in trouble with the law. Grieving may be inextricably linked with the risk of further loss and, thus, may even be more

complicated than initially diagnosed.   Such was the case for one young girl,
Lily, and her treatment team.

Lily

Lily's sadness was palpable to the staff when they met her. She greeted people
with her story, introducing herself with the information that her brother had died,
and the police had taken her away from her mother.   When she came to
residential care, Lily was at first quite open about sharing her story, showing
pictures of her sibling and talking about her experience of the funeral. At some
point, however, this openness and willingness to talk diminished drastically. She
was more and more resistant to talking about her memories relating to the death.
This was a clear departure from her presentation and from earlier sessions with
the therapist in which Lily had initiated conversations and described in detail her
recollections of the event. The team noticed that somewhere in the course of her
treatment, this child began to feel unsafe sharing this heartbreaking loss.

There were a number of factors that were likely contributors to Lily's
closing down, many of which seemed tied to her belief that sharing her loss
would risk greater loss. Around this time, her mother was allowed contact with
her, when earlier there had been a court order denying contact of any kind. Lily
seemed aware of her mother's fear that speaking of the death, the investigation,
a report of abuse, Lily's removal, in a sense "airing the family's laundry," might
have severe consequences. Perhaps the information would be used against the
mother in court. Perhaps Lily would not be allowed to see her mother again if
she disclosed family problems.

The desire to protect their family became a barrier to grief work. Lily's
mother had once stated: "We'll only be able to work on our relationship after
she is home. I don't trust that they'll let her come home if she starts talking
about what's happened." Despite their initial mistrust, Lily and her mother
began to have positive visits and began to work on safety and emotion
management in family sessions. The team felt that they should be allowed
unsupervised visits, and a new visitation arrangement it was granted. Several
months later, after ongoing visitation and a beginning focus on the loss that the
family had faced due to the death of her brother and Lily's removal, Lily's
mother appeared before a criminal court judge regarding charges of abusing
Lily. There had been some miscommunication among lawyers, family court,
criminal court and treatment providers. After months of visitation and family
therapy, the criminal court determined that an order of protection was still in
effect, and that Lily's mother's contact with her daughter was a serious legal
transgression. Further, there was to be no additional contact with her daughter
until the next court date. This drastic turn of events seemed to confirm for both
Lily and her mother that the system could not be trusted. Although the reality

was more complicated, Lily's experience seemed to suggest that when she began to talk about her loss, she was no longer allowed to see her mother.

Other factors also were likely contributors to her refusal to talk about her losses. Few things are more disturbing than the death of a baby, and the staff who worked with Lily acknowledged their discomfort about the baby's death. Over time, most conversations, therefore, addressed Lily's presentation and behavioral issues. It seemed a far easier matter to focus on her demeanor. Treatment more readily addressed Lily's behavior which was presumed to be manipulative and attention-seeking. Although everyone on the team knew the significant losses— death of her sibling, removal from her home, and abrupt severing of maternal contact — these topics were only lightly recounted and inevitably quickly dismissed in conversations. Instead, the team stressed developing behavior plans and arrangements for Lily's discharge to a foster home.

At this juncture, the importance of the SELF framework surfaced. Lily's team met for a quarterly treatment planning conference, and in the course of talking about her progress in the areas of Safety, Emotion management, Loss and Future, they recognized that they had barely addressed the severe consequences of Lily's personal loss. Even though death is often the most obvious form of troubling loss, in Lily's case, her sibling's death was often overshadowed by other issues in the course of her treatment. The team then decided that Lily would be a good candidate for a trauma-specific intervention. With the help, support and agreement of the treatment team, the clinician began using trauma focused cognitive behavioral therapy with Lily. This treatment protocol deploys a gradual exposure to the traumatic event, often through narrative devices[10]. As the work progressed, Lily continued to demonstrate significant resistance to sharing details. Lily had already made the connection that disclosure was equated with punishment. Her experience suggested that her mother's removal from contact was the price of disclosing physical abuse. In sum, talking through loss seemed to trigger a court order denying contact with her mother.

Lily's cognitive behavioral therapy program, however, did offer a process which held a special appeal for the child. This particular trauma-focused cognitive behavioral therapy protocol involves sharing the narrative with an adult. Lily had built a relationship with her previous foster family, and wanted to share her story with her foster mother. She also wanted to share her narrative with the staff of her cottage. Her therapist arranged for sessions in which Lily could read her narrative with her foster parent, and as the protocol suggests, help the foster parent respond to Lily in an affirming and supportive way. The staff also heard her narrative, with Lily's permission, and was immediately sensitized to her

---

[10]Cohen et al, *Childhood traumatic grief.*

experience. The exposure to Lily's narrative and therefore to her loss experience helped change the staff's perceptions of Lily's behavior, framing many of her past actions as reenactments of her painful home situation. They began to recognize that her troubling performance was actually a series of unsuccessful coping responses, not manipulative and attention-seeking actions, as they previously thought. Lily, herself also seemed to change. Her initial resistance began to dissipate and she was able to talk about her future as well as express her ambivalence about living with a foster family and returning home. When Lily began to acknowledge her losses, do some grieving work, and share her experience with adults who could tolerate hearing her pain and be supportive, she was more able to stay safe, manage her emotions and work toward goals related to imagining her future.

Changing Expectations – Facing Loss

Part of the unspoken culture of residential organizations is the inherent and very strong desire to protect the children in care. In part, this may be due to many residential treatment centers' heritage as former orphanages. As agencies, it is common for staff to go to great lengths to ensure that children are well cared for, and that they can have access to trips or material things that they may not have had previously. Staff seek to insulate the children from painful experiences. This often takes the form of overt and perhaps an unconscious response by the staff to collude with children to avoid talking about the children's painful pasts.

With the introduction of the Sanctuary Model, and specifically SELF, in one residential program, staff have been able to create the opportunity to talk openly with the children about loss and grieving. In fact, it has become expected of the staff to do so. Any potential emotional minefield instead becomes and opportunity; crisis can be diffused when the children begin to incorporate the language of SELF into their daily programs. What was once the exclusive domain of therapists and confined to 45 minute sessions once or twice per week has become part of the culture of the community. Treatment has now been imbedded in the milieu of the residences and school in community meetings, therapy groups as well as the daily activities of meal times, recreation and night time transitions. Staff also have found that as part of a treatment community, they can use themselves as models for how to manage emotions regarding losses that are appropriate to share with the larger community. Allowing children to give voice to their losses, having the expectation that they can in fact heal from loss, and expecting that staff members will do the same, are part of creating a functional therapeutic milieu.

Loss for Families with Children in Residential Care

> Part of my frustration with our field is that we seem so determined to locate
> human suffering narrowly while ignoring broader ecological perspectives. In
> family therapy we pride ourselves on having a systemic understanding of
> problems that we need to look not just at the individual, but at the whole family.
> But in some ways this is still very narrow, because the family exists in a broader
> socio-cultural context [11]. (Hardy, 2001)

Like the children who come into residential care with unresolved grief, many
parents suffer from the affects of loss. We often find that parents feel guarded
or mistrusting of the systems that are designed to help them reunite with their
children. The children who come to residential care are often the youngest in a
long line of intergenerational adversity. Whether families have suffered
tangible or intangible losses, we often see the effects of these experiences in
their behaviors. Just as we overlook loss issues in treatment with children, we
are likely to overlook issues of loss for parents and families. In some instances,
it seems that intergenerational loss begins to define a family system and traps it
in chronic reenactments, as it did for a mother named Karen and her children.

Karen

Karen was pregnant with her fourth child when her daughter came into
residential care. Fearful, heartbroken and admittedly mistrusting, Karen
described having lost one child to her husband's family in a custody dispute,
having lost one child to Sudden Infant Death Syndrome and "having lost the
other to the foster care system." Karen talked about the unresolved losses that
were likely contributors to her substance use. She also shared her belief that her
own history of loss played a role in her children's experiences. She shared
various losses endured in her childhood and early adulthood. For example, her
mother had been an alcoholic; their relationship had been very conflicted.
Further her pain was compounded through other serious losses. Karen had been
raped several times, she lost friends to suicide, lost her grandparents who were
her primary caregivers, and eventually lost her childhood home in a legal battle
with her brothers. In sum, she had lost her sense of self. She became
agoraphobic, explaining that she often felt buried alive by her fear. She made a
clear connection between her own adverse experiences, her reactions and the
experiences that her children were having. Some of her children's negative
experiences were directly related to her own reenactments of her trauma history.
Karen shared her wish that her own children would not suffer as she had. She
also realized that her unresolved losses had played an undermining role in her
children's lives.

---

[11] Hardy, *African American Experience*

Karen's unusual insight allowed her to acknowledge the effects of her unresolved grief and determine to work through her losses. She recognized that the death of her baby and the removal of her daughter were the most significant blows. But Karen also identified the ripple effect of those losses. She talked about feeling that her friends felt awkward around her, often seeming to be unsure of how to speak with her, afraid that any mention of her children would upset her too much. Karen also spoke about the loss of her apartment. Her daughter's reunification with her was based on her having a suitable home. For this reason, Karen would need to find a larger place to live. Although she wanted to comply with the court and move to a new home in order to have her daughter returned, she felt conflicted. She was very reluctant to leave her apartment because it was where her son had died. She said,

> I know that some people think it's weird, but I feel safer there. I feel close to him there. There is a little boy who lives upstairs who was born a few months before my son was. I look at him and think about what my son might look like. I look for signs from God like that.

Although Karen struggled with the significant losses in her life, she was like the children who are treated in residential care in her resilience. She spoke about her choice to have an open casket at her son's wake, despite the negative responses she experienced from relatives about her decision. She recalled, "I didn't want people to see a closed box. To me, it just seemed more personal. I had to see him one more time to say goodbye." Karen talked about having made the same decision about her mother's funeral, needing the visual experience of closure. She remarked that she lights a candle at each holiday in order to remember her son and puts up an empty stocking for him at Christmas.

In the course of treatment for her Karen's child, it became clear that grieving and healing from losses would be the work of the entire family, not just the identified client – the child. In this case, and likely in many cases, it is unresolved grief that explains why family systems frequently repeat cycles of violence and reenact trauma.

Karen's sobriety has played a significant role in her work to regain custody of her daughter. Her participation in substance abuse treatment has helped her to grieve in her own way. She talked about her hopes for the future for her family. "I just hope my kids can be happy, that we can come together as a family and be happy. I've been sober for 16 months and I expect my daughter to come home in a few months."

Secondary Losses for Families

Just as the children in residential care face intangible losses related to being part of a marginalized group, families with children in residential care face a multitude of secondary losses. Often, families are allowed limited contact with their children in residential settings in the form of weekly or biweekly visits. When children are allowed weekend or overnight visits with their families, they may maintain some contact with their communities. But they live the rest of the week in another place, going to a different school and remaining separate from their own communities. This separation contributes to a significant secondary loss, one which may be exacerbated when the privilege of visiting one's family is tied to the child's behavior. In residential care, it is common practice to keep children from home visits if they misbehave. This is often done in the service of safety, using the logic that if the child cannot manage his/her behavior in the residence, he/she certainly cannot do so in a home setting in the community. What may be missing from the equation is that the separation from one's family actually may be contributing to the acting out behavior. In this way contact with one's family or community is presented as either a reward or something to be taken away as a punishment. Despite the good intentions of the residential staff to keep the child safe, the child and family may view this protective intervention as punitive.

The SELF model can be effective in managing secondary loss in that it allows a context for discussing all sides of a decision, and the dialogue promotes the involvement of the child. In most residential treatment settings, the conversation is likely to focus exclusively on safety and end there. In using the SELF Model, the context for discussion includes the emotions and management of these emotions for the child, the staff and the family. Conversations organized around the SELF components also acknowledge the loss created by the separation from family and community and offer the possibility that further work on safety and emotion management might lead to a different outcome in the future.

The marginalization of families with children in residential care can manifest in other ways. A family's sense of itself as a self-determining entity may be compromised by residential care. Most families have their own definition of who they are; they may function as autocratic decision-making bodies for themselves. Independently they may choose to accept or disregard advice or criticism from outsiders. When children enter residential care, the sense of family sovereignty and the boundary between who is in the family and who is outside of the family is often breeched. This schism may be further exaggerated by the rules of the child welfare system, especially for those families whose children are removed by the state and placed in residential care.

The break also may be exacerbated by issues of institutional racism and poverty, the secondary losses that Hardy describes. The control over the care of their child is left up to the state, and families are forced to submit to rules and regulations that may seem unfair and infuriating. Because the need to protect children is paramount, and the results of failing to do so can be deadly, social services, the courts, and agencies that contract with them to provide residential treatment must be vigilant in protecting children. These systems, however, often exacerbate the experience of marginalization for families. The family court system, with its participant arrangement (the parent as respondent, the state or county child welfare agency and a legal advocate for the child) often inadvertently sets up an adversarial relationship between parents and the agencies that are trying to help them and their children. It is this very attempt by our legal system to intervene on behalf of children that disrupts the powerbase of many families. This adversarial basis engenders an inherent lack of trust between families and agencies and places agencies in the precarious situation of determining when to allow contact and how trustworthy parents may be with their own children.

Residential settings often describe themselves as being family-centered; they make attempts to include families in various decision-making steps in their treatment programs. Although this may be their intention, residential settings are sometimes hindered by court or state mandates in meeting this goal. Frequently residential resources or manpower also are hindrances. It is common practice for children who have been removed from their families to have only supervised contact with their families. During these supervised visits, an agency worker must sit and observe the family, watching and making note of anything that might be deemed inappropriate. Parents and families in this situation have complained about feeling watched and judged by this process. This, too, represents a loss as the inherent boundaries of the family have been breeched by the addition of a watchful third party.

The limitations on amount and length of content are also contributors to a sense of marginalization for families. With limited resources, many residential settings find it difficult to pull staff members away from their other work in order to supervise a family visit for more than an hour. With the number of children in these programs and the number of times families wished to come per week, some residential settings have found themselves struggling with staffing resources and space to provide visit supervision. Many families and children have reported feeling frustrated by the limited contact and the parameters set for them by social services, the court and residential agencies. The secondary loss of family self-determination is compounded by other restrictive variables: visitation hours, number of visitors, the need to clear family members with social services or the court before contact is allowed.

There may be restrictions, too, on gifts as well as the number and length of phone calls. In light of these restrictions, many parents report a sense that they are being judged for their parenting skills, viewed as incompetent or criminal. In some cases, explosive or rageful behavior on the part of a parent in response to staff limit-setting can be traced to these feelings of marginalization and intangible loss which are created by the systems that serve children. Without understanding the context of this anger and acting out by parents in the context of secondary loss, many of these interactions become reenactments of the persecutor, victim, rescuer dynamic. The traumatic experiences are reenacted between the family and the service providers.

Again, because of the unsafe experiences many residential children have had with their families, the restrictive interventions are done in the name of safety. There are many parents who need the guidance of a trained staff person to help them interact appropriately with their children or to help them manage their children's behavior during a visit. However, a parent's perception of this is marginalizing is heightened when these interventions are viewed as punitive rather than as helpful. Fortunately, working through the components of SELF with parents along with their children can be a way to acknowledge the loss that occurs when the nucleus of the family is compromised while emphasizing the need to manage emotions around the loss. Working toward achieving physical, social, psychological and moral safety during visits and phone calls can ensure that family self-determination is restored in the future.

Resiliency

Families are incredibly resilient, and in fact most of the workers in the child welfare system are smart, well-intentioned and kind. When these workers are able to recognize the conflicts that the child welfare system creates and can think about the long term safety and needs of the children— rather than the short-sighted fixes that some policies mandate—they are able to help children and families overcome significant loss, while working toward reunification. The adoption of the SELF framework by a social services worker and residential team in the case of Leah and Chris was one such example.

Leah and Chris

A young sibling pair, Leah and Chris, were physical opposites of each other. Leah was small and stout next to her brother's lanky frame. Their physical differences highlighted their differences in personality, Leah an outgoing chatterbox and Chris a reserved boy. The children had been living with a pre-adoptive foster family for several years and had been freed for adoption. Their adoption had not been finalized, but there were a number of other children in the home who had been successfully adopted from foster care. Leah and Chris had come to residential care after being removed from their pre-adoptive parents when it was learned by local authorities that the oldest of the adopted children had been downloading pornography from the internet and taking provocative photos of his teenage sisters. This child, a teenager himself, was removed from the home and referred for treatment. Because the other children in the home had already been adopted, they were allowed to remain in the care of the parents, but the youngest two were removed from the home. Because their adoption had not been finalized, the county workers had to reconsider whether this home was suitable as a permanent place for Leah and Chris. The parent's ability to supervise the children appropriately and care for these two siblings was in question.

The state had the best interest of these children in mind, but also faced the dilemma of managing the legal issues that the situation presented. From one perspective, it appeared that the parents had been negligent in supervising their teenage children; after all, they were unaware that their oldest son might be a sexual predator. From another perspective, it seemed that these parents, and more significantly, that these two children, were being punished for the sexual curiosity of a teenage boy. The caseworker was able to appreciate both perspectives, and worked with the family and the treatment team at the residential treatment center to determine the best course of action. Had she only looked at the facts of the case, the worker quite possibly may have begun looking for an alternative placement for Leah and Chris. Safety outweighs almost every other consideration in determining placement, but the treatment team and the social services worker were able to explore multiple definition of safety in making plans for this family.

The treatment team, which included the parents and the social worker from social services, was able to look at physical, psychological, social and moral safety as factors in their decision. Physical safety was the easiest for all parties to understand and work around. Physical safety meant making sure that the children would not be exposed to a sexual perpetrator or be at risk for sexual or physical abuse. It meant that their corporeal needs would be met through appropriate housing and availability of resources. Psychological safety involved creating an environment that allowed appropriate expression of emotions, tolerance for strong emotion coupled with the ability to manage strong emotion without hurting oneself or others. A psychologically safe environment is free from neglect, humiliation, blaming, shaming and fear of reprisal. Social safety represents the ability to feel secure within one's social group or family, and that one will not be ostracized or rejected for being oneself. A socially safe environment is free from abusive attachment, isolation, abusive uses of power, weak boundaries or tolerance for inappropriate behaviors. Moral safety allows for people to feel safe to make ethical decisions and choices. A morally safe environment is free from dishonesty, injustice, discrimination and perpetration.

The team agreed that the decision to remove the children and disrupt the adoption process seemed to provide a certain level of physical safety for the children. The problem with the decision was that it had greatly interfered with the emotional, social and moral safety of the children and family system. The sibling pair had a very strong and secure bond with the parents and the other children in the home, therefore their sense of emotional connection and sense of family was disrupted by the removal. This was one in many betrayals and disruptions for them, including their abandonment by their birth parents and their subsequent disrupted placements in other foster homes. The decision also marked a departure from social safety since it took two children who had identified as full members of a family, and placed them in a system where they felt vulnerable and isolated. Their placement reinforced their belief that they were not real or true members of a family they had lived with for years. The decision also presented a lack of moral safety; it seemed to demonstrate to the children and family that it was acceptable to punish people because of the mistakes of others.

When the treatment team and social services worker were able to reframe the issue of safety to include all of the dimensions, the team decided to work toward returning the children to this home. The family was able to change the layout of the house so that the children would be more easily supervised to provide better physical safety. Most importantly, the family met together to talk about what had happened. These discussions opened the door to more healthy communications about boundaries for the younger children and sexuality for the older children, making significant progress in both psychological and social safety.

These conversations were also a way of creating a dialogue about the losses that the children had experienced in their lives. Discussions framed in the SELF components helped address past losses in order to create a future that would not recapitulate these losses. The team and family were able to better understand Leah and Chris' separations from previous families, their identity as children of color, traumas they had experienced prior to placement as well as the traumatic experience of being interviewed by the police, and learning of their siblings' involvement in inappropriate sexual activity. Their removal from their pre-adoptive family presented a potential trigger for some of the problematic behaviors they were presenting. To help restore the family's sense of self, the team encouraged them to talk about loss. This emphasis was more constructive than previous discussions focusing strictly on diagnosing the issues at hand. Together, the team, social service worker and family sought to repair relationships rather than cause a painful emotional schism by removing the children permanently.

Losses for Residential Treatment Settings as Systems

The solidarity of a group provides the strongest protection against terror and despair, and the strongest antidote to traumatic experience.
—Judith Lewis Herman, Trauma and Recovery

Organizational systems face multiple significant losses all the time. There is the loss of residents and students as they graduate out of the residential system, return home or are placed with foster parents. There is the loss of students who cannot return to facilities because they require hospitalization or require a different level of placement. Tragically, there is the loss of former residents to suicide, prison or accidental death. Residential settings also face the loss of staff, those who leave to care for own families or for new positions. Job burnout in residential care is a significant source of loss. At times, the weight of all of these losses is overwhelming. It interfaces with an individual's

inability to bear the core triad of grief, fear and despair that (are) the source of much of our individual and collective emotional ills[12].

Just as families may suppress grief particularly when there are multiple losses, organizations also suffer from the effects grief suppression. Perhaps mental health professionals are especially avoidant because these losses are things that cannot be "fixed or cured"[13]. In the context of loss for families, McGoldrick and Boundy suggest that the lack of acknowledgement of loss has "immediate implications for that family's development over its life cycle and long term effects across generations". The enduring after effect "is that failure to adequately mourn losses results in enduring maladaptive patterns"[14].

Organizations, much like individuals and families, may demonstrate these maladaptive patterns in response to un-mourned loss, becoming immobilized, depressed, and expressing reenacting behaviors. As a result of this organizational immobilization, residential settings often settle for treating behavior rather than connecting behavior to its source. Workers in residential care risk becoming detached, focusing on order rather than repairing attachment by being attuned to an individual's complex needs. Because residential systems are as vulnerable to the effects of loss as the children and families they

---

[12] Greenspan, *Healing Through the Dark Emotions.*
[13] Boss, *Loss, Trauma and Resilience,* p.4
[14] McGoldrick and Boundy, *The Legacy of Unresolved Lodd*

serve, the SELF model can be used to help organizations address their system-wide experiences of grief and loss (see Bloom, *this volume*)..

Sadly, many agencies have experienced suicides and even homicides. When these tragedies occur, staff members are often so preoccupied and overwhelmed by trying to regain safety for their residents, talking to the press, and responding to investigations, that they may become numb and exhausted. As a result, frequently these institutional traumas are buried and not discussed. But, as organizations have used the SELF assessment, old painful memories are unearthed and the unresolved grief and shame are faced.   Using SELF, the organizational community can find a way to be open about past losses and even memorialize a tragedy symbolically. For example, a tree or garden has been planted at some residential agencies after a suicide as a way of recognizing the loss of life and acknowledging the loss of that child's potential to be healed.

Another limiting aspect of coping with loss for residential care workers is that they are precluded by who they may talk to about work related tragedies. If the loss is related to one of organization's children or their families, the pledge of confidentiality prevents their discussing the situation in the way that other workers might typically process the loss. This is similar to the issue of "Coming Home"[15] for Iraq and Vietnam War Veterans. A veteran of Iraq in recalling a devastating mortar attack on the chow hall of her unit (and the re-experiencing of the attack) later said: "It's stuff you can't talk about in the civilian world..."

The gap between home and work can be enormous. For example, in the work lives of staff in residential treatment, it is common to hear trauma histories of children that involve murder, rape and torture. These staff arrive home where family members more readily are able discuss their daily upsets or seek escape by tuning into *American Idol*. Being able to distance oneself from the job in a meaningful fashion is often too big a leap for many. The result? At times those who work in residential care may feel alienated from the normal support of their families.

Combat survivors refer to this sensation as feeling much like outsiders when they return home. Some maladaptive ways of coping as an outsider may be reflected in the use of substances and in broken family relationships. Numbing is an occupational habit reflected in organization stress, but this alienation can be addressed by the constant attention to the L of the SELF Model. The need to focus on organizational loss was evident for one residential treatment center when one of its former residents, Brenda committed suicide shortly after her discharge to another facility.

·

---

[15] Simon, *Bringing the War Home,* p.32.

Brenda

Brenda had struggled in with despair and many instances of self harming while in residential treatment. She had lost her family of origin, had failed foster care placements and was beginning to age out of the foster care system. The team had valiantly struggled to find a placement for this child and had finally succeeded. An adoption had gone through and the team had seen and heard reports of the benefits of her being adopted by a loving family. Her adoptive family was mindful and compassionate about the maturational needs of this former resident. Many of the older students at the agency knew her, and some of them had stayed in touch with her. Naturally, when the news of the suicide reached the agency, both staff and students were devastated.

Several staff proposed scheduling a series of L groups for the staff of the cottage where Brenda had lived. Other staff who had worked with this child were to be included. Some of the leaders in the organization thought it would be burdensome to an already profoundly sad group. They suggested L groups might decrease their ability to keep the structure of the residential unit and care for their current residents. Others persevered, recognizing that if they did not face the loss, then they would not be able to function in the present. Equally limiting, without facing loss, it would be impossible to move into the future.

The group that had worked with this child assembled. As they sat down, a staff member from another residential unit walked in, asking to join as a supportive participant for those who had worked with the deceased child. The positive impact of a sympathetic group who were there to offer support was palpable. As they talked about the loss, the more affected members of the staff recognized the benefits of having their colleagues express care and concern for *their* loss. This could easily have been a forgotten moment as the staff soldiered ahead in their day to day duties of caring for children who have been afflicted with many adversities and traumatic experiences. The staff group experienced first hand what is was to have care and support. Bereaved staff members did not have a sense of alienation; they had colleagues who were there to offer support, to help them discuss the loss. All colleagues—those who were mourning the loss of this young adult as well as those there to offer support—personally understood the value of loss work in a extremely unique and meaningful new context.

Conclusions

Not everything that is faced can be changed. But nothing can be changed until it is faced.
– James Baldwin

Coping with loss requires relationships and connection to others. In the past, grief work in many residential settings was limited to individual psychotherapy sessions. Many now see that this work often is most effective and best done in groups. One of the benefits of residential care is its congregate nature and therefore its ready availability of groups. With other participants and mourners, there is the opportunity to normalize the experience of loss. This dynamic reduces isolation and builds emotional connections with others who have experienced a similar loss. Holding loss groups in a residential unit or school offers the benefit of emphasizing community and cooperation by demonstrating that "classrooms can become places where (youth) learn to think about themselves as members of a whole that is greater than themselves" [16].

Aside from loss or bereavement groups, psychoeducational groups are another very effective way of helping children and families understand the effects of exposure to trauma and adversity and ways that the SELF Model can serve as a framework for addressing these effects. Children in several residential settings that use the Sanctuary Model have described the surprising ease with which children understand the concepts of SELF and the effects of trauma. In the Sanctuary Model psychoeducation curriculum for children [17] these concepts are conveyed through short lessons and participatory exercises, such as music and film clips. "In these sessions youths learn how healing from loss is connected to safety and emotions and how this is connected to a better future, how difficult it is to grieve, how people can get stuck when they are not able to grieve their losses, and how people need support when they are grieving so their safety can be maintained." [18].

For parents with children in residential care, education about the impact of intangible losses serves to empower and can facilitate the healing process for families. As part of treatment, parents can be encouraged to process the intangible losses they may have faced – losses of childhood, a sense of safety in the world, attachment relationships, the ability to manage emotions like other people, self esteem, capacity to establish healthy, nourishing relationships, good role models, conflict resolution skills, loss of ability to individuate, ability to let go of past, and a sense of wholeness. When families begin to acknowledge and understand the propensity to recreate these losses in their own lives and those of their families through reenactment, they can begin to interrupt that cycle of loss. Groups, individual and family work that focuses on loss can contribute to the development of the therapeutic community as more whole and humanized.

---

[16] Hardy and Laszloffy, p. 200
[17] See Sanctuary Leadership Development Institute, www.andruschildren.org
[18] Rivard et al, Preliminary Results of a Study, p.82

That need to humanize and create community also extends to the staff of residential treatment centers and the systems themselves. Allowing for opportunities to acknowledge institutional losses and community grief can serve to disrupt the perpetuation of traumatic loss for the organization and the clients they serve. Adopting the understanding that a residential treatment system is in many ways an organism that is vulnerable to the effects of trauma can help leaders and staff members treat each other and their organization with the same compassion that they show their clients.

Residential treatment centers are, by nature, grounded in loss. From the children served to the staff who serve, to the environment in which the organization exists, loss is an inextricable part of residential care. Despite this reality, loss is easily lost when there is so much emotional intensity in the lives of the children, the families and within the system. One residential treatment staff member recently shared a story about the pain and vulnerability of facing our losses, understanding that working through loss is a painful but necessary process for healing. He shared a moment of truth with his own daughter. She had cut her leg in a household accident. When her parents took her to the hospital for stitches, both mother and father were dreading seeing their child in pain. Despite the anesthesia, his daughter cried, "Daddy it hurts". At first he was speechless, then he heard himself say, "Honey, sometimes it's got to hurt so it can get better." With this understanding, residential settings will continue in the work of creating Sanctuaries where children and those who care for them can face their hurts in order to get better and move into a future with fewer burdens from the past.

References

Bloom, S. L. *Creating Sanctuary: Toward the Evolution of Sane Societies*. New York: Routledge, 1997.

Bloom, S. L., J. F. Foderaro, and R. A. Ryan. *S.E.L.F.: A Trauma-Informed, Psychoeducational Group Curriculum*: Available at www.sanctuaryweb.com, 2006.

Boss, P. *Loss, Trauma, and Resilience: Therapeutic Work with Ambiguous Loss*. New York: W. W. Norton, 2006.

Cohen, J.A., A.P. Mannarino, T. Greenberg, S. Padlo, and Shipley C. "Childhood Traumatic Grief: Concepts and Controversies." *Trauma, Violence and Abuse* 3, no. 4 (2002): 307-27.

Greenspan, M. *Healing through the Dark Emotions: The Wisdom of Grief, Fear and Despair*. Boston: Shambhala, 2004.

Hardy, K. V., ed. *African American Experience and the Healing of Relationships in Family Therapy: Exploring the Field's Past, Present and*

Possible. Edited by D. Denborough: Dulwich Centre Publications http://www.dulwichcentre.comau/kenhardyarticle.html, 2001.

Hardy, K. V., and T. A. Laszyloffy. *Teens Who Hurt: Clinical Interventions to Break the Cycle of Adolescent Violence.* New York: The Guilford Press, 2005.

McGoldrick, M., and D. Boundy. *The Legacy of Unresolved Loss: A Family Systems Approach.* New York: NewBridge Professional Programs, 1996.

Rivard, J.C., S. L. Bloom, D. McCorkle, and R. Abramovitz. "Preliminary Results of a Study Examining the Implementation and Effects of a Trauma Recovery Framework for Youths in Residential Treatment." *Therapeutic Community: The International Journal for Therapeutic and Supportive Organizations* 26, no. 1 (2005): 83-96.

Simon, C. "Bringing the War Home." *Psychotherapy Networker* January/February (2007): 32-33.

Chapter Seven

Loss in Human Service Organizations

Sandra L. Bloom, M.D.

All changes even the most longed for, have their melancholy; for what we leave behind us is a part of ourselves: we must die to one life before we can enter into another!
—Anatole France, *The Crime of Sylvestre Bonnard*

Introduction

I enjoy writing and over the course of the last fifteen years I have written dozens of articles, columns, chapters and even several books. So, I was a little perplexed – and more than a little frustrated with myself – when I just could not get this chapter started. After spending an inordinate amount of time gathering material, looking through books in my library, interviewing a number of organizational leaders, starting web searches, and making notes, a few weeks ago I took every available opportunity to sit down in front of the computer and begin to compose my thoughts. But each time, I would get distracted by a phone call, or an email that had to be immediately answered, or a task that demanded urgent attention – like cleaning my kitchen drawers. The dog needed to be walked, papers need to be filed, bills needed to be paid. As they do, new work tasks kept arriving and demanded my attention. The final straw came earlier today when I left my desk for a luncheon engagement and was sitting comfortably in the restaurant when I realized that I was actually twenty-four hours *early* for my appointment. With this, I had to confront the enormity of my own largely unconscious avoidance of this topic, despite my conscious willingness to write about the subject and the torturous preoccupation about writing this chapter that has dominated my thoughts for weeks.

In fact, loss in both the personal and professional sense has been a recurrent theme in my life for decades and I don't like it. I don't like being sad, disappointed, angry or overwhelmed. Like other human beings, I prefer to avoid pain. I don't want to revisit – even indirectly – the losses that are now part of my history, and that I like to think are over and done with.

Work with survivors of a vast array of adversity and trauma has taught me that try as we might, there is no avoiding loss and it is largely unnegotiated loss that compels reenactment, or as we say in our loss groups, repeating one's negative life patterns is *"never having to say goodbye"*. Trauma survivors have also taught me that safety in the world is significantly influenced by our ability to manage the painful emotions that accompany loss. They also taught me that sometimes, the place to begin, a place that offers us the courage and hope to fortify us in the journey through our own existential darkness, is a vision of a future positively changed as a result of committing ourselves to safety, learning to more effectively manage painful feelings and negotiating loss.

The other authors in this volume have offered a glimpse into the pain, suffering and healing - the loss, hurt and hope - of children and families who come into some level of care in order to get the help they need to lead better lives. This chapter focuses on the organizations that are charged with providing that care and the leaders whose job it is to assure that the job is accomplished appropriately, competently, expediently – and successfully.

My experience working with very traumatized children, adults and families within the context of stressed and traumatized organizations is embodied in the theory and practice of the Sanctuary Model, a trauma-informed, whole systems approach to organizational development [1]. The fundamental operating tool of the Sanctuary Model is called "S.E.L.F.", the four letters representing the key domains of recovery: Safety, Emotional management, Loss and Future. My colleagues and I have developed a Sanctuary Leadership Development Institute (SLDI) and our experience with many social service environments has demonstrated that the aspects of organizational trauma and loss that are covered in this chapter are virtually universal to the human social service field. Many of the participants of the SLDI and other organizations that I have collaborated with willingly shared their organizational experiences with me and their comments are included in this chapter as illustrations of some key points.

I make a very basic and somewhat unusual assumption about organizations and that is, that they are living beings, that when we come together over time to achieve specific tasks, something emerges out of our shared experience that cannot be attributed solely to the individual psychology of the combination of individual members that comprise that organization. A conceptual framework that sees organization as having *emergent* qualities has been discussed in other settings, particularly in the world of business, and allows a conversation about such things as organizational learning,

---

[1] Bloom. *The Sanctuary Model of Organizational Change for Children's Residential Treatment;* Bloom, *The Sanctuary Model: A Trauma-Informed Systems Approach to the Residential Treatment of Children.*

organizational memory, organizational culture, and of course, organizational loss[2].

Human beings are group animals before we become individuals, and every time we become part of a group, our individual identity is impacted by whatever subsequently affects the group identity. Loss is a profoundly transformative experience for individuals and so too is loss distinctively meaningful for organizations as small as families and as large as whole societies. This chapter explores the territory of loss within organizations, a subject that encompasses the normative losses that accompany change as well as the losses that accompanies chronic stress and collective trauma. The concept of "parallel process" is helpful in explaining why attending to creating healthier organizational processes is so important to successful treatment. It is important to understand the variety of reasons and expressions of loss in the workplace and what it tells us about the ways in which the organization is functioning. The chapter concludes with some recommendations for managing organizational loss so that growth and learning rather than stagnation and decline become possible.

Group Behavior, Living Systems and Loss

Individual Identity and the Group

Individualism has long dominated our philosophical, and to a large extent, our psychological premises for understanding human behavior. But human beings are intensely social animals. The latest breakthroughs in neuroscience are demonstrating something that attachment theorists and group therapists have been noticing for several centuries:

> Neuroscience has discovered that our brain's very design makes it sociable, inexorably drawn into an intimate brain-to-brain linkup whenever we engage with another person. That neural bridge lets us affect the brain – and so the body- of everyone we interact with, just as they do us…. To a surprising extent our relationships mold not just our experience but our biology….nourishing relationships have a beneficial impact on our health, while toxic ones can act like slow poison in our bodies[3].

There is a growing body of evidence to suggest that groups are a basic form of social and cognitive organization that is essentially "hard-wired" into our species and that our 'group-self' is the core component of our sense of

---

[2] Bloom, S.L., *Organizational Stress as a Barrier to Trauma-Sensitive Change and System Transformation*

[3] **Goleman** *Social Intelligence: The New Science of Human Relationships*, p.5

personal identity[4]. A new paradigm has been emerging about the interactive and dynamic components of individual and group identity:

> Through human interaction the inner life becomes transformed into social experiences and systems and, conversely group experience comes to be personally and internally represented. The two dimensions of inner and group life are linked by an interface, a network system consisting of verbal and non-verbal interactions linking members of a group … The individual and the group emerge from a primal unity through the creation of a boundary which distinguishes one from the other [5].

Emergence and Organizational Culture

The paradigm that has dominated group life – and therefore individual existence – for at least the last two hundred years is a model that sees organizations as machines that operate more or less like clocks with interchangeable parts, lacking feelings, able to perform their function without conflict – regular, predictable, ordered and controlled. In contrast, *"groupmind"* is the word that has been used to describe the controversial concept of a supra-individual nature and independence of the collective mind of a social group. The concept goes back at least to the German philosopher Hegel and Durkheim, but it was the social psychologist McDougall who became convinced that a society is more than the mere sum of the mental lives of its units and he concluded that "a complete knowledge of the units, if and in so far as they could be known as isolated units, would not enable us to deduce the nature of the life of the whole"[6].

Increasingly, organizations are being recognized as alive, possessing the basic requirements of a living system[7]. In the organizational development literature, the idea of the organization as alive has been steadily emerging. As one investigator noted:

> The prevalence of life cycle and ecological models of change in organization science has produced several generations of theorists who think and write about organizations in terms of life metaphors. According to many accounts, organizations are born, grow up, age to adolescence and maturity, become set in their ways, and eventually die. Although organizations certainly are not alive in any meaningful biological sense, few people question the use of these metaphors

---

[4] Ettin, Fidler, and Cohen, *Group Process and Political Dynamics*
[5] Ibid, p.13, p17
[6] McDougall, *The Group Mind*, p. 7.
[7] DeGeus, *The Living Company*; Gantt and Agazarian, *Systems-centered Emotional Intelligence*.

in describing organizational life cycles.... Our metaphors strongly condition how
we think about organizations. Theorists are preoccupied with when organizations
are "born", what species they are (their forms), and when they have changed
enough to be termed dead [8].

We didn't wake up one day and decide we would take tougher kids. There has
been a whole change in the overall climate. Over the last twenty years we have
gone from being a very child-like place, to being an adolescent and then in the
last few years I think we have grown up. The previous CEO had been here for
over twenty five years and when he left it was as if Dad left and there were
mixed feelings about that. We [the present CEO and COO] are not the parents he
was. There is a very different feel to the place and I am sure there are people
who miss it the way it was – and sometimes I do too.
—C.O.O., Residential child-care facility

  Some of the most useful explorations of organizations as collective and
living organisms derive from the study of *organizational culture*. Organizational
culture has been defined as a *"pattern of shared basic assumptions that a group
has learned as it solved its problems...and that has worked well enough to be
considered valid and taught to new members"* or "How we do things around
here". Organizational culture matters because cultural elements determine
strategy, goals, and modes of operating[9].

  The current concept that may hold the most theoretical and practical
promise for understanding group process is that of complexity theory in which
an organization is viewed as a complex adaptive system that is self-
organizing[10]. In complexity theory, one way of understanding how collective
phenomenon could arise and be different than the components that comprise it is
through the concept of *emergence*. The simplest way of understanding
emergence is that it occurs whenever the whole is greater than – or smarter than
– the sum of the parts. It is about understanding how collective properties arise
from the properties of parts and the relationship between them [11]. As
neuroscientist John Holland has written in his book on the topic,

we are everywhere confronted with emergence in complex adaptive systems –
ant colonies, networks of neurons, the immune system, the Internet, and the
global economy, to name a few – where the behavior of the whole is much more
complex than the behavior of the part[12].

---

[8] Hager, *Tales From the Grave*, p.52.
[9] Schein, *The Corporate Culture Survival Guide*
[10] Goldstein, *The Unshackled Organization*
[11] Johnson, *Emergence*
[12] Holland, *Emergence*, p.2

In the business world, unlike the social service sector, a new paradigm for understanding groups has been itself emerging in part due to the enormous pressures of globalization. Some strong proponents of this emerging point of view in the business world, Peter Senge among them, have claimed that *"the 20th century gave birth to a new species – the global corporation… a life form that can grow, evolve, and learn"[13]*. In this new paradigm, individual consciousness becomes even more – not less – important so that *"the key challenge is to apply inner knowledge, intuition, compassion and spirit to prosper in a period of constant and discontinuous change)"[14]*. As organizational development expert Peter Drucker notes,

> The organization is above all, social. It is people. Its purpose must therefore be to make the strengths of people effective and their weaknesses irrelevant. If fact, that is the one thing only the organization can do – the one reason why we have it and need to have it[15].

If organizations are living entities, and if the purpose is to maximize people's strengths and minimize their weaknesses, then the psychological knowledge gained in the last hundred years and more about human development, human developmental failures and human systems should help us imagine how to maximize organizational function, beginning with an understanding of how living systems work.

Human Service Systems as Systems

A system is a set of interconnected elements that are *interdependent* so that changes in some elements or their relations produce changes in other parts of the system. A system is comprised of a set of components that work together for the overall objective of the whole[16]. Unlike a machine - like your car, or your vacuum cleaner – any environment that delivers human services is a living system – open, complex, and adaptive. It is comprised of the staff, administrators, boards, clients, and their families. It is rooted within the mental health, juvenile justice, or child protective systems that are components of the social service system of a county and state, and all are set within a country that is embedded within a global civilization.

---

[13] Senge et al, *Presence,*p.7.
[14] Ibid, p. 6
[15] Drucker, *Introduction, The Organization of the Future*
[16] Haines, *The Manager's Pocket Guide to Systems Thinking and Learning;* Jervis, *Systems Effects*

The past history of any service program, like the histories of the individual clients and staff, and the systems they are embedded within, continue to determine present behavior and in every moment, present behavior is playing a role in determining the future. All of these components – individual, group, organization, local government, national government, global influences, past, present and future – all are interacting with and impacting on each other in complicated ways, all of the time – that's what makes things so *complex*. It is this complexity that compels the usual oversimplification that occurs whenever an individual or a group of individuals encounters the apparently overwhelming complexity of changing systems.

Living systems are *open systems* because they accept input from their environment, they use this input to create output, and they then act on the environment. Living systems are adaptive because they can *learn* and based on that learning, they can adapt to changes in their environment in order to survive. As a living system, the human service system and every component of that system has an identity, a memory, and has created its own processes that resist changes imposed from above, but will evolve and change naturally if the circumstances are conducive to change.

> What has been clear to me – and that's one of those transitions from being little to big – when you came to work here twenty years ago each person had regular contact with the CEO, department managers and as a result of personal contact, new staff got indoctrinated into the organizational values in a very real way. As we got bigger we made the assumption that this informal system was still working but in fact we need a much more vigorous process for how we orient people, get them up to speed. I think we have gotten better in real time talking about those issues and at the last general staff meeting that is what we talked about – loss and change, the idea that so much has changed here and that everyone has lost something, everyone is grieving. I talked about the organization I loved, the campus program, and as much as people in the other divisions think they have lost, so have we all.
> —C.O.O., *Residential child-care facility*

Living systems are not entirely controllable by top down regulation. Like the human body, a living system functions through constant feedback loops, flows of information back and forth. In the body, there certainly are hierarchies but these hierarchies are "democratic hierarchies" – power distribution is circular [17][16]. Regulation comes through feedback mechanisms and changes constantly over time, adjusting and readjusting to internal circumstances that have been altered and reacting and adjusting to external changes in the environment. Information from below in the hierarchy has as

---

[17] Ackoff, *The Democratic Corporation*

much influence as control mechanisms higher in the hierarchy. (If you find this difficult to believe, just try focusing your own intellectual attention on something when even your little toe is throbbing with pain.) A living system evolves, regenerates, and self-organizes to adapt to changing circumstances. Living systems learn and use that new information to alter present and future behavior. A living system is constantly balancing and rebalancing to maintain homeostasis. And in a living system there is no such thing as an absolute state of "health" – health is a relative term. You cannot feed a living system and then leave it alone - it must be fed and maintained all the time.

The Individual, the Group and Loss

A central position of this chapter is that, not only are individual staff members and administrators of our human social service system vulnerable to the emotions, attitudes and behaviors typical of trauma, loss and mourning, but so too are the organizations as a whole because they are alive and because all living things cycle developmentally from birth to death. When individuals become a member of an organization, the individual surrenders some of his or her own individuality in service of the organization. As a result, losses to the organization are likely to be experienced individually as well as collectively. For the same reason, failures of the organization to live up to whatever internalized ideal the individual has for the way that organization should function, is likely to be experienced individually and collectively as a betrayal of trust, a loss of certainty and security, a disheartening collapse of meaning and purpose. As workers in this field have determined, *"the relationship between employee and organization are: deep-seated; largely unconscious; intimately connected to the development of identity; and have emotional content"*[18]. Because of this connectedness between individual and collective identity, and because all change involves loss, organizational change and individual grieving tend to go hand-in-hand.

> I think for everyone there has been the loss associated with the changes from what the organization used to be to what it is now. Even ten years ago it was very different than now. We have had to give up security, stability, smallness, ease in problem solving, and a high level of resources to spread in a narrow way. For those of us who have been here throughout we feel that what we have gained is greater and we are happy to let some of that narrowness go. But still it is a loss. When I first came here I knew every staff member, every child, and every family by name. That is gone – that sense of closeness and familiarity is lost. We had a major leadership change – the CEO who had been here for 28 years left

---

[18] Ibid, p. 429

three and a half years ago after a five year process – but that was a very wrenching change for some people. The school, some of the old time staff that liked the way he did things – that was a change. For those of us who have been here for a number of years, we have all lost the jobs we used to do and in doing that other people have lost us and the way we used to be with them. We've been trying to strengthen the leadership quality we have and working styles, so we have changed over some positions, brought in new people, created some new positions, but a number of people feel a little off balance. We've lost the kinds of kids we used to work with. We work with far more challenging children now.
—C.E.O. Child care agency

Parallel Processes in Organizations

The concept of parallel process is a useful way of offering a coherent framework that can enable organizational leaders and staff to develop a way of thinking "outside the box" about what *has* happened and *is* happening to their clients, themselves, their treatment and service delivery systems, as well as to the world around them[19]. Identifying a problem is the first step in solving it. The notion of parallel process derives originally from psychoanalytic concepts related to transference and has traditionally been applied to the psychotherapy supervisory relationship in which the supervisory relationship may mirror much of what is going on in the relationship between therapist and client [20].

In their work with organizations, investigators have recognized that conflicts belonging at one location are often displaced and enacted elsewhere because of a parallelism between the conflicts at the place of origin and the place of expression. Other authors have used the notion of parallel process to illustrate this largely unconscious individual and group interaction[21]. An even older conceptualization of this process derives from the original sociological studies of mental institutions in the 1950's describing "collective disturbance" [22]. More recently, the idea of parallel process has been described as:

When two or more systems – whether these consist of individuals, groups, or organizations – have significant relationships with one another, they tend to develop similar affects, cognition, and behaviors, which are defined as parallel processes .... Parallel processes can be set in motion in many ways, and once initiated leave no one immune from their influence. They can move from one level of a system to another, changing form along the way. For example, two vice presidents competing for resources may suppress their hostility toward each

---

[19] Bloom, *Neither Liberty Nor Safety, Parts I-IV;* Bloom, *Societal Trauma.*
[20] McNeill and Worthen, *The Parallel Process in Psychotherapy Supervision.*
[21] Alderfer and Smith, *Studying Intergroup Relations Embedded in Organizations;* Sullivan, *Finding the Thou in the I*
[22] Stanton and Schwartz, *The Mental Hospital*

other and agree to collaborate interpersonally, but each may pass directives to her or his subordinates that induce them to fight with those of the other vice president. Thus, what began as a struggle among executives for resources become expressed by lower-ranking groups in battles over compliance with cost-cutting measure [23].

It is the contention of this chapter that parallel processes are at play that significantly interfere with the ability of the human service system and its components to address the actual needs of children, adults and families who present to them for help. Instead, because of complex interactions between traumatized clients, stressed staff, pressured organizations, and a social and economic environment that is frequently hostile to the aims of recovery, our systems often recapitulate the very experiences that have proven to be so toxic for the people we are supposed to treat[24]. Destructive unconscious group parallel processes are more likely to occur as a result of organizational exposure to collective trauma, chronic disaster, and chronic stress.

Collective Trauma

In his seminal work on community disasters, Kai Erikson has described collective trauma as

a blow to the basic tissues of social life that damages the bonds attaching people together and impairs the prevailing sense of communality. The collective trauma works its way slowly and even insidiously into the awareness of those who suffer from it, so it does not have the quality of suddenness normally associated with 'trauma'. But it is a form of shock all the same, a gradual realization that the community no longer exists as an effective source of support and that an important part of the self has disappeared... 'I' continue to exist, though damaged and maybe even permanently changed. 'You' continue to exist, though distant and hard to relate to. But 'we' no longer exist as a connected pair or as linked cells in a larger communal body [25].

Trauma occurs in the workplace is individually experienced by those members of the organization most closely associated with the traumatic event, but the events are also experienced collectively. Organizations under severe stress can manifest traits similar to stressed individuals. As anyone knows who has worked in a setting facing some kind of threat, everyone's attention becomes riveted on the latest rumor and little productive work is accomplished.

---

[23] Smith, Simmons and Thames, *Fix the Women*, p. 13.
[24] Bloom, *Organizational Stress as a Barrier to Trauma-Sensitive Change and System Transformation*
[25] Erikson, *A New Species of Trouble*, p.233

Because human beings are "hard-wired" for social interaction, a threat to our social group can be experienced as a dangerous threat to our individual survival and can evoke powerful responses.

> I will never forget the day I opened up the paper and read what people were saying about the place where I work. It was bad enough that a child had died, but the newspaper made it sound like we are all sadists who don't care at all about the kids. They made it sound like a barbaric place. I don't work on that particular unit, but now everybody I know acts like I should be ashamed or something. It's embarrassing and it just isn't true. Sure, we aren't perfect but I don't know anybody that doesn't care about the kids.
> —Therapist, Residential treatment center

Patient deaths and injuries – from natural causes, accidents, and most particularly homicide, suicide, and deaths while in restraints; staff deaths or injuries; accusations of sexual abuse; sudden death of leaders or other members of the community - all are examples of situations that create a crisis and all are likely to be overwhelming not just for the individuals involved but for overall organizational function. Deaths by suicide or homicide are acutely traumatic, particularly to a mental health or social service setting where the guilt, fear of recriminations for a failure to anticipate or prevent the deaths, affixing of blame, and glaring media exposure may be major components of the event as it is experienced by the members of the organization.

A crisis is a condition where a system is required or expected to handle a situation for which existing resources, procedures, policies, structures, or mechanisms are inadequate[26]. It describes a situation that threatens high priority goals and which suddenly occurs with little response time available [27]. In a crisis, the things that people are used to doing and comfortable doing, are not working and the stage is set for the possibility of disaster or new learning – or both.

An organizational crisis will be sensed by everyone in the sphere of influence of the organization almost instantaneously regardless of how strenuously leaders attempt to contain the spread of information. Emotional contagion –without cognitive input – occurs within one-twentieth of a second and although employees of an organization may not know what the problem is, they will indeed know that there is a problem [28]. Tension literally fills the air. Within minutes or hours of a particularly disturbing piece of gossip, news, or

---

[26] **Boal and Bryson**, *Charismatic Leadership*
[27] **Jick and Murray**, *The Management of Hard Times*
[28] **Hatfield, Cacioppo and Rapson**, *Emotional Contagion*

crisis, everyone in an organization will be in an alarm state with all that goes along with that, including compromised thought processes.[29]

Organizations respond to crisis in observable ways. When a crisis hits, most managers want to do the right thing. But one of the things that makes a crisis a crisis is that no one really knows what to do for certain, yet everyone expects the organizational leaders to know what to do. Different leaders will respond in different ways but this is often the time when a charismatic leader exerts the most influence either by creating a different frame of meaning for followers, by linking followers' needs to important values and purposes, through articulation of vision and goals, or by taking actions to deal with the crisis and then moving to new interpretive schemes or theories of action to justify the actions [30].

> I guess what makes a crisis a crisis is that you are not really prepared to deal with it. When my colleagues and I received the calls about the woman who had killed herself, I felt like the floor dropped out from under me. I had no idea what to do except to get back to the program and meet with my friends. I remember just feeling so sick and scared. When we arrived, all the other clients were flipping out and we had to immediately prioritize what to do. I had to listen not just to my head but to my heart as well. Obviously, there were some people more acutely distressed than others so we attended to them first and then began to rank order what we needed to do and divide up the tasks. I was so glad I didn't have to face this thing alone.
> —Medical Director, mental health unit.

At such a time, every person throughout the system is under stress, so everyone's ability to think complexly will be relatively compromised. Stress increases a person's vigilance towards gathering information, but it can also overly simplify and perceptively distort what we see or hear. Negative cues are usually magnified and positive cues are diminished or ignored altogether. Furthermore, the stress of an event is determined by the amount and degrees of change involved, not whether this change is good or bad [34]. Under these conditions, command and control hierarchies usually become reinforced and serve to contain some of the collective anxiety generated by the crisis. Command hierarchies can respond more rapidly and mobilize action to defend against further damage. In times of danger, powerful group forces are marshaled and attachment to the group radically increases. Everyone in the organization is vulnerable to the risks the organization faces as a whole – everyone feels vulnerable[31].

---

[29] Bloom, *Neither Liberty Nor Safety, Part I*
[30] Boal and Bryson, *Charismatic Leadership*
[31] Hirschhorn, *Reworking Authority*

Just as the encroachment of trauma into the life of an individual client is an insidious process that turns the past into a nightmare, the present into a repetitive cycle of reenactment, and the future into a terminal illness, so too is the impact of chronic strain on an organization insidious. As seemingly logical reactions to difficult situations pile upon each other, no one is able to truly perceive the fundamentally skewed and post-traumatic basic assumptions upon which that logic is built. As an earthquake can cause the foundations of a building to become unstable, even while the building still stands, apparently intact, so too does chronic repetitive stress or sudden traumatic stress destabilize the cognitive and affective foundations of shared meaning that is necessary for a group to function and stay whole[32].

Human Services and Chronic Disaster

For decades, state mental health systems have been burdened with ineffective service-delivery programs and stagnant bureaucracies. Their operations have become rote, spurred to change only by crises. Combined with ever-increasing fiscal pressures, this situation has precluded innovation and kept most systems from incorporating the new and more effective interventions developed in recent years. As a result, patched-up state mental health systems have all but disintegrated, falling ever farther from the ideal of accessible, effective services that promote meaningful community membership[33].

An organization, or an entire system, can be traumatized by acute events or by chronic conditions. Kai Erikson has defined a "chronic disaster" as one that:

gathers force slowly and insidiously, creeping around one's defenses rather than smashing through them. People are unable to mobilize their normal defenses against the threat, sometimes because they have elected consciously or unconsciously to ignore it, sometimes because they have been misinformed about it, and sometimes because they cannot do anything to avoid it in any case" (p.21). In individuals this manifests as "a numbness of spirit, a susceptibility to anxiety and rage and depression, a sense of helplessness, an inability to concentrate, a loss of various motor skills, a heightened apprehension about the physical and social environment, a preoccupation with death, a retreat into dependency, and a general loss of ego functions" [34].

---

[32] Bloom, *Organizational Stress as a Barrier to Trauma-Sensitive Change and System Transformation*
[33] Bazelon Center, *Disintegrating Systems*, p.5
[34] Erikson, *A New Species of Trouble*, p. 21

The impact of dramatic changes in mental health care and social service funding and operations can be thought of as a chronic, slow-rolling disaster to the human service system as a whole, directly impacting the organizational culture of every component of the system and the system as a collective. Since every organization has its own culture, each culture can be traumatized.

When crisis unrelentingly piles upon crisis - frequently because leaders leave the organization, burnout, are fired, or fail - an organizational adjustment to chronic crisis occurs. Chronic fear states in the individual often have a decidedly negative impact on the quality of cognitive processes, decision making abilities, and emotional management capacities of the person. Impaired thought processes tend to escalate rather than reduce, existing problems so that crisis compounds crisis without the individual recognizing the patterns of repetition that are now determining his or her life decisions.

In similar ways, significant problems arise in organizations when the crisis state is prolonged or repetitive, problems not dissimilar to those we witness in individuals under chronic stress. Organizations can become chronically hyperaroused, functioning in crisis mode, unable to process one difficult experience before another crisis has emerged. The chronic nature of a stressed atmosphere tends to produce a generalized increased level of tension, irritability, short-tempers and even abusive behavior. The urgency to act in order to relieve this tension compromises decision making because we are unable to weigh and balance multiple options, arrive at compromises, and consider long-term consequences of our actions under stress. Decision-making in such organizations tends to deteriorate with increased numbers of poor and impulsive decisions, compromised problem-solving mechanisms, and overly rigid and dichotomous thinking and behavior.

Organizations under stress may engage in a problematic emotional management process that interferes with the exercise of good cognitive skills, known as "group think". The social psychologist, Janis looked at how groups make decisions, particularly under conditions of stress. He reviewed studies of infantry platoons, air crews, and disaster control teams and felt that this work confirmed what social psychologists had shown on experiments in normal college students, that stress produces a heightened need for affiliation, leading to increased dependency on one's group. The increase in group cohesiveness, though good for morale and stress tolerance, could produce a process he saw as a disease that could infect otherwise healthy groups rendering them inefficient, unproductive, and sometimes disastrous. He observed that certain conditions give rise to a group phenomenon in which the members try so hard to agree with each other that they commit serious errors that could easily have been avoided. An assumed consensus emerges while all members hurry to converge and ignore important divergences. Counterarguments are rationalized away and dissent is seen as unnecessary. As this convergence occurs, all group members share in the sense of invulnerability and strength conveyed by the group, while the decisions made are often actually disastrous. At least temporarily, the group experiences a reduction in anxiety, an increase in self-satisfaction, and a sense of assured purpose. But in the long run, this kind of thinking leads to decisions that spell disaster. Later, the individual members of the group find it difficult to accept that their individual wills were so affected by the group[35].

In a crisis unit, or an acute care inpatient setting, groupthink is easily observable. Staff members are under stress to admit patients, diagnose them, stabilize them and get them out on the streets again. Under such conditions, the staff is likely to develop a high level of cohesiveness which helps them handle the stress more adequately, but the result may be that the group is so intent on supporting each other that the group members never engage in meaningful, task-related conflict surrounding the diagnosis or the treatment of the patients.

A psychiatrist who had worked for years in inpatient settings in the early 1990's decided to move from outpatient work back into inpatient work because private practice had become so lonely and he wanted to work with a team again. He was appalled and disheartened by the changes that had occurred in the inpatient program where he had previously worked, despite the fact that some of the same people he knew as social workers and members of the nursing staff were still working there. He was frustrated by the nature of the patient information in the charts. Apparently, because of the excessive regulation instituted by the combined forces of managed care and increased risk management, the charts had become, as he put it "dumbed down" to such an extent that they were largely worthless in providing any useful clinical information about the client. That is not to say that the charts were empty of paper. In fact, if anything the charts had expanded in size but not in meaningfulness. What he found was a great deal of detailed reporting about exactly what the patient said, detailed charting of their bathroom and dietary habits, particularly when they were on some kind of special monitoring. What was lacking was any assessment or synthesis of what the information meant. There was no case formulation, no evidence of a thought process, no true clinical assessment. He found that the staff appeared unable to *think*, and instead just wanted him to tell them what to do, give them a set of directions, point them in the direction of a manual they could use. They were unable to individualize treatment but instead wanted rules that would apply to everyone.

---

[35] Janis, *Decision Making Under Stress.*

Another significant group emotional management technique that is particularly important under conditions of chronic stress is conformity. Another social psychologist, Solomon Ash, demonstrated that when pressure to conform is at work, a person changes his opinion not because he actually believes something different but because it's less stressful to change his opinion than to challenge the group. In his experiments, subjects said what they really thought most of the time, but 70% of subjects changed their real opinions at least once and 33% went along with the group half the time[36]. If a psychiatric setting is dominated by norms that, for instance, assert that biological treatments are the only "real" medicine that a patient needs, or that the only way to deal with aggressive patients is to put them into four-point restraints, or that "bad" children just need more discipline, then many staff members will conform to these norms even if they do not agree because they are reluctant to challenge the group norms.

It has been so difficult to change the behavioral management system that has been in place here for a long time, even though from what I can see, it doesn't really change these kids behavior. The staff want to respond to everything with some punitive consequence and from my point of view, it just seems to reinforce the kind of treatment the kids have received their entire lives. But when I even try to bring this up, that it isn't working and that it may be hurting the kids, the pressure to go along with the rest of the staff is enormous. It's intimidating for me. They make me feel that any change in a different direction will make them less safe and it will be my fault.
—Childcare worker, Residential treatment facility

Specialists in the corporate world have looked at the impact of chronic fear on an organization. Just as exposure to chronic fear undermines the ability of individuals to deal with their emotional states and to cognitively perform at peak levels, chronic fear disables organizations as well. Lawsuits, labor unrest, the formation of unions and strikes are typical signs of a high-fear environment. A lack of innovation, turf battles, social splitting, irresponsibility, bad decisions, low morale, absenteeism, widespread dissatisfaction, and high turnover are all symptoms of chronic fear-based workplaces[37].

In all these instances, the hidden factor may be an absence of group cohesion and commitment and the presence of unbearable tensions which create particular stresses for the individual. In these circumstances, the workplace is experienced as unsupportive, threatening to the emotional and physical well-being of the

---

[36] Forsyth, *Group Dynamics*
[37] Ryan and Oestreich, *Driving Fear Out of the Workplace*

employee. At its worst, the workplace becomes a paranoid-schizoid environment, a nightmare existence[38].

Organizations have culture and organizational culture helps to determine the health and well-being of the individual worker. Organizational culture arises out of the history, memory, experiences and formal structures and personnel of the organization. As organizational research has demonstrated, uncertainty is a main contributor to the perception of stress, and there is nothing so uncertain in corporate life as organizational change. As one author from the world of business has noted

> the combination of economic scarcity, the recession of the late 1980s and early 1990s, the widening gap between demand and resources in public services such as health and education, and the rampant influence of technological change has produced a deeply uncertain organizational world which affects not just organizations in their entirety but groups and individuals at all levels of the organizational matrix"[39].

The literature clearly demonstrates that this combination of uncertainty and the imminence of change, both favorable and unfavorable change, produces stress and, ultimately, affects perceptions and judgments, interpersonal relationships, and the dynamics of the organization itself [40]. In the mental health field for the last two decades, change has been steady and certain only in its tendency to be unfavorable to the practice of the mental health professions.

As multiple investigators have pointed out, services for children are in even worse disarray than those for adults, with children stuck for days and even months in emergency rooms waiting residential programs [41]. According to a report requested by Senators Waxman and Collins, about 15,000 children with mental illnesses were improperly incarcerated in detention centers in 2003 because of a lack of access to treatment, and 7% of all children in detention centers remain incarcerated because of a lack of access to treatment. In addition, the report found that 117 detention centers incarcerated children with mental illnesses younger than age 11. The report also found that 66% of detention centers said they incarcerated children with mental illnesses "because there was no place else for them to go," Some witnesses who testified at the hearing said that children with mental illnesses often are incarcerated in detention centers

---

[38] Nitsun, *The Anti-group,* p. 250.

[39] Ibid, p. 253

[40] Marks and Mirvis, *Merger Syndrome*

[41]Bazelon Center, *Disintegrating Systems*

because their parents do not have access to treatment in schools or lack health coverage for such treatment[42].

In observing the fact that spending for mental health care had declined as a percentage of overall health spending throughout the 1990's, former Surgeon General Satcher noted that although some of the decline in resources for mental health relative to total health care could have been due to improvements in efficiency, he concluded that it also could reflect increasing reliance on other (non-mental health) public human services and increased barriers to service access a conclusion which has been born out by subsequent reports[43].

Even the most dedicated mental health people and programs cannot function providing free service. As one astute observer pointed out,

> So poorly are psychiatrists, clinics and hospitals compensated for the treatment they render that relying on insurance payments for patients' care is often literally a losing proposition.

The response has been the closure of psychiatric inpatient units, service cutbacks at clinics and an inability of psychiatrists and other mental health professionals to support their practice with insurance payments. The existing problems have been vastly compounded by the utilization-review practices of the managed care industry and taken together the result is *"a critical inability of patients to access needed psychiatric care"[44]*. Adding to the burden is that current incentives both within and outside managed care generally do not encourage an emphasis on quality of care[45].

Although an extensive research base has been documenting the enormous implications of previous exposure to trauma, violence and abuse to the physical, emotional, and social health of the nation for over twenty-five years, only now is the issue of trauma beginning to be addressed by both the private and public health systems, and that largely due to the insistence of the consumer recovery movement and some very diligent and persistent mental health providers and administrators[46]. Most mental health programs and substance abuse programs are still only minimally addressing the issue of trauma and public systems are only now receiving pressure to become trauma-informed. Although, there are other reasons for resistance to incorporating the

---

[42] Kaiser Daily Health Policy Report
[43] Satcher, *Mental Health*
[44] Kanapaux, *Vision Offered to Overhaul Nation's Mental Health Care System*
[45] Satcher, *Mental Health*
[46] Jennings, *The Damaging Consequences of Violence and Trauma;* Blanch, *Developing Trauma-Informed Behavioral Health Systems;* Huckshorn, *Six Core Strategies for Reducing Seclusion and Restraint.*

issue of trauma, particularly because it is so fundamentally disturbing to the underlying mental models upon which mental health practice is based, the most obvious cause for this resistance is the lack of innovation and creativity that is typical of both stressed individuals and stressed systems.

> I think people want to be more productive but the way we do business works against that – no centralized scheduling as an example. Underneath that – and this gets to the issue of mental models – professionals have an idea of what treatment is, for an example, and for them treatment is long-term treatment. Because that is the greatest good it is the only good and they can't get their head around anything else. So when we talk about short-term, sessions instead of cases, they can't even comprehend what you are talking about. It is a different language and it doesn't connect to the way this work needs to be done as far as they can see. It's most obvious there because I am most disconnected there [from the outpatient setting]. On the campus, it's harder for me to see because I am so connected there. Another example is the idea of not restraining kids – people see that as just not possible and maybe even harmful. It's the way we have always done things and we are a good place. So it's habitual. In this way, the system works against the change and our own experiences work against it. In the literature on organizational change one of the things that keeps organizations from changing is their own success.
> —*C.O.O., Residential child-care facility*

The mental health system as a whole and each individual element of that system have had all they could manage to simply contend with the enormity of the changes they have undergone. The capacity to innovate, experiment, evaluate innovations, and tolerate the uncertainty of trying new things is simply not possible under the conditions described by this paper. Worse yet, innovation that was burgeoning in the private psychiatric system in the 1990's was virtually completely eliminated by the managed care environment. Dozens of programs specializing in the treatment of trauma were created in the early 1990's and almost all were closed by the beginning of the new century – not because of a lack of clients seeking services but because the loss of beds and the tightening of budgets meant that beds could be filled with far less expense by eliminating all specialty care[47]. More recently, many isolated examples exist of exemplary programs but as the Bazelon Center report illustrates, these are rarely brought to scale and made available to significant numbers of people in need. These successful programs, often funded with demonstration dollars for limited periods, are overshadowed by the disintegration of the system as a whole [48].

---

[47] Bloom, *The System Bites Back*
[48] Bazelon Center, *Disintegrating Systems*

The Organizational Impact of Chronic Stress and Unresolved Loss

Just as the lives of people exposed to repetitive and chronic trauma, abuse, and maltreatment become organized around the traumatic experience, so too can entire systems become organized around the recurrent and severe stress of trying to cope with change and the losses that accompany change. When this happens, it sets up an interactive dynamic that creates what are sometimes uncannily parallel processes. The clients bring their past history of traumatic experience and unresolved loss into the mental health and social service sectors, consciously aware of certain specific goals but unconsciously struggling to recover from the pain and loss of the past. They are greeted by individual service providers, subject to their own personal life experiences with loss. Given what we know about exposure to childhood adversity and other forms of traumatic experience, the majority of service providers have experiences in their own backgrounds that may be quite similar to the life histories of their clients, and that similarity may be more-or-less recognized and worked through[49]. In addition, all service providers have had and are likely to still be having professional experiences with what is often cataclysmic system change as described above. And all are deeply embedded in entire systems that are under significant stress. As two substantive reports have concluded, at least about the mental health system,

The public mental health system is in shambles[50].

The overall infrastructure is under stress, and access to all levels of behavioral health care is affected[51].

Our institution has had to adjust to so many changes in just the past year and some of these changes have had both positive and negative implications. Managed care came to our state about ten years ago and that has produced an unrelentingly negative change. The HIPPA law and its perceived and real limitations on the sharing of information has been a mixed blessing. The Federal and State emphasis on the reduction and elimination of restraint and seclusion has been an overall positive process shifting the culture of the organization and has been positive for the children and families in our care, but it has multiplied the amount of stress on a staff that was already experiencing the limitations of a managed care environment. We have moved to a computerized medical record

---

[49] Felitti et al, *Relationship of Childhood Abuse and Household Dysfunction to Many of the Leading Causes of Death in Adults;* Edwards et al, *Relationship Between Multiple Forms of Childhood Maltreatment and Adult Mental Health*
[50] President's New Freedom Commission
[51] National Association of Psychiatric Health Systems, *Challenges Facing Behavioral Health Care*

which has stressed everybody, and is great when it works. But when the technology breaks down, it can also cause breakdowns in people's relationships with each other because so much of our connecting with each other now is through electronic communication. Locally, the closing of a number of psychiatric hospitals and the downsizing and realignment of others has adversely affected the care of everyone in our region. And we are all embedded within statewide organizations and each election brings someone new and different who lacks the institutional memory of what has preceded them.
—C.O.O, Residential program for children

For many institutions the end result of these complex, interactive, and largely unconscious parallel processes is that the clients – children and adults – enter our systems of care, feeling *unsafe* and often engaging in some form of behavior that is dangerous to themselves or others. They are likely to have difficulty managing *anger* and *aggression*. They may feel *hopeless* and act *helpless*, even when they can make choices that will effectively change their situations, while at the same time this chronic *helplessness* may drive them to exert methods of control that become pathological. They are chronically *hyperaroused* and although they try to *control* their bodies and their minds, they are often ineffective. They may have significant *memory problems* and may be chronically dissociating their memories and/or these feelings, even under minor stress. They are likely therefore to have *fragmented* mental functions. The clients are not likely to have ever learned very good *communication* skills, nor can they easily engage in *conflict management* because they have such problems with emotional management. They feel *overwhelmed, confused* and *depressed* and have *poor self-esteem*. Their problems have emerged in the context of disrupted attachment and they do not know how to make and sustain healthy *relationships* nor do they know how to *grieve* for all that has been lost. Instead they tend to be revictimized or victimize others and in doing so, repetitively *reenact* their past terror and loss.

Likewise, in chronically stressed organizations, individual staff members - many of whom have a past history of exposure to traumatic and abusive experiences – do not feel particularly *safe* with their clients, with management, or even with each other. They are chronically frustrated and *angry* and their feelings may be vented on the clients and emerge as escalations in punitive measures and humiliating confrontations. They feel *helpless* in the face of the enormity of the problems confronting them in the form of their clients, their own individual problems, and the pressures for better performance from management. As they become increasingly stressed, the measures they take to "treat" the clients tend to backfire and they become *hopeless* about the capacity for either the clients or the organization to change. The escalating levels of uncertainty, danger and threat that seem to originate on the one hand from the clients, and on the other hand from "the system" create in the staff a chronic level of *hyperarousal* as the environment becomes increasingly crisis-oriented. Members of the staff who are most disturbed by the hyperarousal and rising levels of anxiety, institute more *control* measures resulting in an increase in *aggression, counter-aggression, dependence* on both physical and biological restraints, and punitive measures directed at clients and each other. Key team members, colleagues, and friends leave the setting and take with them key aspects of the *memory* of what worked and what did not work and team learning becomes impaired. *Communication* breaks down between staff members, interpersonal *conflicts* increase and are not resolved. Team functioning becomes increasingly *fragmented*. Staff members experience *multiple losses* but there is no time for grieving, no recognition that dealing with a wide variety of workplace loss experiences is even necessary. As this happens, staff members are likely to feel *overwhelmed, confused,* and *depressed,* while emotional exhaustion, cynicism, and a *loss of personal effectiveness* lead to demoralization and burnout.

And how are these parallel processes manifested in organizational culture? Under these circumstances, the organization becomes unsafe for everyone in it. Emotional intelligence decreases and organizational emotions, including anger, fear, and loss are poorly managed or denied. The crisis-driven nature of the hyperaroused system interferes with organizational learning. When the organization stops learning it becomes increasingly helpless in the face of what appear to be overwhelming and hopelessly incurable problems. Radical changes in reimbursement and regulation force radical changes in staff, positions, and role descriptions. People and programs depart and the organization begins to suffer from the consequences of organizational amnesia. Communication networks breakdown and error correction essentially stops and instead errors begin to systemically compound. Leaders respond to the perceived crises by becoming more controlling, more hierarchical, and more punitive. In an effort to mobilize group action, leaders silence dissent which further diminishes active participation and essentially ends innovative risk-taking. As participatory processes are scaled back, decision making and problem solving processes are deeply ravaged. As a result, decisions tend to be oversimplified and may create more problems than they solve, despite the leaders' best efforts. Staff respond to the control measures by various forms of aggressive and passive-aggressive acting-out. Interpersonal conflicts escalate and are not resolved, further sabotaging communication. Systemic function becomes ever more fragmented and stagnant. Ethical conflicts abound, organizational values are eroded, and hypocrisy is denied. If this process is not stopped, the organization steadily declines and may, in the way organizations can, die sometimes by dying through closure, sometimes by committing

organizational suicide, and sometimes by continuing to function but
demonstrating a permanent failure of mission and purpose[52].

> As a whole organization, we had so many losses in the past decade. We had
> several executive directors who came and left. We lost programs, funding, staff
> and perhaps most critically, we lost a sense of previous purpose, safety,
> continuity and reputation. We went from being a kind of national "flagship"
> organization, pioneers in what we do to being a place that people in the
> community could no longer trust. Our reputation plummeted and we all felt it.
> As that was happening, everyone felt abused- the clients, the staff, and the
> managers.
> —Executive Director, Domestic violence shelter for families

The effects of stress in organizations and within whole systems are
cumulative. A series of small, unrelated, stress-inducing incidents can add up to
a mountain of stress in the eyes of people that work there and receive services
within these settings. Therefore, the distinction between minor and major stress
may be irrelevant; minor stress can multiply into often irresolvable dilemmas[53].
Everyone in the organization experiences repetitive and compounded losses
which are rarely addressed largely because of the continued need to adapt, cope
and continue to function.

Loss in the Workplace

> In the norms of the world of work, all losses become disenfranchised, because
> emotions and feelings are discounted, discouraged, and disallowed... Even
> mourning as it relates to death is severely constrained by narrowly defined
> policies that govern acceptable behaviors[54].

Attachment and Loss

Wherever there is attachment behavior, there is the potential for loss of
attachment. One of John Bowlby's great contributions was to recognize that
attachment behavior is a fundamental part of our evolutionary heritage and
therefore has high survival value. Primates – including humans – need to attach
from "cradle to grave" and any disruption in normal attachment relationships,

---

[52] Bloom, *Organizational Stress as a Barrier to Trauma-Sensitive Change and System Transformation*
[53] Appelbaum, *Anatomy of a Merger*
[54] Stein and Winokur, *Monday Morning,* p. 92.

particularly those being established in early childhood, is likely to cause developmental problems[55].

> Grief and mourning occur in infancy whenever the responses mediating attachment behavior are activated and the mother figure continues to be unavailable .... The experience of loss of mother in the early years is an antecedent of relevance in the development of personalities prone to depressive and other psychiatric illnesses and that these conditions are best understood as sequelae of pathological mourning[56].

Bowlby studied the reactions of very young children to separation from their mothers. He developed an outline of what was observed as a result of this separation and found that the description also applied to adults who suffered loss[57]. In Phase I the person experiences numbness and shutdown which may last for hours or weeks and can be interrupted by intense distress and/or anger. In Phase II, protest involves protesting the loss and attempting to recover what was lost. There is a yearning for what is loss, anxiety, wishful thinking, denying or avoiding the painful reality of loss. In Phase III, the person experiences disorganization and despair as hope for recovery of what was lost fades. This is accompanied by longing, apathy, hostility, and sadness. Phase IV is characterized by detachment and reorganization. The grieving person begins to let go of the attachment bond as it used to be and energy then becomes available for new beginnings. He identified four main variants of pathological responses by bereaved adults: 1) anxiety and depression, which he saw as the persistent and unconscious yearning to recover the lost person, originally adaptive because it produced strong motivation for reunion in a vulnerable child separated from his or her mother; 2) intense and persistent anger and reproach expressed towards others or the self and originally intended to achieve reunion with the lost relationship and discourage further separation; 3) absorption in caring for someone else who has also been bereaved, sometimes amounting to a compulsion; and 4) denial that the relationship is permanently lost [58]. It is possible to observe many of the behaviors related to attachment and loss in the workplace, not only in the clients but in the staff as well.

Normal Bereavement

Bereavement is the state of deprivation or loss itself. *Loss* is the separation of an individual or group of individuals from a loved or prized object

---

[55] Bowlby, *Attachment and Loss, Volume III*
[56] Bowlby, *Grief and Mourning in Infancy and Early Childhood*, p. 9-11
[57] Ibid
[58] Bowlby, *Pathological Mourning and Childhood Mourning*

which may be a person or group, a job, social position, status, an ideal or fantasy, or a body part. *Grief* is the set of responses to a real, perceived, or anticipated loss, responses that usually include physical, emotional, cognitive and psychological components. *Mourning* is the cultural response to grief[59]. Bowlby's description of grief responses that proceed through protest, despair, detachment and finally personality reorganization holds true for many different kinds of losses because any significant loss is likely to arouse childlike fears of loss of attachment regardless of our age or life experience.

> I went to a bereavement counselor and when I called there and spoke to the director, and I said, "I can't even take care of myself, much less anyone else – that's why I can't go into a support group". It was one of the best things I could have done and was very different from treatment experiences I had in the past. Bereavement counseling was all focused on reality, on acknowledging the loss, finding the things that would work for me, and was totally non-judgmental. Whatever it is – in grieving – it just is. There are no "shoulds or shouldn'ts". I told her my biggest fear for a long time was that I wouldn't be able to get up in the morning and she said, "What would be so terrible if you did that?" My own experience was so catastrophic and overwhelming that I walked around just feeling like I had electric charges running through me for months, hypersensitive to things. We did do some training with all of the leadership staff and I took every opportunity I could to bring home the experience of loss and how that impacts others and the responsibility we have to help others. I think that we have more language for communicating with the children so that when something does happen I think we can spring into action.
> —*C.E.O, program for children*

Although there are no clear "stages of grief" that people inevitably work their way through, nor is there likely to be anything like "closure" after a significant loss, there do appear to be tasks of grief work. The first task is to accept the reality of the loss. After a sudden or traumatic loss people are likely to be "in shock", an acute state of denial that buffers people from the reality of the loss and gives them the time to adjust to this reality. Different people need different amounts of time to make this adjustment. In many situations, denial may serve the needs of survival in the moment and so accepting the reality of loss may be delayed.

> Daniel had been the Executive Director for years and was loved and admired. We were shocked when we learned he only had a few months to live and when he died within weeks of this announcement. I am not sure any of us ever had a chance to really grieve for his loss. There was so much to do just to keep the organization together that we had no time. We went to the memorial service, of

---

[59] Zinner and Williams, *When A Community Weeps*

course, but I know I for one was focused on how I was going to do the job I
wasn't really ready to do yet. I think we can still see evidence of unresolved loss
throughout our organization.
—Executive Director, Foster care agency

Grieving is – by definition – painful, both physically and emotionally
and may be accompanied by a number of other distressing emotions including
anger, shame, and guilt. The mourner must adjust to life without whoever or
whatever is missing and lost and then must emotionally relocate whatever or
whoever is gone and move on with his or her life. Grief occurs within a
sociocultural context which varies greatly from culture to culture and will be
affected by a number of factors including the extent of the loss and the damage
to the community as a whole. There is no set timetable for grief; everyone
grieves in a different way, and every new loss opens the door again onto every
other loss that has ever occurred. Organizations that do not grieve for their
losses can remain stuck in the past, unable to adequately adapt to the present and
create a better future.

My mom passed away four years ago and that was a difficult time. Then my
wife's mom passed away last year and that was challenging. But the death of our
CEO's son was more challenging than either of those losses for me. I had my
own deeply personal and longstanding affection for her, so I was affected by her
son's accidental death because I saw what she was going through and I knew her
son. I still remember the night of the morning it happened. I went to her home
that night and was just, "oh my God" - She has always been solid and I was
looking at someone in pieces. I said to my wife, "I don't know how you come
back from this. How does she put this back together?" I don't think I have ever
seen anyone that shattered. The loss was so devastating for her that she just
wasn't able to do her job for quite some time and I had to pick up the slack while
I was still figuring out what my own job was supposed to be because it happened
in our early transition only a year after the former CEO had retired. I remember
thinking, "Oh my God, what if she doesn't come back from this? I'm not ready
for this". For a year there were things that were grossly wrong and that she
wasn't managing and I didn't have the authority to manage. We were hanging on
by our fingernails. I just had faith that eventually we would get it back and we
have.
—C.O.O., Residential child-care facility

Complicated Mourning

The concept of "complicated grief" applies to people and situations
where bereavement exceeds the expected norm and creates additional problems.
The subject has been extensively covered by Theresa Rando and she highlights
seven high-risk factors that predispose individuals to complicated mourning.

These include: sudden, unexpected death especially when traumatic, violent, mutilating or random; death from an overly lengthy illness; loss of a child; the mourner's perception of the death as preventable; a premorbid relationship with the deceased that was markedly angry or ambivalent, or dependent; prior or concurrent mourner liabilities such as other losses, stresses or mental health problems; and the mourner's lack of social support. All of these factors result in greater numbers of people experiencing complicated mourning [60].

> When I first came here, I was shocked to discover how much the entire atmosphere of the shelter – and the behavior of each individual staff members - was being affected by the past history of the place. Five executive directors had come and gone in a decade, each one unable to extricate themselves from the problems of the previous directors. Ten years before I started, a document had been written reporting on the problems in the environment and the report was damning in its criticism. This report had profoundly impacted the way subsequent directors had dealt with the staff, even though the staff had no idea about what was actually written in this report. In order to start getting the agency back on track I had to enlist a number of core people – and eventually the whole staff - in reviewing the past, expressing painful feelings, and honoring all the past losses before we were able to move on. As I see it, the organization had to grieve.
> —Executive Director, family shelter

Childcare organizations and the employees that work in them are at risk for complicated bereavement when a death of a child occurs while the child is in the care of the organization. Children who enter residential treatment facilities are likely to arrive there after multiple experiences with disrupted attachment and as a result of complex physical, emotional, cognitive, and social problems. These children have much to grieve for and few internal resources available to them. They have a history of unsafe behavior which is the usual precipitant to intensive treatment environments. They have profound difficulties managing distressful feelings and a history of unresolved loss. With little ability to envision a better future for themselves these children may be a threat to themselves or to others. The fundamental job of the treatment environment is to keep these children safe. And sometimes they fail.

In rare occasions, children succeed in seriously harming themselves, others, or even dying from being forcibly restrained or from suicide. In virtually all of these cases, government officials, regulatory agencies, and the providers themselves will perceive these injuries or deaths as unexpected, horrific, and preventable. The staff members involved are likely to experience significant

---

[60] Rando, *Treatment of Complicated Mourning*

guilt and are likely not to receive much social support throughout the course of the legal and sometimes criminal investigations that follow.

> The Executive Director of a residential program for kids asked me to come and do a consultation with the staff. We set a date that was mutually agreeable but I didn't discover until I arrived that it was the date of the two-year anniversary of the death of a child who committed suicide while in the institution. At the time of the death, the staff was instructed by the hospital attorneys to stop all conversation about the incident. There was, of course, an investigation but other than those immediately involved, no one seemed to know what the outcome of the investigation had been and although rumors abounded, no one appeared to have accurate information. Staff members who spoke to me, however, had become firmly convinced that nothing had been the same at the place since that child had died, and all still worried about what had gone wrong, who was to blame, and whether or not it could happen again.
> —Consultant, residential treatment program

Ambiguous Loss

Ambiguity means being driven in at least two ways at once, or experiencing two conflicting and apparently unsynthesizable feelings. Pauline Boss has extensively explored the concept of "ambiguous loss":

> My basic theoretical premise is that ambiguous loss is the most stressful kind of loss. It defies resolution and creates long-term confusion about who is in or out of a particular couple or family. With death there is official certification of loss and mourning rituals allow one to say goodbye. With ambiguous loss, none of these markers exist. The persisting ambiguity blocks cognition, coping and meaning-making and freezes the grief process [61].

> I think this notion of ambiguous loss is particularly important when it comes to relationships between management and staff. There have been times when I have had to fire staff as a result of some significant violation of boundaries or indiscretion on their part but I couldn't share the information with the other staff members because of privacy concerns related to the staff member involved. But from their point of view, losing someone they care about is a significant loss and it appears to be without a satisfactory explanation or reason – the person is just suddenly not there. The staff members left behind don't know the whole story and it can lead to a lot of resentment and distrust. For awhile, it's like the person that is fired is there, but not there. He or she seems to keep exerting an influence even though they are gone. It's really hard to know what to do about it, or how to make it better.
> —Human resources director, psychiatric facility

---

[61] Boss, *Loss, Trauma and Resilience,* p.xvii

Boss defines two main groups of ambiguous loss: 1) when loved ones who are physically absent but are kept psychologically present, especially when the loss is not verified by evidence of death, such as when someone is missing in action, or the their body has never been found, but also applies to cases of adoption, divorce, or work relocation; and 2) when people are physically present but psychologically absent as when their affliction is denied and they are expected to act as they were, as in the case of dementia, chronic mental illness, addiction, head injuries and obsessive preoccupations. According to Dr. Boss, her premise is that ambiguity coupled with loss creates a barrier to working through loss and leads to symptoms such as depression and relational conflict that erode human relationships.

> I remember the time that one of our staff was accused of sexual abuse by a very disturbed child who had a history of sexual abuse. It was a horrible experience for all of us because when the accused staff member was forced to go home, we were short-staffed, all of the children suffered another loss, we all worried about whether or not it was true or not, and whether we should support the child or the staff member or both – and how to do that. Then, when the staff member was cleared, and the child had admitted that it hadn't happened, we never talked about it again. But I have never felt safe with those kids ever since that experience. I think we all lost something and have never gotten it back again.
> —Child care staff member, group home

Disenfranchised Grief

Disenfranchised grief has been defined as grief that is deemed as inappropriate, that cannot be publicly acknowledged, openly mourned, and socially supported and which is thereby refused the conditions for normal resolution through the work of grieving. Examples of disenfranchised grief include examples such as when someone has been involved in what is considered an illicit affair and the lover dies, or in many cases, when a homosexual partner dies[62].

> We have begun changing our organizational policies to manage loss more effectively. One thing we recently did was to expand our definitions of "family" and "significant other" because previously these definitions had been very conservative in nature.
> —Program Director, Childcare agency

---

[62] Doka and Davidson, *Living With Grief*

This term has been extended to apply to the workplace in general, serving to indicate that any loss becomes disenfranchised if we are not allowed to express grief in the one place where most of our waking hours during the week are spent – on the job. This is particularly important since at any point in time, 16% of the workforce experiences a personal loss within a given year.

Grieving in the workplace represents decreased individual productivity and anything that inhibits the grieving process and thus causes the mourning period to be lengthened, more severe, or entirely postponed, is likely to negatively impact the organization. Nonetheless, little attention has been paid to this issue[63]. In fact, grieving in the workplace has been actively discouraged. Typically, the amount of grieving in the workplace that is "allowed" is determined by the perceived closeness of the relationship. On the average, organizations give employees about three days off to grieve for the death of a loved one and after that time they are expected to get back to work and resume normal activity.

It's over fifteen years ago and I still have never really recovered from that death of that child on my watch. When I got the call that he had been killed, it was like time stood still and the world dropped out underneath me. I had to identify the body, call the family, go through multiple investigations, support the staff, calm down the executives above me, represent the institution in the media. It was a nightmare and I still worry about something like that happening every day. I orchestrated ceremonies, rituals, and a memorial for the child, but nobody ever really helped me work through my grief and that still makes me really angry when I think about it.
—Program Director, Residential facility for children

And the amount of allowable grief may be determined by the person's role in the organization. Leaders are expected to go on working as if nothing had happened in their private lives. People who deal with life and death issues all the time are expected to keep tight control in their workplace. Losses that are a result of suicide, homicide, substance abuse, or "preventable" accidents may be stigmatized and become losses that are disenfranchised – never discussed, never aired, and consequently never worked through[64].

The problem, of course, is that grief often refuses to comply with the organizational timetable. Grieving is not linear and does not decrease steadily over time. The more normal grief is inhibited and the longer the grieving process is postponed, the more likely it is to become problematic and even pathological. When this happens and performance is affected, corrective

·

---

[63] Bento, *When the Show Must Go On,* p.35
[64] Ibid

measures are often directed at the symptom rather than the cause and the individual may become increasingly alienated from the organization[65].

Unresolved grief can result in an idealization of what has been lost that interferes with adaptation to a new reality. Individual employees and entire organizations may distort memories of the past as individuals can. Organizations may selectively omit disagreeable facts, may exaggerate or embellish positive deeds, may deny the truth and engage in what has been termed "organizational nostalgia" for a golden past that is highly selective and idealized and when compared to the present state of affairs, surpassingly better. It is a world that is irretrievably lost, with all of the sense of inexpressible grief associated with such loss and the present is always comparably poorer, less sustaining, less fruitful, less promising. In this way the organizational past – whether accurately remembered or not – can continue to exert a powerful influence on the present. The failure to grieve for the loss of a leader may make it difficult or impossible for a new leader to be accepted by the group. In fact, one author has noted that

> Nostalgia is not a way of coming to terms with the past (as mourning or grief are) but an attempt to come to terms with the present[66].

> I didn't realize how much I was in the grip of nostalgic feelings and years of unresolved loss until a new Medical Director joined us who was young and just out of her training. One day, after listening once again to all of us reminisce about the way things used to be in out treatment program, she interrupted us and said "You know I can about all of you, and I admire the work you have done, but really…. I just can't stand one more discussion about "the good old days"! I have to make the most of what is here NOW."
> —Former Medical Director, psychiatric inpatient program

Loss of Attachment in the Workplace

Many people spend at least as much time in the workplace, with workplace colleagues, as they do with their families. The result is that workplace relationships assume a vital part of each worker's support network and any loss of that support is likely to result in reactions typical of anyone who has a real or threatened loss of an attachment bond.

In the protest phase, employees may hold on to what was lost through a wide variety of real and symbolic behaviors[67]. They may try to hold on to old work equipment, resist a move to a new office location, go out to lunch only

---

[65] Ibid
[66] Gabriel, *Organizational Nostalgia*, p. 132
[67] Jeffreys, *Coping with Workplace Grief*

with former colleagues, file grievances or other actions to stop change, and engage in other forms of written and vocal protest.

The CEO had worked long and hard to achieve a long-held dream of a new school. Finally the new facility was ready. It was gorgeous – all new structures, new equipment, and lots more space. She was perplexed then after the move, when the staff seemed to do little except complain about missing the old, broken down and decrepit building they had left. No one had thought about bringing a symbolic part of the old, well-worn and highly remembered building with them to the new facility.

For as long as they possibly can they may deny that the change that is anticipated is really going to occur. When the prospective changes are brought up, employees typically change the subject, continue to use old forms, old procedures, and old labels. Employees may attempt to bargain with their supervisors, trying to hold on to previous attachments, *"can I keep my desk, can I stay in my office"*, *"can we use the old software"*, *"can I go to lunch at the same time?"*

When new people are added to the organization as part of the change, or veterans may keep their distance from new people. These behaviors must be understood as reluctance to let go of what has been so much a part of who we are regardless of whether that is other co-workers, a sense of safety and trust, predictable routines and familiar surroundings.

> To let go is to let a part of ourselves die. This is painful and we want to delay it, push it away, and pretend it isn't happening. We hope for a last-minute rescue, a change of heart by the Board of Directors, or a miraculous new contract[68].

Individual reactions to loss will be influenced by experiences of previous loss.

> Change can be so hard. People I liked a lot have left and as a person and a friend, I have felt very bad about those changes at times. But in my position of leadership, my "love" can't be unconditional. If a person isn't meeting the needs of the organization – and that is to serve the welfare of the children – then that person has to go, regardless of my personal feelings about them. So when someone leaves, or is forced out, I end up feeling a mixture of confusing feelings – relief that the problems they were causing are over, sadness because someone I care about has left the organization and guilt because I had to make decisions that were not happy ones for the other person – at least not at the moment. It's always hard for me too because as things are changing, those steady and predictable relationships that I felt I could rely on change as well and you can't be sure where it is all going until it goes.
> —C.O.O., Residential child-care facility

---

[68] Ibid, p. 38

Despair and disorganization may be seen in decreased work effort, many complaints, and active expression of distress including feelings of anger, hurt, fear, guilt and shame. When any kind of attachment bonds are broken people experience an aching emptiness. The physical and emotional pain of grief that occurs along with anger is a part of the process.

> For people who have made their work and the workplace social environment the most important part of their lives, the loss or threat of loss of what has been can result in devastating pain[69].

Because fractured attachments are experienced at a gut level as a threat to survival, the result may be fear rising to the level of panic and even terror. Employees may express fears about security and their future. Trying to contain fear and anxiety may lead to an increase in both physical and emotional symptoms.

Rage, resentment, bitterness, sabotage, violence can represent anger phase of loss and grief. Anger may be displaced onto someone else – old management, co-workers, family, family pet. Anger may be directly expressed through hostile attitudes, words or behaviors or through grumbling, excessive questioning, complaining, angry facial expressions, arguing, fighting, insubordination, destruction of property, theft, and in the worst cases physical violence. Other people may express their distress through passive expression: lateness, absenteeism, work slowdown, less teamwork, poor communication, increased errors, decreased cooperation, lack of follow-through, and diminished self-direction. *"Take a title, desk, parking space, job security, workplace friend, or feeling of trust away from an employee and anger is a natural reaction"[70]*. We express anger whenever we are denied something we want or we perceive obstacles to our goal. Frustration converts to anger very quickly and is a natural, normal release of an inner emotional state. Depression may characterize the whole environment. People may withdraw from normal routines, relationship patterns and give off non-verbal signals that say "just leave me alone".

> After my son died I felt many things but no anger. It was a tragic accident and there was no one to direct anger at. But several years later a situation presented itself at work. Someone in a key management position for many years had a variety of interpersonal problems and I had been apologizing for his behavior for a long time. As the organization changed, he appeared to become increasingly unable to cope with the changes and it culminated when he behaved quite inappropriately to me and to the Board. I felt an enormous sense of betrayal. We had to terminate his employment which was difficult given our long-term

---

[69] Ibid, p. 46
[70] Ibid, p. 45

relationship. But what was particularly disconcerting was the enormity of my rage at him. I could not stop replaying the incident in my mind, could not sleep, began having terrible dreams and felt like I was in danger all the time. My husband, who had been like a rock up to this point, began becoming very frustrated with my preoccupation. I was angry at everyone. I called my bereavement counselor and told her that I thought the magnitude of my anger had to be related to my son's death in some way but I couldn't figure out how. In talking it over with her, I came to a fundamental realization that I was angry at the manager I had terminated because he had taken away my life for the moments that I had to deal with his perfidy. I realized that for me to live my life I have to devote a certain amount of my time to mourning for my son. It made me realize that if we are talking about loss we have to be talking about anger and aggression. It made me wonder who else might be running amok because they have not dealt with this aspect of loss?
—C.E.O. Child care agency

Both managers and line staff may feel guilt, the former over the role they may be playing in the decisions that are resulting in change, and the latter over surviving the changes when some of their colleagues have not. Deep feelings of shame may dominate the employee who is demoted or otherwise loses status in the organization. When the mourning process is neither complicated nor delayed, employees can then begin to envision an end to the transition and begin to develop a new identity and a new set of skills. They may not be entirely happy with the changes but they are beginning to accommodate to the changes. They are likely to reconcile themselves cognitively before they completely work through the loss emotionally.

Organizational Change and Loss

Losing the comfort of a safe and reliable work environment creates an ongoing sense of the loss of trust. Loss is the factor that determines our grief. Loss – whether from a death or a death-like change in our life circumstances – hurts[71].

In the mental health and social service literature, there is very little recognition of the ways in which these forces are playing themselves out across our horizons. Caught in the grip of monumental assaults upon the systems, few people have had the time or energy to step back and begin to look at the system-as-a-whole through a trauma-informed lens. The effects of downsizing, mergers, hostile takeovers, cuts in program funding, changes in roles, increased and burdensome demands of insurance companies all may be experienced as

---

[71] Ibid, p.27

examples of more "chronic disasters" that insidiously impact and change a system.

The losses associated with organizational change are significant and impact the lives of the individuals within the organization as well as the organization-as-a-whole. Organizational change can be a result of downsizing, mergers, restructuring, reorganization, and transitions secondary to traumatic events. Some employees describe the constancy of organizational change as "permanent white water"[72].

> This place really was a family when I first got here. It was very intimate. We only did residential care and many of the kids were higher functioning than the children we see today. We used to do staff parties, a Kris Kringle luncheon and have 45 staff members with the kids. You could have 6 people watch 45 kids. Now, with 150 kids you need 150 staff to watch them. The whole climate has changed. The people who are "old timers" remember it when everyone new everyone – but those days are gone forever. It's not a product of choice and people don't get that. The industry changes and we have to respond to that or close the doors. What we were is no longer there. We are different.
> —C.O.O., Residential child-care facility

What are the losses that employees experience? Losses include changes in organizational structure that means adjusting to new managers or supervisors, changes in employment status and job description, changes in physical locations, salaries, benefits, job security, dependable colleagues, resources. As one author has pointed out, *"Whatever we left behind after we went through the transition represents loss. Even if the new situation is a desired change – promotion, new office – we still lose the way it used to be, and the reaction to this loss is grief"[73]*. Organization restructuring may mean that people with whom other people have bonded are suddenly gone. One's status in the organization may suddenly be changed. Familiar procedures, surroundings and trusted reporting relationships may be lost. Employees may lose the ability to do the work they were trained to do and be spending more time doing paperwork than they are developing relationships with clients. The result of all this may be the loss of safety, security, control and some basic assumptions about what they can expect from the organization which jeopardizes the sense of basic trust [74].

> Systems are funny. Every time you add something you lose something. We added a diagnostic center and a day treatment program and after all the planning, we – the administrators – were excited about the new programming. But the primary programs felt like there was someone else leeching of them, depriving

---

[72] Ibid
[73] Ibid, p. 15
[74] Ibid

them of their resources, and the new programs felt like second class citizens. You are always contending with that – the new people feel like stepchildren and the old people think the new kid is taking up their space.
—C.O.O., Residential child-care facility

Downsizing has been called *"a pervasive form of organizational suicide"*. According to previous research, 80% of the organizations studied that were involved in downsizing suffered morale problems. Under such circumstances, people feel insecure and their organizational commitment is decreased. They fear taking any risks and thus innovation is dampened. They have to work harder for the same pay or frequently, pay cuts. Anger over the loss of colleagues may lead to grieving with possibly a false sense of hope that the lost co-worker will eventually come back or will be rehired. The emotional toll is high on everyone [75]. As one executive reported,

while layoffs may provide a short-term boost to profits, over the long run downsizing begins a cycle in which companies falter because of loss of talent and a decay of morale that constrain economic performance for years afterwards[76].

There are so many things in the system that end up frustrating your efforts to change and many different kinds of things. We all say we embrace change, yet we don't really, even though we feel like we are. There is the issue of habits and routine that keeps us from changing. For example, if I decide I want to go out into the cottage tomorrow and talk to people and see how things are going, that's fine until some crisis arises that pulls me back to my office. There are so many things that change during the day. Doing something that is not part of the routine means making a plan, really thinking about it ahead of time and letting nothing interfere. That just doesn't happen.
—C.O.O., Residential child-care facility

It is clear that the ways in which grief, loss, and termination are handled have a significant impact on employee attitudes. There is evidence that when employees are given permission to grieve for the "end of what was", the readjustment to new conditions is likely to be less problematic[77]. But unfortunately, in the human service sector, time to grieve for losses in the workplace has become a rarity that has enormous consequences:

Our society in general, and the business world specifically, has typically not granted enough permission for people to grieve. As a result, many grieving employees are given little time to be off balance, sad, angry, scared,

---

[75] Appelbaum, *Anatomy of a Merger*
[76] Hubiak and O'Donnell, *Downsizing,* p. 31
[77] Buono and Bowditch, p.18

unmotivated, and unproductive. When there is a lack of time to mourn what was, employees are less free to bond to the new situation[78].

As I see it now, everyone reacts differently to loss. One of our key organization leaders has been acting out a lot, being arbitrarily divisive and obstructing everything I try to do. She is questioning things that she would not have questioned before and being just difficult about things she doesn't need to be difficult about. Interestingly, she is not even someone who is affected by the things she is questioning. This is all started after I hired someone as my V.P. and to whom she must now report. As I think about it, I think this is the way she is demonstrating the losses she has had, including the reporting relationship to me, and that has never really been addressed.
—C.E.O. out-patient mental health provider

Costs of Not Addressing Normal and Complicated Loss

There is a high price to be paid individually and collectively when the process of grief is inhibited or arrested. The grief does not go away but instead turns into feelings and attitudes that can severely disrupt productive work. An overall feeling of distrust and resentment toward the organization may lead to hostile acts, counteraggression, destructiveness, stealing, poor work product, and chronic anger. Shame and an inclination to "play it safe" can lead to stagnation, an unwillingness to take any creative risks, avoidance and isolation. Chronic fear lowers creativity and increases stress related physical and emotional problems. As one authority states it,

> Unresolved anger can lead to chronic bitterness, self-hatred, grudges, and on ongoing sense of helplessness. It some cases, it can also lead to physical aches and pains, symptoms of stress, depression, and other emotional disorders[79].

Under these circumstances, similar to their repetitively and chronically stressed clients, employees may overreact to even minor provocations.

In the beginning of working through the loss of my son, I was numb. After the first few months, I couldn't get affectively engaged with the petty stuff anymore. There wasn't much that was emotionally charged. But then when I started to be able to engage affectively again it didn't come out right. It was either too much or not enough. I would be over-reactive or under-reactive. And then gradually it started to even out.
—C.E.O. Child care agency

---

[78] Jeffreys, p.16
[79] Ibid, p.68.

On the other hand,

Anger that is constructively managed can fuel productive change and bring about motivation to develop new skills and to complete important tasks [80].

Feelings that are not allowed appropriate expression through grieving are unavailable for productive purpose and productive work is likely to plummet with morale sinking and errors compounding.

Organizational Defenses

Psychodynamically-oriented investigators who have looked at the human social organization and institutional development have pointed out one underlying and largely unconscious motivation beneath organizational function and that is the containment of anxiety. Human beings are particularly vulnerable to overwhelming fears of disintegration, nothingness, annihilation, disorder, chaos, loss and underlying all – death. We organize our social institutions to accomplish specific tasks and functions, but we also utilize our institutions to collectively protect us against being overwhelmed with the anxiety that underlies human existence. We are, after all, the only animal that knowingly must anticipate our own death.

The collective result of this natural inclination to contain anxiety becomes a problem when institutional events occur that produce great uncertainty, particularly those events that are associated with death or the fear of death. Under these conditions, containing anxiety may become more important than rationally responding to the crisis, although because of our relative ignorance and denial about our unconscious collective lives, this is likely to be denied and rationalized. As a result, organizations may engage in thought processes and actions that may serve to contain anxiety but that are ultimately destructive to organizational purpose[81].

Like individuals, institutions develop defenses against difficult emotions which are too threatening or too painful to acknowledge. These emotions may be a response to external threats such as government policy or social change. They may arise from internal conflicts between management and employees or between groups and departments in competition for resources. They may also arise from the nature of the work and the particular client

---

[80] Ibid, p. 45.
[81] Lawrence *The Presence of Totalitarian State of Mind in Institutions;* Pyszcznski, *What Are We So Afraid of?,* p.827; Pyszcynski, Solomon and Greenberg, *In the Wake of 9-11.*

group[82]. Managing countertransference in situations where suicide, homicide or injury has occurred is difficult as an organizational leader. The need to find fault and punish is strong and may make situations much worse as defensive routines are employed, premature closure is encouraged, and silence about the incidents is mandated by organizational attorneys.

> The CEO and the COO had previously worked closely together, although always in subordinate positions, and had developed a close personal and professional relationship. When the CEO moved up, she became more distanced from her talented COO geographically and practically. Neither of them expressed their experience of personal loss over these changes, nor was any attempt made to process organizationally what it meant to have the CEO so distanced from the daily operations that she had so lovingly and carefully managed before. When a client murdered another client shortly after leaving the institution and not long after these major management changes had occurred, the CEO conveyed a mixture of feelings to the COO but mostly anger, frustration and disappointment that he hadn't done a better job in keeping the institution safe. The COO was already feeling severely wounded by the reality of the situation he had to deal with but compounding this was a sense of betrayal and overwhelming loss at not being able to turn to his friend for support. Over the next several years, the performance of the COO declined, he was demoted and ultimately, he left the field entirely.

> Organizations produce organizational defensive routines (in the form of policies, practices and norms) that inhibit individuals, groups, and organizations from experiencing embarrassment or threat and, at the same time, prevent the actors from identifying and reducing the causes of the embarrassment or threat. The use of defensive routines learned early in life is reinforced by the organizational cultures created by individuals implementing strategies of bypass and cover-up. These strategies persist because organizational norms sanction and protect them[83].

Isabel Menzies, building on the work of Jacques, described the ways in which mental health systems create "social defense systems". She described how systems develop specific and static protective mechanisms to protect against the anxiety that is inevitably associated with change. The defense mechanisms she describes sound uncannily like those that we see in victims of trauma - depersonalization, denial, detachment, denial of feelings, ritualized task-performance, redistribution of responsibility and irresponsibility, idealization, avoidance of change[84].

---

[82] Halton, *Some Unconscious Aspects of Organizational Life*
[83] Argyris, *Knowledge and Action*
[84] Menzies, *A Case Study in the Functioning of Social Systems as a Defense Against Anxiety*

This social defense system plays itself out at every level within the institution. For example, in the nursing staff in a hospital who:

> develop some form of relationship that locates madness in the patient and sanity in themselves, with a barrier to prevent contamination. Such an arrangement allows the nurses to stay in the situation without feeling that their minds are being damaged. It justifies the use of control by the nurses, entitles patients to care and refuge, and is a virtual guarantee that they will continue to be thought ill and therefore will not be sent outside[85].

This social defense system can be seen operating in psychiatrists who spend more time deciding on the diagnosis that most adequately fits the DSM-IV-R and then based on the diagnosis, prescribing the "proper" medication, then they spend actually talking to the client. It is operating in childcare workers who focus on a point system and setting up punitive consequences for children because lacking professional training, understand the problems these children present is an overwhelming task. It is also operating in the institution as a whole, when that institution provides services that are called "treatment" but which are more accurately designed to control or "manage" the individual patient on behalf of the society. The conflict between "controlling" the mentally ill for the sake of society and helping the mentally ill by empathizing with and empowering them to make positive change is a source of chronic conflict. And this conflict is a source of chronic, unspoken, unrealized stress for everyone working within virtually any social service institution. It is also major barrier to the goals of the consumer-recovery movement[86]. As long as the mental health system is responsible for the legal and social containment of mental illness, it will be exceedingly difficult and perpetually stressful for the staff of institutions to offer the kind of care sought by many advocates of the recovery movement.

Over time and as a result of collusive interaction and unconscious agreement between members of an organization, this agreement becomes a systematized part of reality which new members must deal with as they come into the system. These defensive maneuvers become group norms, similar to the way the same defensive maneuvers become norms in the lives of individual patients and then are passed on from one generation to the next. Upon entering the system each new member must become acculturated to the established norms if he or she is to succeed. In such a way, an original group creates a group reality which then becomes institutionalized for every subsequent

---

[85] Spillius, *Asylum and Society,* p. 604
[86] Szegedy-Maszak, *Consuming Passion*

group[87]. This aspect of the "groupmind" becomes quite resistant to change, rooted in a past that is forgotten, now simply the "way things are"[88].

Unresolved Organizational Loss and Systemic Reenactment

The great American poet, W. H. Auden, has pointed out the importance of enactment in human functioning,

> Human beings are by nature actors, who cannot become something until first they have pretended to be it. They are therefore to be divided, not into the hypocritical and the sincere, but into the sane, who know they are acting, and mad who do not. We constitute ourselves through our actions[89].

We were actors long before we were talkers in our evolutionary history, and enactment remains a nonverbal form of communication with others of our kind.

Traumatized individuals frequently are subject to "traumatic reenactment", a compulsive reliving of a traumatic past that is not recognized as repetitive and yet which frequently leads to revictimization experiences. Reenactment is a sign of grief that is not resolved and instead the trauma and the losses associated with it is experienced over and over relentlessly. Reenactment means "never having to say goodbye".

An organization that cannot change, that cannot work through losses and move on will, like an individual, develop patterns of reenactment, repeating past strategies without recognizing that these strategies may no longer be effective. This can easily lead to organizational patterns that become overtly abusive. Corporate abuse comes in many forms including discrimination, demotion without cause, withholding of resources, financial manipulation, overwork, harassment, systematic humiliation, and arbitrary dismissal[90]. With every repetition there is further deterioration in functioning. Knowledge about this failing is available but it tends to be felt before it is cognitively appreciated, but without the capacity to put words to feelings, a great deal of deterioration may occur before the repetitive and destructive patterns are recognized. Healthier and potentially healing individuals enter the organization but are rapidly extruded as they fail to adjust to the reenactment role that is being demanded of them. Less autonomous individuals may also enter the

---

[87] Menzies, *A Case Study in the Functioning of Social Systems as a Defense Against Anxiety*
[88] Bloom, *Every Time History Repeats Itself the Price Goes Up*
[89] Driver, *The Magic of Ritual*
[90] Wright and Smye, *Corporate Abuse*

organization and are drawn into the reenactment pattern. In this way, one autocratic and abusive leader leaves or is thrown out only to be succeeded by another, while those who have been involved in the hiring process remain bewildered by this outcome[91].

> After the founder of the organization died, we couldn't seem to find someone adequate to run the place. We would interview people, they would look good on paper but when it really came down to it, every successive manager seemed to make things worse. They would come in, try to "lay down the law" to the staff, and when it didn't work, each one would leave and it would start all over again. I don't think any of them ever asked us to review the past history of the organization or took a particularly sympathetic approach to the staff.
> —Board Member, family shelter

Reenactment patterns are especially likely to occur when events in the past have resulted in behavior that arouses shame or guilt in the organization's representatives. Shame and guilt for past misdeeds are especially difficult for individuals and organizations to work through. The way an organization talks to itself is via communication between various "voices" of the organization. If these voices are silenced or ignored, communication breaks down and is more likely to be acted-out through impulse ridden and destructive behavior.

> I have been trying so hard to get the staff to stop putting the kids into holds. It's clear to me that they do it many times when the kids should be dealt with in an entirely different way, but instead they escalate the problem. Every time I push them, it comes back to the same discussion about the kid who seriously injured a staff member a number of years ago and they aren't taking any chances of that happening again.
> —Clinical director, children's crisis center

But in the workplace - although employees may indeed be constantly reliving the losses they have experienced - there is likely to be little time or attention given to the need to provide individual employees the sustained social support they require, Nor is it likely that a stressed organization will pay attention to the losses it sustains and allow any natural ritualized forms of working through organizational loss to unfold. The mental health system has sustained enormous losses over the past decade as leaders and staff have left, programs have been dissolved, communication networks destroyed, and meaning systems abandoned. Yet there has been little discussion of the unrelenting signs of unresolved grief that now plagues the system. Instead what remain visible are abundant signs of organizations in decline.

---

[91] Bloom, *Neither Liberty Nor Safety, Part III*

An outpatient organization with a variety of different programs decided to work on better integrating their overall system. To serve this goal, the consultant urged the group to review their long history. One of the conflicts that surfaced was a generalized but nonspecific fear and suspicion of the financial department in the organization that seemed to make no sense in terms of present operations. The consultant asked the most long-term members of the organization to form an inner circle to talk about the past and the other members of the group sat in a wider circle around them. What surfaced was a part of their history that many people in the room knew nothing about. Thirty years before there had been a financial crisis that almost caused this venerable institution to shut its doors. Financial specialists – one of whom was still running the department – were called in to attempt to rescue the situation. At the time, everyone felt enormous pressure but particularly the newly hired financial people. The organizational grapevine warned everyone about "staying away from finance" and some personal vignettes about short-tempered responses from the people in finance reinforced this warning. Although the situation had long since righted itself, the "word on the street" was still "stay away from finance". The current leader had known nothing about this piece of the history so had not been able to do anything to correct the misapprehension that targeted one lonely – and isolated – department until this fragment of organizational memory was retrieved.

Organizational Decline

According to a worker who wrote about the issue of organizational decline forty years ago, organizations attempt to anticipate and adapt to environmental changes but the larger, more rapid, and harder to predict the changes are, the more difficult it is for the organization to adapt. This failure to adapt then leads to organizational decline and possibly, dissolution.

> Decline begins when an organization fails to anticipate or recognize and effectively respond to any deterioration in organizational performance that threatens long-term survival[92].

When the new medical director took over he first noticed that the physical condition of the program had radically altered. The place was dark and dingy. The carpets were stained and the furniture was battered and dirty. Regardless of what the cleaning staff did, the place never really looked clean. Many of the patients were dressed in hospital gowns, rather than street clothes. Likewise, some of the other psychiatrists insisted on wearing white coats and all that was missing was a stethoscope around their neck to convey the medical

---

[92] Weitzel and Jonsson, *Decline in Organizations*, p.94

nature of the program. The unit, previously unlocked was now carefully locked and off-duty policemen were often called in to manage "security" problems, sometimes wearing their weapons. The staff had come to view a patient restraint as a form of treatment and congratulated themselves when a restraint went well – and they had frequent opportunities to exercise their skills. On one of the charts there were careful recordings about what a woman said about her compulsion to self-mutilate. In the social service history there was brief mention that this woman had been repeatedly sexually abused as a child. But nowhere was any connection made between the sexual abuse and the self-mutilation, nor was there any formulation that the two problems could be related. For the medical director, these examples and many other experiences helped him to recognize how previous standards of care had deteriorated dramatically, although none of these negative changes were reflected in existing standards of quality assurance. The unit had just passed JCOAH and state inspections with flying colors. He attributed this decline in the whole process of treatment as signs of unresolved grief in a system that had numbed itself to the anger, sadness, shame, and despair associated with downsizing, loss of resources, and loss of status. He said,

> I feel like I have gone into a time warp and am back in the early 1950's before the ideas of milieu treatment, systems theory, and psychodynamics had permeated the system. It is a terrible thing to see the extent of regression that has occurred in our field and no one seems to be willing to talk about it. They don't even seem to notice. But this unit still passes all the inspections – what in the world are these regulatory agencies calling quality care at this point!?

One of the most pronounced effects of decline is to increase stress and under stressful conditions, managers frequently do the opposite of what they need to do to reverse decline: relying on proven programs, seeking less counsel from subordinates, concentrating on ways to improve efficiency, and shunning innovative solutions. Their causal explanations for what is causing the problem dictate their response alternatives and their causal explanations are likely to be incorrect or inadequate because the causes are frequently so complex. Just when people need to be pulling together, interpersonal and intraorganizational conflict increases and becomes difficult to resolve and thus goal-setting, communication, and leader-subordinate relationships decline[93].

Critical events and organizational failure change us and change our organizations, but without memory we lose the context. Some modern philosophers believe that all memories are formed and organized within a collective context. According to them, society provides the framework for

---

[93] Whetten, *Organizational Decline*

beliefs, behaviors, and the recollections of both[94]. Later, present circumstances affect what events are remembered as significant. Much of the recording and recalling of memories occurs through social discussion. This shared cohesiveness of memories is part of what defines a culture over time. Shared language also helps a society organize and assimilate memories and eventually, forget about the events. Similarly, there is reason to believe that maintaining silence about disturbing collective events may have the counter effect of making the memory even more potent in its continuing influence on the organization or society much as silent traumatic memories continue to haunt individuals[95].

> We had had a positive reputation in the distant past. But we went through this period of decline, verging on failure, there were other agencies just waiting for us to fail. We cleaned up the leadership and the quality of services improved enormously but other organizations still look at as us as if we were the way we were in the past instead of seeing us as we are now. We still have to prove ourselves more than other organizations have to. Every misstep, every miscommunication – just the stuff that can happen in the course of managing a human service organization – becomes a source of scrutiny and there is a kind of attitude that comes out at meetings and in interagency communications that says "see, I knew you hadn't really changed". It's been hard coming back from that loss of reputation in the community, hard to once again feel safe in the larger environment.
> —Program Director, Family shelter

Studies have shown that institutions, like individuals, have memory and that once interaction patterns have been disrupted these patterns can be transmitted through an organization so that one "generation" unconsciously passes on to the next, norms that alter the system and every member of the system. But without a conscious memory of events also being passed on, organizational members in the present cannot make adequate judgments about whether the strategy, policy, or norm is still appropriate and useful in the present[96]. This process can be an extraordinary resistance to healthy organizational change[97]. Organizational decline is said to be caused by a dysfunction in organizational learning and organizational learning is seriously impaired by failures of organizational memory as discussed earlier. Regression may occur so that previous levels of achievement, knowledge, training, and

---

[94] Halbwachs, *On Collective Memory*

[95] Bloom, *Neither Liberty Nor Safety, Part III;* Pennebaker, Paez, and Rimé, *Collective Memory of Political Events*

[96] Menzies, *A Case Study in the Functioning of Social Systems as a Defense Against Anxiety*

[97] Drucker, *Introduction*

service delivery are no longer remembered and appear to play little if any role in the organizational culture.

Many dysfunctional behaviors characterize organizational decline. Increases in conflict, secrecy, scapegoating, self-protective behaviors, loss of leader credibility, rigidity, turnover, decreases in morale, diminished innovation, lowered participation, nonprioritized cuts, and reduced long-term planning are common problems associated with periods of decline[98]. All of these behaviors can be seen as inhibitors of organizational learning and adaptation – both necessary if the decline is to be reversed[99].

Successful or Permanent Failure

When discussing organizations as living systems,

> theorists are preoccupied with when organizations are "born", what species they are (their forms), and when they have changed enough to be termed dead[100].

Organizational death can be more difficult to define than biological death. It may come when an organization ceases to operate, when it loses its corporate identity, when it loses the capacity to govern itself, or it experiences any combination of these situations. An organization may die when it successfully merges with another organization, so that organizational death may not be equated with failure[101].

It is odd that some organizations seem to be "permanently failing", yet continue to operate for years on end[102]. This may be because the society prefers "successful failures" when the true, albeit unconscious motivation is *"to keep a troubling issue out of the public eye and create the illusion that something is being done"[103]*. It is this kind of "successful" and "permanent" failure that perhaps best defines large components of the existing mental health and social service system. Abused and neglected children, the mentally ill, the poor, the homeless all bring up distasteful reminders of what is wrong in our present social system and arouse anxiety about life's uncertainties.

It is this unseen but real "successful" failure that most confounds people who dedicate their lives to the mental health and social service professions. When young professionals first enter the helping professions, they

---

[98] Cameron, Whetten and Kim, *Organizational Dysfunctions as Decline*

[99] McKinley, *Organizational Decline and Adaptation*

[100] Hager, *Tales From the Grave*, p. 52

[101] Ibid

[102] Meyer and Zucker, *Permanently Failing Organizations*

[103] Seibel, *Successful Failure*

are motivated by a desire to serve, a willingness to sacrifice financial gain for the satisfactions they assume to be found in helping other people get well, seeing people change, and bettering the lives of suffering humanity. What they frequently find instead are bureaucratic systems designed to "control the behavior" of children and adults rather than systems designed to facilitate healing and empowerment.

Kai Erikson sums up what that can feel like to the people involved

> the mortar bonding human communities together is made up at least in part of trust and respect and decency and, in moments of crisis, of charity and concern. It is profoundly disturbing to people when these expectations are not met, no matter how well protected they thought they were by the outer crust of cynicism our century seems to have developed in us all....The real problem in the long run is that the inhumanity people experience comes to be seen as a natural feature of human life rather than as the bad manners of a particular corporation. They think their eyes are being opened to a larger and profoundly unsettling truth: that human institutions cannot be relied upon[104].

Advice For Working With Loss in Organizations

Human beings historically have used ritual and social support to work through the process of loss toward recovery. Scheff has defined ritual as the

> potentially distanced reenactment of situations of emotional distress that are virtually universal in a given culture[105].

Indigenous healing groups deal with the experience of suffering, misery, and healing through staged reenactments of the traumatic experience and a reenactment of the great myths of the tribe. The healing ceremony is almost always a public and collective procedure involving family, tribe, and members of a special healing society. In tribal cultures these ceremonies are often quite large and may involve the entire social group. They are publicly open and often egalitarian, reflecting the traditional ethos of foraging societies. They tend to be repetitive and ongoing, occurring often throughout the year. The participants in the group use techniques designed to greatly increase the level of emotional arousal and alter consciousness. In such states, the participants are permitted the leeway to say or do things that under normal social conditions would be prohibited. In most healing groups, the healed are expected to become healers. The reliving of the traumatic experience or loss occurs in precise detail, and the pain is integrated into a meaningful whole by giving it a meaning in a

---

[104] Erikson, *A New Species of Trouble*, p. 239.
[105] Turner, *From Ritual to Theater*

larger mythical system. There is a re-labeling of the complaint, a reduction in fear through the ability to maintain some degree of control while social relations and subjective experience are brought into harmony[106].

For human beings, grieving clearly is a social experience. It would appear, that on an evolutionary basis we are set for reenactment behavior and that this behavior has important signal importance to our social support network. The nonverbal brain of the affected individual signals through gesture, facial expression, tone of voice, and behavior, that something is amiss, that there is some rift in the social fabric that connects the individual to the social group, a rift that must be healed. The behavior of the individual triggers a ritual response in the group in order to help the individual tell the story, re-experience the affect, transform the meaning of the event, and reintegrate into the whole, while simultaneously the group can learn from the experience of the individual. The amount of social support that is offered is often enormous, with an entire group participating in escorting the injured party back into the fold through any means necessary to do so[107].

The human need to work through loss in order to form new attachments has not changed in the millennia of human existence. But what has changed, at least in our culture, is the willingness of groups of people to address this need. In order to process traumatic loss and the more normative losses associated with change, organizations must be willing to utilize their inherent social structure to help the individuals within the group and the group-as-a-whole to heal and move on.

> We had a person suicide in our program that was unexpected and extremely traumatizing. What I mean by unexpected was that we didn't even know the man was suicidal – he was leaving the next day to go home. So when it happened, we were all devastated and so were all the other patients in the program. But we remembered what we had all learned about responding to disasters so we provided information to everyone as we had it, supported people – patients and staff – in supporting each other, and over the course of 48 hours held a number of community meetings to talk about safety, to plan and implement rituals that might help all of us, and to express a mixture of feelings about the whole incident. By the end of that time, the patients told us that they were ready to get back to their own work and there were no further displays of aggression or suicidal behavior during the time those patients were in the program. In fact, it was one of the best and most mutually supportive communities we ever had. Interestingly, in the rest of the hospital, as word got out about what happened, there were a number of "copycat" behaviors that everyone attributed to what had

---

[106] Bloom, *Every Time History Repeats Itself the Price Goes Up;* Scheff, *Catharsis in Healing;* Turner, *From Ritual to Theater;* van der Hart, *Rituals in Psychotherapy*
[107] Bloom, *Every Time History Repeats Itself the Price Goes Up*

happened in our program, but none of the other units had done anything to
process the incident – that was universally known within hours because of the
grapevine – in the rest of the hospital.
—Clinical Coordinator, inpatient unit

There are three large categories of intervention that organizational
leaders should be knowledgeable about in order to deal with the inevitable
losses associated with organizational existence: becoming prepared to deal with
organizational change and loss on a regular basis; what to do when change or
loss occurs, and how to help people adjust to life after change and loss[108].
Consistent with the notion of parallel process, many of the suggestions offered
here apply just as readily to the clients in our care. When initiating a process to
review and eventually shelve, old losses, it is useful to use a S.E.L.F. framework
to help an organization recognize the intimate, interactive, and cyclical nature of
keeping oneself safe, managing distressing emotions, particularly emotions
surrounding loss, and doing this work in service of creating positive change
aimed at the future. Using S.E.L.F. as a regular part of any psychoeducational
environment brings the issue of loss into regular and routine usage[109].

Preparing to Deal with Organizational Change and Loss

It is vital that every individual in the organization becomes aware of
their own individual vulnerability in attending to issues of trauma and loss from
their own personal and professional past and the ways in which these issues may
become activated again in the present. Knowledge about normal and traumatic
bereavement, and the more normative losses that accompany change should
become a part of routine activity and everyday function and should become part
of the orientation program for new staff and clients. In team meetings and
management meetings, issues surrounding losses - those that are tangible and
those that are symbolic – need to be a part of every clinical and management
conversation. Organizational leaders should communicate with peers about how
they have dealt with issues of loss and bereavement in their institutions and
learn from the things they did well, the mistakes that were made, and the
learning that they experienced. Listen for the ways in which your organization
has dealt with loss in the past and make yourself familiar with the landscape of
organizational loss. Likewise, evaluate the organization for signs of unresolved
trauma and traumatic loss.

---

[108] Jeffreys, *Coping with Workplace Grief*
[109] Bloo, Foderaro, Ryan, *S.E.L.F. A Trauma-Informed Psychoeducational Group
Curriculum*

If you are in a position to do so, consider initiating a conversation about these past losses, making sure to honor past adaptations while simultaneously allowing whatever has not been finished to emerge. Have everyone make a list of the loss-related reactions they see in themselves and each other and ask them to review their previous experience with workplace change, including exploring what was negative and positive about the changes. Assess what the existing cultural norms are for dealing with loss and if the normative expression is denial, set about changing that norm.

Recognize in advance that grief reactions to change will occur, are natural and normal regardless of how much advance preparation is done. As any change is anticipated, provide a continuous flow of information to everyone affected by the change. You will never be able to prepare for every contingency, but create plans to deal with emergencies, crises, and losses that you can anticipate. Remember that once we are in a crisis, the quality of thinking can be negative impacted, so whatever you can plan for ahead of time is likely to be better thought out.

> The other thing that came out of the experience of personal loss for me was a different level of appreciation of loss in the children. Our CEO was 60 years old and it was her child, but she wasn't dependent on him. She is smart, surrounded by friends and family, had sufficient money to take care of her needs, was in a sustaining marital relationship and despite all that she was completely shattered. It made me think about what happens to the kids in care. Frankly, far worse things have happened to them and it took her a year before I thought she was ok. We get kids fresh out of horrible situations and expect them to "buck up". The fact that they get up in the morning is pretty impressive. When I saw what it did for someone with incredible resources and then thought of our kids who have nothing, it hardly seemed fair. The reason she had a year was because she had supports and these kids don't. That for me was one of the major lessons from it – this stuff takes a lot out of you.
> —*C.O.O., Childcare Agency*

When Change or Loss Occurs

If you work in an organization, change and loss are inevitable. So be aware of the risk factors for particular individuals and for the organization as a whole. Be especially attentive to previous experiences with trauma and loss. Recognize that different individuals or subgroups are likely to have different levels of exposure when a loss occurs, but everyone in the group will be affected.

> Without question and I think the event that initially triggered a greater awareness of grief and loss for us happened almost four years ago. We had a devastating

experience when someone in our middle management level had his older son murdered in a local incident by just being at the wrong place at the wrong time. We had all seen this young man grow up and he was a really good kid. Our manager was very invested in being a father, did a lot of extra duty and lived on campus. We knew in a very visceral way the level of devotion he had invested in his son. So it was shattering for all of us and especially significant because he was in charge of the diagnostic unit and through that program we had become particularly sensitive to the issue of loss in those abused kids. This came at the beginning of the time we were looking at trauma and loss in a new way. And this was not clinical, something that happened to the kids – it was happening to all of us. And then about a year and a half later my son was killed in an accident. He was older, on his own, and an accident not an act of violence and that too was devastating. And then seven months later a senior person, a department head, lost his son-in-law - a brand new father running in a race when he had a sudden heart attack and died. So here in a short space of time three very important people in the structure and history of the organization had experienced the loss of a child that for most people is an unimaginable loss. It's not compatible with life to think about that happening. Speaking for myself I know it changed my understanding of trauma and loss. Working in an environment that is itself sensitive to this issue and field with people who are sensitive to these issues helped. But it changed my understanding that if I as a mature person with a lot of resources and skills can be so devastated utterly – take that experience and place it in the mind and heart of a young child.
—*C.E.O, Childcare agency*

When an event occurs, one of the risk factors in how much it is likely to impact the group will also be determined by the degree of "social offensiveness" of the loss[110]. Incidents of sexual abuse, suicides, homicides, and criminal behavior are all indicative of social offenses and may be even more difficult for people to talk about. If an event occurs that causes people or subgroups to be physically dislocated, there will be real and symbolic losses that may not seem important to you but are expressions of grief to those who have lost parking spots or office space, or privacy. The greater the extent of helplessness over change, the more difficult adjustment is likely to be. To the extent you can, help people exert as much control as possible over the changes that occur.

Remember that there are factors that make traumatic loss more traumatic. These include personal contact with death, injury or horrific circumstances; injury or death of a child; sudden or extreme change or loss; prolonged exposure to trauma or loss; and the extent to which everyone in the community is impacted by the change or loss.

---

[110] Jeffreys, *Coping with Workplace Grief*

When a distressing event has occurred, provide as much information as possible about the facts of the event, why it has happened, what is likely to happen next, what steps are being taken, what people can do to help, and what is over and what is not. Accept that people vary greatly in their responses to traumatic events and to any kind of change. Some people respond dramatically and quickly while others may have little response at first and react only over time. While promoting adjustment and adaptation be cautious about setting deadlines to "get over it" – people don't necessary get over things, but they can move on.

Expect and accept a variety of signs of grieving including shock, anger, anxiety, sadness, disorientation, confusion, forgetfulness, and depression and give special attention to those who are the most impacted by an event. Acknowledge losses openly and honestly and do not try to minimize the reality and importance of loss or the losses associated with change. But do not speak in platitudes like "I understand what you are feeling". Be a good listener and do not take personally the feelings that people may express.

Provide as much continuity as possible between the past and the present. Facilitate discussions about the "way things used to be" and help people say goodbye to what has been[1111]. This continuity can be established in a variety of ways: let people take an object that is symbolic of the old way with them into the new situation; find a way to "say goodbye" to the old space, the old way of doing things, the people left behind; write goodbyes down on paper; if people are leaving a specific space, encourage them to take photographs of the old space and bring the pictures with them; create a book of memories and share them at a group meeting; prepare people in advance for the changes in procedures or places that are going to change. Encourage grieving rituals of all kinds and recall cultural methods for dealing with loss and use those methods – burning, burying, eulogizing, memorializing.

If someone's feelings and thoughts get out of control, help him or her seek professional help. Make sure that if employee assistance services exist, that they are confidential and that everyone knows they are available, and guarantee that health care benefits cover the cost of getting help.

Be prepared that periods of grief and loss are associated with decreased productivity, inefficiency and errors. Anticipate this and offer help when needed. If you are an organizational leader it is important to pay attention to your own reactions to trauma, loss and change and allow yourself the time to grieve what you too are losing. Remember that in positions of leadership you have the additional stress of having to role model appropriate and healthy responses to change and loss, including allowing yourself to grieve. Exhibit

---

[1111] Ibid

confidence by treating people as if they can cope and that they are necessary to help the organization to "get through this" successfully.

Helping People to Adjust to Life After Change or Loss

When change has occurred, provide orientation training and whatever information is needed to help people adjust to change. Restore active routines and constructive action as soon as possible after an event as part of "getting through this together" without denying what has been lost. Acknowledge the value of what has been lost and provide as much continuity between the former space/place/situation and the new experience as possible. Encourage the development of new interpersonal bonds and teamwork and recognize the inherent value in the new situation. Organize team-building activities and provide whatever assistance people need to adjust to the new situation. Create new rituals and traditions for team interaction and individual recognition and encourage the development of a new group identity.

Conclusion

September 11, 2001 represents a collective trauma and a shared loss that has had profound effects on the way we all live in America. I would argue that the reaction to September 11 – the Iraq War that began in 2003 - represents a collective failure to fully engage in the grieving process that inevitably follows a traumatic loss. As one observer put it:

> September 11 may go down as one of the most tragic events in modern history not only because of the thousands of deaths it caused but also because it so seriously distorted American perceptions about itself and the world. It has knocked America down into a dank and dangerous cul de sac, making it susceptible to apocalyptic visions of darkness rather than motivating it toward high visions of human possibility[112].

The tragedy of the World Trade Center bombings and the national response to it, are large scale analogues to what frequently happens in the lives of individual children and their individual families, individual staff members within organizations and within organizations-as-a-whole[113]. All too often, anger and aggression substitute for mourning, while shaming and blaming stand-in for a shared recognition of human tragedy. An inability to sit with the reality of loss and move on through that loss inevitably makes us less safe in the

---

[112] Jim Garrison, America as Empire: Global Leader or Rogue Power?, p.45
[113] Bloom, *Neither Liberty Nor Safety, Part I-IV*

world, whether we are an individual child, a family, an employee, an organization, or a whole culture and unleashes powerful and contagious negative emotions that can readily lead to individual and collective disaster.

Loss is an inevitable part of individual and organizational life. We only have two choices: we can either remain stuck in the past or we can keep moving into the future and only if we can share a vision of a better future can we safely transform our losses into a better life.

> After all the losses we have experienced I think we are coming out the other end. I think it's already happening. This notion of Future is what I think is happening. This is the first time in my 20 years here that I think, starting with me and the CEO, that we are really saying, what could come. We are finally getting a vision that this could be an amazing place and we could do some amazing stuff. I would hope that down the road change will be just what we do. For a long time we have been what we are and haven't challenged that vision. Longevity and dedication have been the paramount values. But it's not just dedicated people you need but talented people. I think that whole paradigm is shifting and I am hoping that 5-10 years from now we will have made radical or at least semi-radical changes. In reality if you don't change, you are going to get run over and you will never be safe. For people who are really professionally hungry and want to grow, learn, and keep being renewed it is a much more exciting place to work – more demanding, but more exciting. I think we feel more useful because the children and families need us much more than before. There is that sense of accomplishment that we are providing a vital service. I think the growth in the organization gives us a different kind of presence in the community that has helped us build a stronger collaboration and feel more connected to the community. We have a growing sensitivity to trauma and loss and some new treatment modalities have been internally rewarding. For those who are committed to influencing the way care and services are provided, it is a better place.
> —C.O.O., Child Care Agency

References

Ackoff, R. L. *The Democratic Corporation: A Radical Prescription for Recreating Corporate America and Rediscovering Success.* New York: Oxford University Press, 1994.

Alderfer, Clayton P., and Ken K. Smith. "Studying Intergroup Relations Embedded in Organizations." *Administrative Science Quarterly* 27, no. 1 (1982): 35.

Appelbaum, S. H., J. Gandell, B. T. Shapiro, P. Belisle, and E. Hoeven. "Anatomy of a Merger: Behavior of Organizational Factors and Processes Throughout the Pre- During and Post-Stages (Part 2)." *Management Decision* 38, no. 10 (2000): 674-84.

Argyris, C. *Knowledge and Action: A Guide to Overcoming Barriers to Organizational Change*. San Francisco: Jossey-Bass, 1993.

Ashbach, C., and V. Schermer. *Object Relations, the Self, and the Group: A Conceptual Paradigm*. London: Routledge, 1987.

Bazelon Center for Mental Health Law. *Disintegrating Systems: The State of States' Public Mental Health Systems*: Bazelon Center for Mental Health Law, 2001.

Bento, Regina F. "When the Show Must Go On: Disenfranchised Grief in Organizations." *Journal of Managerial Psychology* 9, no. 6 (1994): 35.

Blanch, A. "Developing Trauma-Informed Behavioral Health Systems: Report from Ntac's National Experts Meeting on Trauma and Violence." Alexandria, VA: U. S. Department of Health and Human Services, Substance Abuse and Mental Health Services Administration, 2003.

Bloom, S. L. *Creating Sanctuary: Toward the Evolution of Sane Societies*. New York: Routledge, 1997.

———. "Every Time History Repeats Itself the Price Goes Up: The Social Reenactment of Trauma." *Sexual Addiction and Compulsivity* 3, no. 3 (1996): 161-94.

———. "Neither Liberty nor Safety: The Impact of Fear on Individuals, Institutions, and Societies, Part I." *Psychotherapy and Politics International* 2, no. 2 (2004): 78-98.

———. "Neither Liberty nor Safety: The Impact of Fear on Individuals, Institutions, and Societies, Part I I." *Psychotherapy and Politics International* 2, no. 3 (2004): 212-28.

———. "Neither Liberty nor Safety: The Impact of Trauma on Individuals, Institutions, and Societies. Part I." In *Psychotherapy and Politics International*, 78-98, 2004.

———. "Neither Liberty nor Safety: The Impact of Trauma on Individuals, Institutions, and Societies. Part Iii." *Psychotherapy and Politics International* 3, no. 2 (2005): 96-111.

———. "Neither Liberty nor Safety: The Impact of Trauma on Individuals, Institutions, and Societies. Part Iv." *Psychotherapy and Politics International* 3, no. 2 (2005): 96-111.

———. "The Sanctuary Model of Organizational Change for Children'S Residential Treatment." *Therapeutic Community: The International Journal for Therapeutic and Supportive Organizations* 26, no. 1 (2005): 65-81.

———. "The Sanctuary Model: A Trauma-Informed Systems Approach to the Residential Treatment of Children." *Residential Group Care Quarterly: Child Welfare League of America* 4, no. 2 (2003): 1, 4-5.

————. "Societal Trauma: Democracy in Danger." In *The Politics of Psychotherapy*, edited by N. Totten, 17-29. New York: Open University Press, 2006.

————. "The System Bites Back: Politics, Parallel Process, and the Notion of Change." *Therapeutic Community: The International Journal for Therapeutic and Supportive Organizations.* 26, no. 4, Silver Jubilee Issue (2005): 337-54.

Bloom, S. L., M. Bennington-Davis, B. Farragher, D. McCorkle, K. Nice-Martini, and K. Wellbank. "Multiple Opportunities for Creating Sanctuary." *Psychiatric Quarterly* 74, no. 2 (2003): 173-90.

Bloom, S. L., J. F. Foderaro, and R. A. Ryan. "S.E.L.F.: A Trauma-Informed, Psychoeducational Group Curriculum." Available at www.sanctuaryweb.com, 2006.

Bloom, S.L. *Organizational Stress as a Barrier to Trauma-Sensitive Change and System Transformation, White Paper for the National Technical Assistance Center for State Mental Health Planning (Ntac), National Association of State Mental Health Program Directors.* http://www.nasmhpd.org/publications.cfm, 2006.

Boal, K.B., and J.M. Bryson. "Charismatic Leadershp: A Phenomenological and Structural Approach." In *Emerging Leadership Vistas*, edited by J. G. Hunt, B.R. Baliga, H. P. Dachler and C.A. Schreisheim, 5-34. Lexington, MA: Lexington Books, 1988.

Boss, P. "Loss. Trauma, and Resilience: Therapeutic Work with Ambiguous Loss." New York: W. W. Norton, 2006.

Bowlby, J. *Attachment and Loss, Volume Iii: Loss, Sadness and Depression.*, 1980.

————. "Grief and Mourning in Infancy and Early Childhood." *The Psychoanalytic Study of the Child* 15 (1960): 9-52.

————. "Pathological Mourning and Childhood Mourning." In *Journal of the American Psychoanalytic Association*, 500-41, 1963.

Buono, Anthony F., and James L. Bowditch. "Ethical Considerations in Merger and Acquisition Management: A Human Resource Perspective." *Advanced Management Journal* 55, no. 4 (1990): 18.

Cameron, Kim S., David A. Whetten, and Myung U. Kim. "Organizational Dysfunctions of Decline." *Academy of Management Journal* 30, no. 1 (1987): 126.

Carr, Adrian. "Understanding Emotion and Emotionality in a Process of Change." *Journal of Organizational Change Management* 14, no. 5 (2001): 421-34.

de Geus, A. *The Living Company: Habits for Survival in a Turbulent Business Environment.* Boston: Harvard Business School Press, 1997.

Doka, K., and J. Davidson. *Living with Grief: Who We Are, How We Grieve.* Washington, D.C.: Brunner/Mazel, 1998.

Driver, T. F. *The Magic of Ritual: Our Need for Liberating Rites That Transform Our Lives and Our Communities.* San Francisco: HarperSanFrancisco, 1991.

Drucker, P. "Introduction." In *The Organization of the Future*, edited by F. Hesselbein, M. Goldsmith and R. Beckhard, 1-5. San Francisco: Jossey-Bass, 1997.

Edwards, Valerie J, George W Holden, Vincent J Felitti, and Robert F Anda. "Relationship between Multiple Forms of Childhood Maltreatment and Adult Mental Health in Community Respondents: Results from the Adverse Childhood Experiences Study." *American Journal of Psychiatry* 160, no. 8 (2003): 1453-60.

Erikson, K. *A New Species of Trouble: The Human Experience of Modern Disasters.* New York: W.W. Norton, 1994.

Ettin, M. F., J. W. Fidler, and Cohen B. D., eds. *Group Process and Political Dynamics.* Madison, CT: International Universities Press, 1995.

Felitti, V. J., R. F. Anda, D. Nordenberg, D. F. Williamson, A. M. Spitz, V. Edwards, M. P. Koss, and J. S. Marks. "Relationship of Childhood Abuse and Household Dysfunction to Many of the Leading Causes of Death in Adults. The Adverse Childhood Experiences (Ace) Study." *Am J Prev Med* 14, no. 4 (1998): 245-58.

Forsyth, D.R. *Group Dynamics, Second Edition.* Pacific Grove, CA: Brooks/Cole, 1990.

Gabriel, Y. "Organizational Nostalgia - Reflections on 'the Golden Age'." In *Emotion in Organizations*, edited by S. Fineman, 118-41. Thousand Oaks, CA: Sage Publications, 1993.

Gantt, Susan P., and Yvonne M. Agazarian. "Systems-Centered Emotional Intelligence: Beyond Individual Systems to Organizational Systems." *Organizational Analysis* 12, no. 2 (2004): 147-69.

Goldstein, Jeffrey. *The Unshackled Organization.* Portland, OR: Productivity Press, 1994.

Goleman, D. "Social Intelligence: The New Science of Human Relationships." New York: Bantam Books, 2006.

Hager, M., J. Galaskiewicz, W. Bielefeld, and J. Pins. ""Tales from the Grave": Organizations' Accounts of Their Own Demise." In *When Things Go Wrong: Organizational Faiilures and Breakdowns*, edited by H.K. Anheier. Thousand Oaks, CA: Sage Publications, 1999.

Haines, S. *The Manager's Pocket Guide to Systems Thinking and Learning.* Amherst, MA: HRD Press, 1998.

Halbwachs, M. *On Collective Memory*. Chicago: University of Chicago Press, 1992.

Halton, W. "Some Unconscious Aspects of Organizational Life: Contributions from Psychoanalysis." In *The Unconscious at Work: Individual and Organizational Stress in Human Services*, edited by A. Obholzer and V. Z. Roberts, 11-27. Routledge: London, 1994.

Hatfield, E., J. Cacioppo, and R. L. Rapson. "Emotional Contagion." New York: Cambridge University Press, 1994.

Hirschhorn, Larry. *Reworking Authority: Leading and Following in the Post Modern Organization*. Cambridge, Mass: MIT Press, 1997.

Holland, J. H. *Emergence: From Chaos to Order*. Reading, MA: Addison-Wesley, 1998.

Hubiak, William A, and Susan Jones O Donnell. "Downsizing: A Pervasive Form of Organizational Suicide." *National Productivity Review* 16, no. 2 (1997): 31.

Huckshorn, K.A. *Six Core Strategies for Reducing Seclusion and Restraint Use*: http://www.advocacycenter.org/documents/RS_Six_Core_Strategies.pdf, 2005.

Janis, I. L. "Decision Making under Stress." In *Handbook of Stress: Theoretical and Clinical Aspects*, edited by L. Goldberger and S. Breznitz, 69-87. New York: Free Press, 1982.

Jeffreys, J. S. *Coping with Workplace Grief: Dealing with Loss, Trauma, and Change, Revised Edition*. Boston, MA: Thomson Course Technology, 2005.

Jennings, A. "The Damaging Consequences of Violence and Trauma Facts, Discussion Points, and Recommendations for the Behavioral Health System." http://www.nasmhpd.org/general_files/publications/ntac_pubs/reports/Trauma%20Services%20doc%20FINAL-04.pdf. Washington, D.C.: National Association of State Mental Health Program Directors, 2004.

Jervis, R. *System Effects: Complexity in Political and Social Lfe*. Princeton, NJ: Princeton University Press, 1997.

Jick, T.D., and V.V. Murray. "The Management of Hard Times: Budget Cutbacks in Public Sector Organizations." *Organization Studies* 3, no. 2 (1982): 141-69.

Johnson, S. *Emergence*. New York: Ballantine Books, 2001.

Kaiser Daily Health Policy Report. *15,000 Children Incarcerated Because of Lack of Mental Health Treatment in 2003*, *http://www.Kaisernetwork.Org/Daily_Reports/Rep_Index.Cfm?Dr_Id=2460 6, July 8* 2004 [cited.

Kanapaux, W. "Vision Offered to Overhaul Nation's Mental Health Care System." *Psychiatric Times* XX, no. 8 (2003), http://psychiatrictimes.com/showArticle.jhtml?articleID=175803022.

Lawrence, W. G. "The Presence of Totalitarian States-of-Mind in Institutions." Paper presented at the Paper read at the inaugural conference on 'Group Relations', of the Institute of Human Relations, Sofia, Bulgaria, 1995. Accessed November 23, 2006 at http://human-nature.com/free-associations/lawren.html 1995.

Marks, M. L., and P. Mirvis. "Merger Syndrome: Stress and Uncertainty." *Mergers & Acquisitions* Summer (1985): 50-55.

McDougall, W. *The Group Mind*. ed. New York: G. P. Putnam's Sons, 1939 (1920).

Mckinley, William. "Organizational Decline and Adaptation: Theoretical Controversies." *Organization Science: A Journal of the Institute of Management Sciences* 4, no. 1 (1993): 1.

McNeill, B. W., and V. Worthen. "The Parallel Process in Psychotherapy Supervision." *Professional Psychology: Research and Practice* 20, no. 5 (1989): 329-33.

Menzies, I. E. P. "A Case Study in the Functioning of Social Systems as a Defense against Anxiety." In *Group Relations Reader 1*, edited by W. H. Bexton. Washington, D. C.: Rice Institute Series, 1975.

Menzies, I.E.P. "A Case Study in the Functioning of Social Systems as a Defense against Anxiety." In *Group Relations Reader 1.*, edited by A.D. Colman and W. H. Bexton. Washington, D.C.: A. K. Rice Institute Series, 1975.

Meyer, M., and L. Zucker. *Permanently Failing Organizations*. Newbury Park, CA: Sage Publications, 1989.

National Association of Psychiatric Health Systems. "Challenges Facing Behavioral Health Care: The Pressures on Essential Behavioral Healthcare Services." Washington, D.C.: National Association of Psychiatric Health Systems, 2003.

Nitsun, M. "The Anti-Group: Destructive Forces in the Group and Their Creative Potential." London: Routledge, 1996.

Pennebaker, J.W., D. Paez, and B. Rimé, eds. *Collective Memory of Political Events*. Mahwah, NJ: Lawrence Erlbaum, 1997.

President's New Freedom Commission on Mental Health. *Interim Report* 2002 [cited September 17 2005].

Pyszczynski, T., S. Solomon, and J. Greenberg. *In the Wake of 9/11: The Psychology of Terror*. Washington, D.C.: American Psychological Association, 2003.

Pyszczynski, Tom. "What Are We So Afraid Of? A Terror Management Theory Perspective on the Politics of Fear." *Social Research* 71, no. 4 (2004): 827.

Rando, T. A. "Treatment of Complicated Mourning." Champaign, IL: Research Press, 1993.

Ray, M. "What Is the New Paradigm in Business?" In *The New Paradigm in Business: Emerging Strategies for Leadership and Organizational Change*, edited by M. Ray and A. Rinzler. New York: G. P. Putnam's Sons, 1993.

Rivard, J.C., D. McCorkle, M.E. Duncan, L.E. Pasquale, S. L. Bloom, and R. . Abramovitz. " Implementing a Trauma Recovery Framework for Youths in Residential Treatment." *Child and Adolescent Social Work Journal* 21, no. 5 (2004): 529-50.

Ryan, Kathleen, and Daniel Oestreich. *Driving Fear out of the Workplace: Creating the High Trust, High Performance Organization.* San Francisco: Jossey Bass, 1998.

Satcher, D. "Mental Health: A Report of the Surgeon General." Rockville, MD: U. S. Department of Health and Human Services, Substance Abuse and Mental Health Services Administration, Center for Mental Health Services, National Institutes of Health, National Institute of Mental Health, 1999.

Scheff, T. J. *Cartharsis in Healing, Ritual and Drama.* Berkeley: University of California Press, 1979.

Schein, E. H. *The Corporate Culture: A Survival Guide. Sense and Nonsense About Culture Change.* San Francisco: Jossey Bass, 1999.

Seibel, W. "Successful Failure: An Alternative View of Organizational Coping." In *When Things Go Wrong: Organizational Faiilures and Breakdowns*, edited by H. K. Anheier, 91-104. Thousand Oaks: Sage Publications, 1999.

Senge, P., C. O. Scharmer, J. Jaworski, and B. S. Flowers. *Presence: Human Purpose and the Field of the Future.* Cambridge, MA: The Society for Organizational Learning, 2004.

Smith, K.K., V. M. Simmons, and T.B. Thames. ""Fix the Women": An Intervention into an Organizational Conflict Based on Parallel Process Thinking." *The Journal of Applied Behavioral Science* 25, no. 1 (1989): 11-29.

Spillius, E. B. "Asylum and Society." In *The Social Engagement of Social Science, Volume I: The Socio-Psychological Perspective*, edited by H. Murray, 586-612. London: Free Association Books, 1990.

Stanton, A. H., and M.S. Schwartz. *The Mental Hospital: A Study of Institutional Participation in Psychiatric Illness and Treatment.* New York: Basic Books, 1954.

Sullivan, Chatham Clarke. "Finding the Thou in the I: Countertransference and Parallel Process Analysis in Organizational Research and Consultation." *Journal of Applied Behavioral Science* 38, no. 3 (2002): 375.

Szegedy-Maszak, M. "Consuming Passion:The Mentally Ill Are Taking Charge of Their Own Recovery. But They Disagree on What That Means." *U.S. News and World Report*, June 3 2002.

Turner, V. *From Ritual to Theatre: The Human Seriousness of Play.* New York: PAJ Publications, 1982.

van der Hart, O. *Rituals in Psychotherapy: Transition and Continuity.* New York: Irvington Publishers, 1983.

Weitzel, William, and Ellen Jonsson. "Decline in Organizations: A Literature Integration and Extension." *Administrative Science Quarterly* 34, no. 1 (1989): 91.

Whetten, David A. "Organizational Decline: A Neglected Topic in Organizational Science." *Academy of Management Review* 5, no. 4 (1980): 577.

Wright, L., and M. Smye. *Corporate Abuse: How "Lean and Mean" Robs People and Profits.* New York: MacMillan, 1996.

Zinner, ES, and MB Williams. *When a Community Weeps: Case Studies in Group Survivorship.* New York: Brunner/Mazel, 1999.

Tips For Coping with Organizational Change and Loss

Preparing To Deal With Organizational Change and Loss

- Be aware of your own vulnerability to issues of trauma and loss from your own personal and professional past and maintain an awareness of the ways in which these issues may be activated by present circumstances.
- Maintain a knowledge base about the impact of loss on individuals, families, and groups. Integrate an understanding of grief and loss into everyday function.
- In team meetings and management meetings, make sure that the loss implications of every change are thoroughly addressed.
- Prepare as much as possible for emergencies, crisis, and potentially adverse situations with preparedness plans.
- If you can, talk to your predecessor (s) or colleagues who hold positions similar to yours in other organizations. Ask them about their own experiences of loss in the job and within the organization.
- Treat the past with respect, honor previous contributions, and learn about the organizational history and culture
- Discover the organizational history of trauma and loss and evaluate the ways in which these experiences may be still affecting organizational function.
- If you are in a position to do so, consider doing an organizational debriefing, asking participants to assess the amount of change and loss that has occurred to them individually and as a group.
- Have everyone make a list of the loss-related reactions that they see in themselves and each other and ask them to review their previous experience with workplace change and explore what was negative and positive about the changes.
- Recognize that grief reactions to change will occur and are natural and normal, no matter how much advance preparation you do.
- As change is anticipated provide a continuous flow of information to everyone involved.

When Change or Loss Occurs

- Be aware of risk factors for particular individuals and for the organization as a whole. These include:
    - Previous experiences of trauma and/or loss
    - The extent to which individuals/subgroups will have different levels of exposure to loss
    - The extent to which the cultural norm is to deny the impact of loss
    - The extent of "social offensiveness" as a part of the loss (sexual abuse, criminal behavior, homicide, suicide)
    - How much people/subgroups are physically dislocated
    - The extent to which those involved were able to exert a degree of control over the change/loss
    - Contact with death, injury, horror, atrocity,
    - Injury or death of a child
    - The suddenness or extreme nature of the change or loss
    - The length of time that the traumatic event or experience of loss lasted
    - The extent to which the entire community is impacted by the change/loss
- Provide as much information as possible about the reasons for the change/loss, what is likely to occur next, what steps are being taken, what people can do to help, what is over and what is not.
- Accept that people differ greatly in their responses to trauma, loss and change. Some individuals respond dramatically and quickly, while others may have little response at first and may only react over time. Do not set deadlines for "getting over it".
- Expect and accept signs of grieving such as:
    - Shock
    - Anger
    - Bargaining
    - Anxiety
    - Sadness
    - Disorientation
    - Confusion
    - Forgetfulness
    - depression
- Give special attention to those who are the most impacted by the trauma or loss

- Acknowledge losses openly and honestly and do not try to minimize the reality and importance of subjective loss.
- Be an active and compassionate listener and do not speak in platitudes. Do not pretend to "understand what they are feeling" – just listen and do not take personally the anger that may be expressed.
- Provide as much continuity as possible between past and present
- Spend time talking to individuals about the value of the "way thing used to be" and help them say "goodbye" [62]
    o Let people take an object that is symbolic of the old way with them into the new situation
    o Find a way to "say goodbye" to the old space, way of doing things, people that have left, etc.
    o Write goodbyes on paper
    o If people are leaving a specific space, encourage them to take photographs of the old space and/or symbolic objects and bring the pictures or objects to the new locations
    o Create a book of memories and share it at a group meeting
    o Prepare people in advance for the changes in procedure or places that are going to change
- Encourage grieving rituals of all kinds – recall cultural methods of dealing with loss and use those methods, even symbolically – burning, burying, eulogizing, memorializing.
- Recognize that periods of grief and loss are associated with decreased productivity, inefficiency, and errors. Anticipate this and offer help when needed.
- Help people seek professional help if feelings and thoughts get out of control – make sure that if EAP services exist, that they are confidential and everyone knows they are available, and guarantee that health care benefits cover the cost of getting help
- If you are an organizational leader:
    o pay attention to your own reactions to trauma, loss and change – allow yourself the time to grieve what you too are losing.
    o In positions of leadership you have the addition stress of having to role model appropriate and healthy responses to change and loss, including allowing yourself to grieve.
    o Exhibit confidence by treating people as if they can cope and that they are necessary to "get through this" successfully

Helping People to Adjust to Life After Change or Loss

- Provide orientation, training and whatever information is needed to people to adjust to change
- Restore active routines and constructive action
- Acknowledge the value of former experiences and colleagues
- Provide for continuity between the former space/place/situation and the new experience
- Encourage the development of new interpersonal bonds
- Recognize the value inherent in the new situation
- Organize team-building activities
- Provide whatever assistance individuals need to adjust to the new situation
- Create new rituals and traditions for team interaction and individual recognition and the new identity of the group

LIST OF CONTRIBUTORS

Valerie Anderson, M.S.W. is a Parent/Child Specialist at the Health Federation Home Visitation Program in Philadelphia, Pennsylvania.

Sandra L. Bloom, M.D. is the founder of the Sanctuary Model and serves as a Distinguished Fellow at the Andrus Center for Learning and Innovation, a teaching and learning arm of the Julia Dyckman Andrus Memorial in Yonkers, New York.

Theodore J. Corbin, M.D., is an Assistant Professor of Emergency Medicine at the Drexel University College of Medicine in Philadelphia, Pennsylvania. He also serves as Director of the Violence Intervention and Research Program.

Kenneth V. Hardy, Ph.D. is Professor of Family Therapy at Drexel University in Philadelphia, Pennsylvania. He is also Director of the Eikenberg Institute for Relationships in New York, New York.

Kathryn Kehoe-Biggs, L.C.S.W., Ph.D. teaches seminars, runs groups and treats adults, children and adolescents at The Bereavement Center of Westchester in Tuckahoe, New York.

David McCorkle, L.C.S.W. is a Social Worker and Senior Trainer for the Sanctuary Leadership Development Institute at Andrus Center for Learning and Innovation in Yonkers, New York.

Nancy Woodruff Ment, L.C.S.W., is the President and Chief Executive Officer of the Julia Dyckman Andrus Memorial, a not-for-profit organization in Yonkers, New York serving vulnerable children and their families in day, residential and community-based programs.

John Rich, M.D., M.P.H., is Professor and Chair of Health Management and Policy at the Drexel University School of Public Health in Philadelphia, Pennsylvania. He is also the recipient of a 2006 MacArthur Fellowship for his work to improve the health of young men of color through innovative programs, research and policy change.

Sarah Yanosy Sreedhar, L.C.S.W. is the Coordinator of External Training at the Andrus Center for Learning and Innovation, a teaching and learning arm of the Julia Dyckman Andrus Memorial in Yonkers, New York.

Lorelei Atalie Vargas, M.P.P., M.A. is the Director of Policy, Planning and Research at the Julia Dyckman Andrus Memorial in Yonkers, New York.